Wonderlands

Terrace Books, a division of the University of Wisconsin Press, takes its name from the Memorial Union Terrace, located at the University of Wisconsin–Madison. Since its inception in 1907, the Wisconsin Union has provided a venue for students, faculty, staff, and alumni to debate art, music, politics, and the issues of the day. It is a place where theater, music, drama, dance, outdoor activities, and major speakers are made available to the campus and the community. To learn more about the Union, visit www.union.wisc.edu.

Wonderlands

Good Gay Travel Writing

Edited by
Raphael Kadushin

THE UNIVERSITY OF WISCONSIN PRESS
TERRACE BOOKS

The University of Wisconsin Press
1930 Monroe Street
Madison, Wisconsin 53711

www.wisc.edu/wisconsinpress/

3 Henrietta Street
London WC2E 8LU, England

5   4   3   2   1

Printed in the United States of America

"When Will You Be Here Again?" by Michael Lowenthal originally appeared in the *Advocate* (4 March 2003), reprinted by permission of the author; "Girona" by Colm Tóibín previously appeared in *Homage to Barcelona*, revised and updated edition, published by Picador, an imprint of Pan Macmillan Ltd., 2002, reprinted by permission of the author; "Everywhere" by J. S. Marcus originally appeared in *The Art of Cartography*, published by Alfred A. Knopf, 1991, reprinted by permission of the author; "Mohammed" and "The Island in Syria" by Robert Tewdwr Moss originally appeared in *Cleopatra's Wedding Present*, published by Gerald Duckworth & Co. Ltd., 1998, and the University of Wisconsin Press, 2003, reprinted by permission of the publishers; "Reading the Body" by Boyer Rickel originally appeared in *Taboo*, published by the University of Wisconsin Press, 1999, reprinted by permission of the publisher; an earlier version of "Tea with Paul Bowles: From a Tangier Diary, 1991" by Edward Field appeared in *Raritan* (winter 1993), reprinted by permission of the author; "Death in the Desert" by Edmund White originally appeared in *The Married Man*, published by Alfred A. Knopf, 2000, reprinted by permission of International Creative Management, Inc. and Alfred A. Knopf, a division of Random House, Inc.

Library of Congress Cataloging-in-Publication Data
Wonderlands: good gay travel writing / edited by Raphael Kadushin.
p.   cm.
ISBN 0-299-19754-9 (pbk.: alk. paper)
1. Gay men—Travel.   2. Travelers' writings.   I. Kadushin, Raphael.
HQ75.25.W66   2004
910'.86'64—dc22   2003021706

to
ALFRED, SYLVIA, AND GOLDIE

and to
TOMMY

Contents

Contents

 Acknowledgments

First, I'd like to thank all of the contributors. The world of gay lit has shrunk down to a very small one, so many of these people are personal friends, and they've all offered their work and time for virtually no compensation, because *Wonderlands* is intended as a fund-raiser for our Living Out series of gay and lesbian autobiographies. One thing the precarious—really desperate—state of publishing has engendered is a collective sense of generosity, a communal spirit among those still committed to the dying art of the book. This collection is a real demonstration of that spirit.

Second, I'd like to thank Sheila Moermond, my colleague at the University of Wisconsin Press, who did her usual impeccable job pulling *Wonderlands* together. Sheila brings an absolute dedication and the purest kind of intelligence to every book she works on, and there would be fewer press books without her.

Also thanks to Scott Lenz, who still practices an elegant form of editing copy—no longer a dying but now an essentially dead art, except for the very few hold-outs—and to all the friends and colleagues who have been crucial to the success of the Living Out series: co-editors David Bergman and Joan Larkin, Felice Picano, Edmund White, Michael Lowenthal, Charlotte Abbott, David Román, Jim Marks, Tzivia Gover, David Rosen, Tim Miller, Betty Berzon, and many others.

Thanks to Brian Rieselman, my generous twin spirit, who came up with the book title, and to lots of people who have always embodied true friendship, though there's only room here to mention the ones I've always known: Philippe Hornwood, Laurel Fujisawa, Doug Swenson, Joan Rogers, Susana Chavez Silverman, Inge Yspeert, Eddie Spenagel, Barb Schulman, Margaret Walsh, Ricardo Gonzalez, Susan Kepecs, and all the others who know who they are.

Acknowledgments

Finally, I'd like to thank Alfred and Sylvia Kadushin, who aren't just the best parents anyone can imagine, but the models of what real love and an honest life are all about, and to Goldie, who has been there with me from the start. And to Tommy, whom I love always.

Wonderlands

Introduction

Raphael Kadushin

Anthologies have become a cottage industry in the last two decades, and they've succumbed to their own laundry list of conventions. What I hoped to do in *Wonderlands* is avoid most of those conventions.

That's why, starting from the very front of the book, the subtitle doesn't claim this is the "Best Gay Travel Writing." Who knows what best is? All those anthologies that blithely overuse the superlative—e.g. most of them—are promising more than they can offer. And that's inevitable. Anthologies, by their very nature, feature a range of styles and voices, and every reader is going to prefer some pieces to others. Absolutely no one will mistake all of them for the best there is.

Except, maybe, for an overly cocky editor, because ultimately, of course, it's the anthology editor who is imposing his or her taste on the collection. And no one's taste is that consistent, or pristine. Mine leans more toward the elusive, the impressionistic, and the understated, but then I've published some bad books. What I really look for is something with an actual voice, as long as that voice doesn't sound anything like the lazy, flat, platitude-spouting voice that has turned too much contemporary literature into drive-through reading.

In gay terms the generic book can be identified by a few omnipresent homo genres. There is the comedy that depends for its robotic humor on recycled *Brady Bunch* allusions, sit-com gags (no, not every dumped bachelor winds up crying into their Häagen-Dazs), and lots of references to recklessly witty friends whom we have to take on faith, because they never actually say anything funny. Mostly they tend to camp it up in a frenzied, faux-whimsical way that makes an increasingly obvious point. Despite all our self-serving celebrations, our wiggy, invented gay families aren't that much more endearing, or interesting, than our real ones. They're just louder.

The other prevailing homo genre is the minimalist gay tragedy that is so understated it's underwrought. These studies in bathos, which always involve disaffected gays roaming through a nightlife of kink, dope, and dick, usually have more to do with establishing the author's hipster credentials than the love of writing. That's why they all sound like a bad impersonation of Bret Easton Ellis, a really bad impersonator himself. Joan Didion did it first and did it incomparably better.

Where does that leave us? Nowhere, which is the best place any writer can start. It leaves us with a writer falling back on himself. And that, I hope, is what most of the following pieces reveal.

And since these writers are not conforming to any defined style, they're not necessarily conforming to the rules of travel writing either. That's another anthology pretense we're giving up on here—the show of some clearly defined and unified front. What defines travel writing as a genre? Everyone has different standards. The only one that links these pieces, and qualifies them as travel writing, is the fact that they pivot around some sort of journey. Beyond that it's a free-for-all. Some of these pieces are clearly autobiographical, some are semi-autobiographical; some are creative nonfiction and some are obviously fiction. They leap boundaries. The biggest fiction, in the end, is travel writing's own claim to being an objective genre. What does anyone really know about a foreign place that isn't partly his or her own creation? We're always choosing what we see, what we don't see, and whom we meet; we're always inventing our destinations.

If the patchwork of styles makes for an unruly, jumpy collection, shifting between different genres and perspectives, that's fine. The last anthology convention we're dumping is any semblance of order. Collections usually love to divide their eighty-five three-page essays into lots of sections and themes; the order of the pieces seems to be an important subtext. But there's no real way of scooping the following essays and stories into neat piles without imposing a phony construction. At least the haphazard flow of the collection simulates a bumpy trip—the unplanned journey, which means the best kind, because you don't know what's hiding around any given corner.

But none of this means that *Wonderlands* is a random collection. These are good travel stories because they all know how to use the trip as a metaphor, or a frame. And in that sense there are clear camps. A lot of the anthology's most compelling travel pieces are love stories. Trips are usually some form of blind date; we react as strongly to a new place as we do to a new person. We love it, we hate it, or we're indifferent to it; the attraction is instant, compelling, and personal, or it's nonexistent. So the minute we arrive someplace for the first time we're engaged in a kind of romance. And then the journey itself lets us abandon our banal lives for a fresh one, so the risk of the trip can trigger other risks, and allow us to do the things we want. And the thing most of us want to do is fall in love.

So some of my favorite pieces in this collection are really as much love stories as travelogues. Mack Friedman's "The Salmon Capital of the World" is a quietly poignant story that subverts its own swagger. The piece's butch camp—the backdrop of an Alaskan fish factory, as male-bonded a world as any Marine Corp barracks—winds up underscoring the poetic first love that is the work's more authentic refrain, and that becomes all the more moving for its lack of realization. Alistair McCartney's "Aerogrammes"—a series of lovelorn missives to his boyfriend Tim Miller—is a more innocent and straightforward romance, though McCartney's take on the old-fashioned love letter is in some ways just as subversive as Friedman's piece. Not enough gay writers have the courage to write a love story anymore, or reveal the kind of open emotion that is probably the gayest thing about being gay.

And then there is Brian Bouldrey's slightly black romantic comedy—focused on a *rondelle* of lovers chasing each other around a French farmhouse—that, despite its soufflé-light tone, evokes the rules of attraction, and the sadness of infatuation. Edmund White's chapter from *The Married Man*—one of the few reprinted pieces here, and a classic—features a harrowing ride through the Moroccan desert, and catches the beauty of love through its fragility. Philip Gambone's flying leap for romance, which he finds in Hanoi after a literal journey of wanderlust through Beijing, Siena, Florence, and Santa Fe, reveals the courage it takes to make that leap, really more of a free-fall. Even Edward Field's "Tea with Paul Bowles" is a romance; the obligatory tea that every gay writer once drank with Bowles, as an homage, suggests the presence of love through its palpable absence, as does Michael Lowenthal's sad confrontation along the back roads of Scotland.

Other kinds of travel writing center less on the raw emotion a trip can trigger than on the trip itself. The question that seems to consume professional travel writers, and that supposedly gives the genre its universal heft, is a metaphysical one. What drives our need to journey out? What does all our busy coming and going really represent, on a deeper level? The question has been asked a thousand times and thankfully none of the pieces in *Wonderlands* rehash the old cliché about the spirituality of travel, or swoop off into some airy netherworld. But a lot of the pieces here answer the question indirectly, in a more unassuming way, without losing sight of their specific journey. In Robert Tewdwr Moss's chapters from *Cleopatra's Wedding Present,* another classic of contemporary travel writing, the journalist's picaresque odyssey through the deserts, villages, and slums of Syria assumes an almost frantic pitch; his need to resolve the muddle of the Middle East, or at least see all its layers clearly, echoes his need to calm a personal chaos. Wayne Koestenbaum, on his tour through the opera houses of Vienna, and the city's preserves of high Germanic culture, sees the contradictions of a place and the way trips can become a history lesson; this is the rarefied world that also exiled his father, and almost killed him. Colm Tóibín's "Girona" evokes a kind of Spanish Brigadoon, the journey as an excavation of lost worlds, and Mitch Cullin finds something in Japan that he knows he lacks himself.

It's the sense of something missing, finally, that may be the link joining all these travel stories. We're always leaving home because we're partly looking for something else. And usually what we find, in the end, is a gift, a small wonderland that we may only recognize years later, when we're back at home, safe again.

The Salmon Capital of the World

Mack Friedman

The summer I turned twenty I fell in love with traveling and a boy named Sean. We lived in a tent made from plywood and pallets and stolen blue tarpaulins. We worked the same line in an Alaskan fish factory. We watched the river for biplanes and rock cod and swooping black cormorants. We climbed a mountain and stashed red wine in the snow. When we weren't working Sean would take off the only shirt he ever wore. He was a quiet mousy boy about five-five. His mother had recently killed herself. He never told us how. He had shiny white canines, thin black eyebrows, a small short nose, and long hazel eyes. His hair was fine and oily and dishwater blonde and flopped over his face, so he had to wear a hairnet when he excised fish skulls before the tops went on the cans.

That May I'd returned briefly to Wisconsin from a college in Pennsylvania, planning to spend the summer with my parents. My prospects distressed me. I thought I might work pizza delivery again, if only I hadn't crashed my folks' detective-blue Ford into a parked Jeep the previous July while craning out the passenger side to catch an address. You should never keep driving when you're halfway out of the car. The guy who ordered the large pepperoni and mushrooms that had since slid into its own paste also owned the dented Jeep. *The good news is your pizza's here. The bad news is it's a wreck and so's your car.* We settled the score in his backyard for the contents of my apron. I was still unsettled.

And, I figured, I could paint houses but for my penchant for falling off ladders. Soon after retiring from pizza delivery, I sprayed white window trim into a hornets' nest. Flying stinging creatures terrified me. The next house was an old Victorian mansion in a suburb we called White Folks Bay. I was scraping a second-story soffit and stretched too far. You should never paint when you're halfway off a ladder, but anyone can make that mistake. The real trick is to make it all fall on you when you land: stepladder, roller, edging stick, brush, big open bucket of paint. My boss (my friend Trance's big brother) fired me immediately the second time. "We do windows, not fucking shingles and sidewalks," Cuong said sadly, after checking my pulse. It seemed to me that I was more or less out of options.

My sex life was hopeless. The only gay guys I met were the ones in park bathrooms redolent with urinal discs and old piss. Flushing meant a cop or a straight guy was coming. All those rushing toilets made me feel hapless and nervous, wanting more. Two ex-girlfriends from high school had moved on to other cities and boys. I didn't have a lot of friends. The main things I could count on in Milwaukee were mild family dysfunction and drugs.

Trance (officially Tran, my old high school soccer teammate) had been growing hydroponic pot in his basement for several months. We met for basketball in late May, when I was trying to figure out how to spend the next few months. Dewey, a friend from sixth grade, joined us on my old elementary school playground. We played hustle, first to twenty-one wins.

"Want to come over and landscape later then?" Trance asked. "Don't worry, no house painting in the plans." He cracked a fucked-up Mona Lisa with too much sly and not enough coy and drove the hoop.

I let him go, watched his fat ass catch spring sun through blue shorts; then blocked his shit from behind. I thought about depantsing him but worried Dewey would take it the wrong way. Or the right way.

I found the ball and swiveled to locate Dewey's gawky pitchers' frame. When we were twelve in art class I'd longed to run a thumb along the curved track of his angel's mark, the space between his stub nose and wide lips. I wanted to turn him into a statue because he was so quiet most of the time. But when he did talk he'd crack us all up, and even then he had a great hook shot, so I wouldn't have wanted Dew frozen in time for more than a few minutes. Instead I stuck close to his side.

"If you need some help trimming bushes, we're always glad to assist," Dew grinned, shrugging his assent. "Just don't make me move furniture."

"What time ya want us?" I asked and pulled up for a jumper. Trance lunged, his arms around my face. His fingertips stretched to me, our hands almost touching. I just wanted him to hug me so I could find out for sure if his neck smelled like kimchee.

Trance had been sharing an apartment with a punk kid named Adam who'd been hot as shit when he was fifteen but now resembled Jesus. Not really my thing, although He has His following. He was gone that night. Trance took us down to the basement that we could smell from the front door, like the breath of a humid sun beating down after a warm thunderstorm. Golf-green plants bloomed in rows under bright humming tubes. We picked the maturest tendrils we could find, microwaved them, and smoked. Dewey dispensed three white paper squares and we dissolved them together, one under each tongue.

The three of us went out night-driving in the hail-scarred hatchback my parents bought cheap after my incident with the Jeep. We crept through the midnight mists and ghostly dew of Riverside Park. Dewey slid in the Pixies: *This ain't no holiday, but it always works out this way: Here I am with my hand.* I wondered whether men were in the bathrooms jerking off. A cop pulled us over. Trance hid the bong between his legs. I guessed I'd been swerving.

"Funny smell in there," the cop said. I didn't look at him but imagined he was wearing sunglasses in the dead of night. His flashers were pretty and flashy, like an under-twenty-one club. Dewey turned down the volume.

"Yeah, that's true," I agreed.

"Be careful," he said, giving a cursory wave with his flashlight. Trance was green in the backseat. The sky was pink, and Dewey was white like marble. I nodded my head vigorously, and he left. After the cop drove away everything was black and silent, like he'd turned off the TV.

When we got back to the flat Trance popped in a movie. He was talking a lot but it wasn't coherent or I couldn't hear. The only scene I remember was two white men fucking a small black girl with a Coke bottle. My boys were entranced. My stomach walls fended off a series of small explosions and I lurched into the bathroom. Shit bubbled from me like the Milwaukee River, sludgy and pungent. To add certain insult, a wall mirror was set across from the toilet. My face turned mauve in slow waves. I heard the locks and dams of my blood in my ears. I wanted to be more alive than this. I remembered what a college friend had told me about a fishing village in Alaska.

The next afternoon I stumbled out of bed and called the physics department, got dad, and told him I was going to the Southeast Passage, off the coast of British Columbia, to fish for halibut. I tried hard to sound like I knew what I was talking about. He was thinking of gravitational forces held by stars too far away to see by telescope and only known to exist by their absence, the wobble of light around them. He absent-mindedly agreed to advance me his frequent flyer ticket if I paid him market price on my return.

"You are legless," I wrote on a Post-it in my parents' room, "like the old dining room table propped against your bedroom wall, waiting to be moved out." Then I hung up and packed a sleeping bag, an army tent, and lots of T-shirts. A week later I found myself ducking out of a propeller plane onto a sunny runway twenty-six hundred miles away.

Ketchikan was the first stop. The rest of the passengers were going back to other islands, like Sitka, or getting off at the end of the line in Juneau, where the Tongass Narrows, which starts in Prince Rupert Sound, meets the mainland. The narrows was like an enormously wide river, and I was on the wrong side—Gravina Island, home of the jet strip. I hoisted my blue nylon body bag over my shoulder and across the gray planked causeway to Revillagigedo Island. White-capped mountains greeted me, the blue of the narrows, the red brick of the town.

It was a mile walk into Ketchikan. Ships cruised lazily under the bridge, mostly going northwest. A small red tugboat, heading home; an enormous white cruise ship docking into port, the lights of shops beside it; a long gray schooner, as flat and sleek as a kayak; two dark green trawlers with bodies like pick-up trucks, trailing fishnets like racy bridal trains. I watched them slide under the bridge and reemerge and wished I were on one, wrapping thick ropes around bolted brass knuckles. My plan was to pound the pavement and bullshit about fish with handsome, rugged skippers, real men of the sea. I'd never fished before in my life. The lakes at home were poisoned.

I stopped at the first restaurant on the other bank of the Tongass, ordered chili, stuffed a handful of Saltines into my pockets, and asked where the hostel was.

Since I'd come with what I had, about three hundred bucks, I didn't want to pay too long for lodging. In the men's dorm I soon learned from Randy, a scraggly, dog-tagged, stale-jeaned caricature of a Vietnam vet, that one of the local fisheries ran a free tent city. I asked whether he was going to work at the cannery. "I'd kill myself before I worked another factory job," he said and tried to sell me a gun he'd smuggled up from Spokane. Besides, he added with a sort of dismal scorn, the fishermen were on strike, and when the fishermen were striking there wasn't any work from Ketchikan to Kodiak. To shake off these doldrums, I wandered alone into the purpling twilight and made my way to the bars along the narrows.

In my wallet was a fake ID that had served as an amulet since I was sixteen. A friend had painted a posterboard with a red picture box and appropriate stencils; Trance then swiped several Wisconsin laminates from the Department of Motor Vehicles. He sold them for ten bucks each. The resulting product wasn't exactly professional, but it satisfied bartenders' requisite. Though I hadn't even started to shave, nobody back home questioned that I wasn't really a man in his mid-twenties named Peter Turner . . . drinking with a pack of other striplings with the same name. They were just happy for the business.

That first night in Alaska I wasn't even grilled about my birth date. I drank Mezcal and watched the Bulls run through the Lakers in Michael Jordan's first trip to the finals. There weren't any women in the bar or on the streets. The air was warm and musty and flushed and communal with sweat and testosterone and drunkenness. I called my parents from a pay phone outside in the clear twinkling night and told them I was okay and safe under a ceiling of the brightest stars I'd ever seen. It looked like someone had taken a broom to the sky, swept clean the cobwebs, and polished the suns.

When all color was gone from the sky, I returned to the hostel and found the men's bathroom. The shower was running so I brushed my teeth slowly, thoroughly. My heart was jumping out of its cage and I wanted to tear free the curtain and suck off whoever was behind it. I rinsed my mouth several times. Finally the shower stopped; there was humming and drying and the artificial sweet scent of shampoo. A compact young man with blue eyes stepped out, clad in white boxers.

"Hey!" he smiled. "Mike Luciano." His chest was smooth and wet and tight. "From San Diego."

"Mac. From Milwaukee."

We shook. "Hey, hey!" he said. "Here to fish?"

"Looking for anything, really. You staying in the dorm?"

"Just got in today."

"Me too," I replied.

Mike threw on a T-shirt and some sweats and we walked downstairs. Randy was back, and card-players were grumbling. Amid whispers and the smoky tang of men I fell asleep.

The next morning was warm and sunny, and I walked around two sets of docks, moving from pier to pier and admiring the vessels, then amusing a succession of skippers by asking whether I could be their cabin boy. Gulls whooped war cries and dove into the brink. Biplanes bounced two, three, four times onto the skim, then settled, bobbing softly on the waves. I picked up a map of the island at a tourist trap near the Love Boat dock and bought a cup of coffee from a chatty vendor named Greg. I walked to the Department of Motor Vehicles and uneventfully exchanged my fake ID for a real one. My friendly civil servant decided that I was most likely to live in Tent City. "That's where they all wind up," she said, handing me my new identity and address: 735 Stedman Avenue, Ketchikan 99950. On the walk back I pretended I was in the Witness Protection Program.

Downtown, where Tongass Avenue, the two-lane thruway, turns into a square, I saw Mike and Randy sitting with two other guys at a picnic table overlooking Ketchikan Creek. Mike introduced me to Wayne, a tall spindly black man from Fresno, and Sean, a short white kid from Washington State. I ordered a fried fish sandwich from an outdoor vendor and sidled up. Mike and Randy were just leaving, looking secretive. Wayne and Sean were about to scour the fish factories to learn about jobs in the offing. Thinking I might find out where I now officially lived, I agreed to join forces.

Sean had also fruitlessly pounded the docks, and Wayne hadn't had any luck with the fisheries nearby. The processing plants relied on locally caught fish, and the unified fishermen's strike for higher salmon prices had already delayed the start of the high season.

Paralleling the narrows, we walked three miles southeast down

Tongass Avenue, passing a small fish factory, a few churches, and two dozen bars. Wayne's strides were long and deliberate. Sean skipped to keep up, and I kept tripping over my shoelaces. We took a left, up the steep hillside at the base of Deer Mountain, and climbed a set of wooden stairs set into a cliff that led to a Tlingit totem-pole preserve. According to a wooden plaque, Civilian Conservation Corps campers created the monument in the 1930s. The older poles were thirty feet tall and their reds had faded to rust, deities eroded to indistinct faces, their colors soaked too deeply into the wood or bleached out by the sun. A dirt path from the poles wound through feathery Sitka pines into a rambling hillside park. Deer Mountain loomed snowcapped above this grassy plateau. We didn't talk that much, listening to the birds and the sounds our feet made walking through. Another path led back to the road. Wayne and I consulted the map I had picked up, which made a big deal out of tourist shops, grocery stores, and monuments, but wasn't much good for factories. Sean stuck out a thumb on the southeast side of Tongass.

An orange old-style Mack cab squeaked to a stop on the shoulder. "Well, what the hell are you waiting for?" the driver asked, craning his neck out the passenger side. I flinched involuntarily. "Hop in." He turned his whole head to say hello, but only one eye moved. Sean jumped up and in, nestling close to the driver and looking at us with a smirk. Wayne shrugged and joined them in the front seat, saving a sliver of vinyl for me by the door. Our ride revved up slowly and asked where we were headed.

"Stedman Avenue."

"Can't say I know any street names. Sure can't see them anyway. Only got one eye, and we don't know how well that one works! This sucker's from 1973, but don't you think she still looks good?"

"Does he mean the eye or the truck?" Sean asked.

"Rig looks great," Wayne offered.

"She's a steady one, sure as the salmon spawn. What's it near?" he asked.

I watched the plumes of black exhaust spouting from the pipe on the wheel well next to me. Wayne nudged me and I pulled out the map. "Oh. It's a half-mile south of Tatsuda's Supermarket, on the left."

"Well hell, only thing around there's Farwest Fisheries, and that's right here." We lurched to rickety entropy on the gravel shoulder, next to a large, open chain-link fence. The truck door wouldn't open. I had a quick anxiety attack about being drawn and quartered by a man with one glass eye.

"Open it from the outside," Wayne suggested, and in my haste I planted my forearm onto the sizzling vertical exhaust and screamed bloody murder. Sean politely said our thanks. There was an enormous, quiet factory to the right, stretching four hundred yards to the narrows. To the left was a large empty sandlot, its path to the sea broken by a few clapboard buildings and the mobile trailer in front of us designated as the office. Wayne and Sean walked up the trailer stairs as I tried to cover my seeping wound with my T-shirt. The saltwater wind kissed with a jellyfish sting.

Wayne came out and waved toward the sun-streaked sandlot. From the top of the steps, his arms glided higher than the trailer's roof. "That's it," he called to me, dubiously.

Sean burst from the trailer and jumped in the air to see the campsite. "Wow, look, our new home," he said, surveying the dust.

"Did they say they were hiring?" I asked.

"She said they were taking names. If we live here we'll have a better shot getting a job. But they're not planning on starting up until the strike's resolved. And that might be weeks away," Wayne said grimly. "I didn't save all winter to be the only black man on an island and be unemployed for a month."

That night I slipped a quarter into the latch of one of the hostel's more obscure doors: you put the coin between the spring-loaded catch and its holster, preventing the lock from engaging even though the door has shut. It didn't take long to find Mike and Wayne in a bar called the F'o'c's'le. I ordered a Mezcal and a paper towel of ice for my burn and joined them, showing off my great new ID. Proud and quickly drunk, I ambled between their stools and listened to them talk.

"What do you do?" asked Mike. "You're in Fresno, right?"

"I'm studying to be a physical therapist," Wayne answered. "Got another year to go. Thought I might make enough this summer to work only *part*-time when school starts."

"How old are you, boy?" asked a blasted old businessman with greased white hair and a lobster-bisque face who was sagging off the stool to Wayne's left.

"I'm thirty-three." I could sense Wayne prickle and shivered. "So you better watch who you're calling *boy*."

"I'm fifty-three," the businessman responded. "I knew I had some years on you. Be glad the Korean War ended before you came of age. You'd a been dead. You make a big enough fucking target." He gave a demoralized guffaw.

Wayne clenched his jaw, steadied his stool, and moved to stand.

"Whoa, big fella," said Mike, standing on his tiptoes and trying to wrap his arms around Wayne's shoulders. "Count to ten. Turn the other cheek. He'll get his."

"Ignore him, mate," said the bartender, materializing from the basement. Wayne stretched his long arms over his head, clasped the back of his own neck, sighed, and returned a big palm back to his pint.

"What's F'o'c's'le stand for?" I asked the barkeep.

"Short for forecastle," he replied. "On a ship."

The dapper drunk started to gesticulate, mouthing silently in the direction of the buoys hanging from the wood-beamed ceiling.

"What are you here for?" Mike asked me, rolling his eyes.

The ten-to-one male/female ratio didn't seem like the right thing to respond with. "Tuition," I lied. "Adventure. Not being at home!"

I rolled my ankle over something on the floor. Bending down, I saw a wallet: his? I left it alone. Mike followed my actions and his blue eyes gleamed. I ordered a shot of Patrón. The confrontational patron shut his eyes and started humming.

"All right, you've had enough for tonight," said the bartender grimly to the businessman. "Would you guys mind hauling Thing A to the curb?"

"Wait"—I started, but Mike stepped on my foot. "Nothing." Wayne and I took the businessman by each arm, hoisted him off the stool, and walked him to a jitney idling lazily outside. We rejoined Mike, who was busily examining the contents of the man's wallet.

"Your man left you a little present," Mike said to the bartender, leaving the leather on the wooden bar.

The bartender, an oversized load with graying jowls and hoods for eyes, cackled like a jackal finding something to scavenge. "Hey, hey, it's the first of the month! Guy owes me $200. How about I take that, and you guys split what's left. Leave me the carcass and don't swipe the cards." He gave us three rounds and we sneaked into the hostel past curfew, up a crisp hundred. I used to feel guilty when I found extra change in pay phones. Here with Wayne and Mike, I didn't feel any qualms. I thought being a guiltless thief might mean something about becoming a man.

For the next four days, I didn't see much of the guys or the hostel—Tuesday morning I went to a community job meeting and landed day labor, building the foundation of a house on Sunset Way, a mile southeast of Farwest. The wages were decent but the contractor told me straight up he just needed me for the week. That Friday night I got paid and walked to a riverside club with Mike and Wayne. We danced on the hardwood platform with some young local women—"Women! In Alaska?" Mike yelled happily over "Smoke on the Water." Seafarers flailed to the beat in a cloud of dry ice and a pink-and-blue lights-and-laser show. Wayne was shadowed by a troupe of groupies, and Mike was closing in on a thin Filipina with a dazzling smile and long shiny straight black hair. In all the excitement, we lost track of the time, had to sneak into the hostel through the door I had rigged, and promptly woke up the manager, who promised to kick us out in the morning.

We were evicted bright and early and dragged our bags down to the kiosks by the docks. Sean joined us; he could afford to leave his stuff behind. "Thank God I'm not old enough to drink," he laughed. Greg consoled us briefly, but his attention quickly turned to the long line of mainlanders in designer shades and fannypacks; the *Pacific Princess* had just docked. Wayne and Mike debated.

"I'm just thinking about going home," Wayne said. "Scrap this plan altogether."

"C'mon, stay with it," Mike cajoled. "I bet Farwest'll start hiring real soon. And think of the money you'll save without paying lodging."

"I don't know. That sandlot doesn't look too hospitable."

"Just give it a week. See," Mike pointed toward the bank, "salmon are already starting to spawn. Fishermen ain't gonna let that go to waste for long."

Wayne contemplated the seagulls circling the confluence of the narrows and the creek. One zoomed into the blue and hastened to the rocks with a flash of silver thrashing from its beak, attracting a flurry of white wings.

I left to order a breakfast corndog near the rainproof-hat shop. The weather had been perfect all week: sunny, warm, barely a cloud in the sky, Deer Mountain still snowcapped and the sea rich and calm. The cruise-boat tourists had dispersed into the town shops, and Greg ambled toward us, flipping his keys. Those moments without gravity—the plane taking off, the coaster reaching its summit, the still, silver gleam of six keys in the sun—gave me an expectancy of perfection, a feeling that the world was finally tilting into place again. There was no reason to linger. We gathered our things, stuffed ourselves into Greg's bug, and moved on.

Our Tent City shanty took three days to build and two weeks to really get right. We picked a plum spot between the outhouse and the factory; several other tents were already up, making creative use of cardboard and tarpaulin. Wayne, Mike, Sean, and I resolved to build the best one around. It was certainly the tallest; Wayne said he'd only stay if he could stand up without stooping. We started with three abandoned five-foot-square pallets from the fishery and made a foundation. Mike and I borrowed Greg's car and stole lumber and plywood from my construction site in the late afternoon. We held a series of evening stakeouts and copped blue plastic tarps covering small boats parked outside a few hillside homes.

We nailed the plywood to the pallets so we'd have a smooth floor and bolted two-by-fours as corner pillars. Then we ran a second set of pallets, vertically, along the edges of the foundation. We fashioned scrap wood nine feet in the air as an outline of a roof. Through sheer luck, the front pillars were higher than the rear ones, guaranteeing a run-off for rain. We used cardboard to patch up holes in the sides and covered the top with three overlapping blue tarps.

Susie, Mike's great new girlfriend from the disco, brought us big sheets of clear tarp, for our combination window-walls, and her grandfather's old Bunsen burner. Then she took us to the dump to find furniture. We lucked out and scored a pea-green love seat, a chair without legs, and a round wooden coffee table before two black bears spotted us. I grabbed a heavy box of books as we ran back to Susie's car. Inside my find was a dog-eared mix of *Penthouse* and Louis L'Amour. We sectioned the shanty into living and sleeping areas. Our house was so big we could set up our individual tents against the back wall. Sean, who didn't have a tent, elected to sleep on the couch.

We got on the list for Farwest, though the strike still wasn't resolved. "A week, or two, we'll be up and running," said the office woman. "You better be ready."

"We'll be ready," Wayne grumbled.

At the end of the first week in June, it started to rain. We were fast running out of money and decided we would share what food we had. I became adept at swiping cans of salmon from tourist traps when the cruise ships came in. Wayne and Sean went to the library most mornings, and Mike visited Susie. For most of June, we met each other for lunch at the Salvation Army between the docks and the fishery. We waited in a line a quarter of a mile long with striking seafarers, toothless Tlingits, and pregnant teenagers blowing cigarette smoke into their strollers. It was worth the wait for a free Styrofoam cup of broth and a bologna sandwich. I remember being late one day because it had taken me so long to jerk off to the straight porn in the tent, but Mike saved me a seat.

Using Greg as a liaison, we developed quite a business of showing tourists around in exchange for dinner. Retired married couples and single women were our best customers. We dragged them around and regurgitated tourist materials. Before Louis L'Amour, they'd been our only literature, and we'd pretty much memorized them. We dared our company to ask Ketchikan trivia. It was actually kind of fun.

How big is this place? *Why, it's the fifth-largest island in the Tongass Narrows, roughly the size of Connecticut. It has been inhabited by Tlingits, a group of Native Americans, for centuries. The island was found by Russian explorers in 1741 and, soon thereafter, named by Spanish adventurers.*

Where the heck are we? *We are about two hundred miles south of Juneau, at the beginning of the Tongass National Forest. In fact,*

Ketchikan is covered with Sitka pine trees and cedars. Due to the constant bog in any region that averages 155 inches of rain a year, the forests are lined with a soft tussocky muskeg that lightens footfalls.

What is that big mountain over there? *Well, first let's say that this island is part of an archipelago of oceanic mountains, further carved from the coastline by ancient glaciers. That is Deer Mountain, with its Hershey's kiss summit, which dominates the western shore, where Ketchikan sits.*

Did you say there were Indians here? *Yes. Tlingits hunted, trapped, and fished these lands, mostly undisturbed by other settlers until the late 1800s. The town was named after a Tlingit named Kitschk, who settled along the creek infused by the narrows. Kitcxan refers to "Kitschk's creek," which was Anglicized into Ketchikan during the heady days of the Alaskan Gold Rush at the turn of the last century. Though no gold was ever found in the hills of Revillagigedo, the port city of Ketchikan was recognized by frontier Americans for its abundance of salmon, which return here, in their seventh summers, to spawn and die in the gravelly riverbeds of their conception.*

Why are you guys here anyway? *Ketchikan is sometimes called "Alaska's First City." It's the first port of call for northbound ships. But it is better known as the Salmon Capital of the World. Ketchikan's economy thrives on seasonal workers who fill the ships and the canneries during the summer. We're seasonal workers and we're hungry and homeless and unemployed because the fishermen are striking. If you feed us cheeseburgers we'll show you where to get the best deals on T-shirts.*

Sean and Mike always made the pitch; Mike liked to do it and Sean didn't, but Sean had a better success rate. More than one motherly soul fell in love with him.

In the next three weeks before we started working, there were three sunny days. The first day, not knowing any better, we went hiking in lichen-bottomed Misty Fjords Park. The ground was a soft and gentle living thing. Spruce trees bathed in a thicket of permafog. ("Don't get me wrong now, it's as pretty as a teenage girl sleeping," cracked Mike. "But no sun for a week, and we go to the rain forest?") The second sunny day, in mid-June, found us sunbathing on the rocks near the water. Mike and Wayne walked slowly along the bank, giving a scrapped fishing rod a touch-up job and a try. Greg came by to visit and sat with me while I watched Sean scamper around without a shirt, stub his toe, yell.

"What are you thinking about?" Greg asked me. The thick, salty breeze flipped up flaxen hair that was probably white thirty years ago, when he was a boy. Away from the Starbucks stand, Greg looked frail and jumpy, like a pixie. He said he'd come up from Seattle; Starbucks wanted to know whether they should invest in a Ketchikan franchise, and they were paying for Greg's rental car and apartment.

"How did you meet Mike?" I asked him.

"He ordered a coffee. And he seemed normal. Sort of." Greg smiled. "But what are you *really* thinking about?"

Sean. I stalled. "How nice a day it is? There are more ships today. Maybe that's a good sign." We were silent for a minute. "You know how salmon come back to spawn in the waters of their birth and all that?" Greg nodded. "They come back during their seventh summer and fertilize the creeks and then they die. Their olfactory glands lead them back home—their underwater sense of smell tells them where to spawn. But what nobody seems to get," I finished, "is how they know when it's *time*."

"You look sad," he said gently and lit a cigarette.

"Maybe. Maybe I've just been reading too many brochures. Can I have one?"

"Sure."

We smoked and watched Sean leap, bare his teeth in a grin, stretch thin arms to the sun.

"What are you thinking about?" I asked him.

"Kind of homesick," he said. "I miss my girlfriend, Val. And my brothers. I have two brothers, you know."

"Younger or older?"

"They're younger. I'm thirty-three. Jeremy's twenty-four and Zack's twenty-six."

"Do they live in Seattle?" I asked.

"Yeah. And do you know the funny thing? They're both gay." Greg's eyes danced in the sun. "Do you think that's one of those things that runs in the family?"

"I really don't know!"

"You don't have a problem with gay people, do you Mac?"

I couldn't talk, so shook my head, gazed at Sean. A loon bobbed gently on the waves. We watched the castaway in khaki shorts climb carefully toward us.

"Sean's great, isn't he?" Greg asked softly.

"Yeah," I said. "He really, really is. But all you guys are."

Late afternoon found us in a rock quarry down the bank. We built a fire with tinder sticks and pine cones, baked the cod Mike and Wayne had caught on thin ledges of shale resting over the pit.

The next wave of rain came that night, and it was taking its toll. Our tent was always leaking in one place or another; the best we could hope for was a slow drip. We were all unemployed—it wasn't near dry enough to paint Susie's grandpa's house—and broke. Wayne's natural tendency toward reflection had turned into moodiness and closely checked despair. Sean was even more withdrawn than usual. When he'd talk, he'd speak darkly of his mother and the residential lock-in where he'd spent the six months after she committed suicide.

Only Mike was really happy, if only for Susie and Louis L'Amour. A former Sonics girl, Susie was a homebody at heart. She brought us all to an enormous family banquet one night with bottomless silver tankards of white rice and vast gold vats of crispy *limpias*. We were all so hungry then. I supplemented Salvation Army fare by helping myself to the Tatsuda salad bar and eating it on their toilets so I wouldn't have to pay.

One night soon after the family buffet, Susie invited Mike, Wayne, Greg, and me to a house party.

"Can we bring Sean?" I asked. He was in the bathhouse, doing laundry.

"Probably. I just heard about it. I don't really know who's having it."

"Let's give it a shot," said Mike. "Can you drive us there?"

Everyone agreed to go, and we scooped up Sean on the way out; he and I rode with Greg, while Susie took Wayne and Mike. The party was in an oversized trailer out in the Tongass Forest. There was a small cover charge and a tangle of young people. Greg came up to me with a couple of beers and I took one gratefully.

"What happened to Sean?" I asked him.

"I don't know." Greg crowed. "He was right behind me. Want to look for him?"

"Yes!" I said. I must have been pretty enthusiastic, because Greg looked at me hard for a second, then shrugged.

"Okay, you lead." We walked through the four rooms, catching Wayne's deliberate slouch to avoid hitting the ceiling. Mike and Susie had found a quiet corner in the living room. Sean was nowhere to be seen.

We checked outside. Sure enough, Sean was on the wooden stairs by the front stoop, looking forlornly at the darkening pine forest. "Hey dude," I said gently. "Why aren't you inside?"

Sean ignored me, turned slowly to Greg. "How long are you staying?" he asked. "They won't let me in. They asked me how old I was."

"How old are you?" Greg asked.

"Nineteen."

"And you told them that?" I asked, incredulous both that the owners would bother and that Sean would tell them the truth.

"It doesn't matter to me," he said. "I told them I wouldn't drink. No one here believes that."

"Since Ketchikan is 90 percent alcoholics . . ." Greg trailed off. "Maybe I can talk to them." He walked back up the front steps.

"I wouldn't drink if they let me in," Sean told me stubbornly.

"Do you want my beer? But just walk around to the side so they won't see you."

Sean looked puzzled, but I held my plastic cup out and he took it. Then I left to go in. I couldn't look at him anymore without feeling gay. But every twenty minutes I'd go back out and give him a refill.

On the last sunny day in June, Mike and I decided to climb Deer Mountain. I lifted a bottle of red wine from Tatsuda's, hiding it in my jeans leg, and we set out with Sean and Wayne, who'd found an old basketball somewhere. We played a fast game of horse on a cracked asphalt court in the park. Wayne nailed every shot he took, it didn't matter from where. The ball didn't even hit the rim.

"Holy fish fry," said Sean, who couldn't hit the narrows from the bank. "You should join the NBA."

"Too old," said Wayne, swishing another. "I tried. Declared myself for the draft back in '79. Never got picked." Mike shagged his ball, threw it back. "It really burned me to see guys I played with—guys I knew I could beat—get selected. Guess if I'd gone to UCLA instead of UC-Riverside," he continued, dunking effortlessly. "But that's the way it goes."

Mike, Sean, and I continued up the mountain while Wayne loped back to camp to write letters. The path took us through a swath of pine, then a pasture of stumps shorn by logging. We traversed over a lateral moraine of rubble and weeds. Finally we hit snow and more trees and stashed our Merlot in a tangle of roots. After two hours, we made it above the tree line and onto a snowy plateau.

"Time for target practice!" Mike exulted. He pulled out an old Magnum. "Anyone want to join me?"

"When did you get that?" I asked him.

"Your man Randy sold it to me. At the hostel." Mike swiveled the gun's chamber, then retrieved, from the pocket of his jeans, a small package of ammunition. He opened it and slid bullets into slots. "Snub nose," he explained. "Go right through the outer layers and explode inside."

"What are we shooting at?" Sean asked.

"Good question. I got a T-shirt underneath my sweats."

Mike pulled off his sweatshirt and then a sleeveless T. He set it on a snowbank and took us fifty feet away, then pulled the safety. "Only brought one round," he said. "Two shots for each of us. Stand back." He held the gun in two hands, straightened his arms, sighted down the barrel, and fired. A tremendous crack rang through the clearing. "Bullseye!" he yelled. "Shit. Sucker's got a kick. One more." Another shot rang through the thin clear air. "Think I missed that time." Mike handed the gun to Sean and shook out his right hand. Sean took a lot of time preparing and took two shots that looked like they sailed wide. My turn came. I'd never held a revolver before and was surprised by its weight. It took two hands to hold it steady. I eyed Mike's shirt between the metal flanges on the barrel and flicked the trigger. The recoil sent my arms reeling upwards, and my ears wouldn't stop ringing.

"Fuck," said Sean, massaging his slight wrists. "That hurts like hell."

"Good aim, Mac. I think you got it. Take the last one."

I fired again, danced backwards, and handed back the Mag, wishing I could hear anything but echoing reports.

"I think I'm fucking deaf," Sean said. We went to inspect Mike's shirt. There were four small jagged holes, two on each side, like an extra pair of nipples. The white-chocolate Hershey's kiss looked steep, pathless, and daunting, and it was already getting late. We decided to descend. Eventually we found our wine and toasted Alaska. Then Mike toasted Susie.

"Susie can shoot," Mike said. "To girls who can shoot." Sean gulped in laughter.

"You mean, a gun?" I asked.

"No, dude. When she has an orgasm, she shoots! Not across the room or anything, but I've seen her juice fly." He took the bottle from Sean. "Susie's great, but if I had my way, I'd have a harem. I'd have six fourteen-year-old girls at my beck and call." Mike tipped the bottle of snow-cold Merlot into his happy wet mouth.

"I'll drink to that," yelled Sean. "To fourteen-year-old girls." His laugh caromed gaily off the cliffs.

"To fourteen-year-old baby girls!" Mike yelled back. He passed me the bottle. "Toast?"

To what? To fourteen-year-old boys? To Sean? "To making our way back home before dark," I said.

"Hear, hear!" said Mike, who promptly got us off the path and lost. We wandered in the dusky pines for an hour, steadily heading downhill. West was easy to judge until the sun went down. We reached an overhang, pondered, and leaped off, falling ten feet and rolling another fifty down the hillside. Incredibly, the path rose up to meet us. We got back to find Susie and Wayne listening to Roxy Music on an old battery-operated boombox her mom had donated to us for the summer. We spent the rest of the night with Mike's Swiss Army knife, scraping resin from the chambers of my pipe and smoking it by candlelight.

"I only like female vocalists," Sean quietly announced, around midnight. He snuggled halfway into his sleeping bag and sat crosswise on the love seat, his hands behind his head, against an armrest. I was in the chair without legs. Mike and Sue were in Mike's tent, in a rear corner, and Wayne was stretched out on the floor, staring at the dark tarp roof. "Ever since she died."

"Do they remind you of her?" I asked him. Sean was silent for a time. I blew out the tea lights on the old stained barrel. I thought he might be crying.

"I don't know," he whispered. Then, more loudly: "Maybe I just like female vocalists, okay?" His voice cracked, but maybe it was just a puberty holdover. He was silent again and then whispered. "Maybe it's not her I want to be reminded of. She was crazy and depressed so much. She was mentally ill ever since I can remember. So sometimes I think, 'Well, maybe I never really had a mother.'"

Susie or Mike rustled in the corner. Wayne's eyes were closed, his long body stretching down the floor to the door. I didn't know what to say.

"But there were times when she could take care of me," Sean continued in his grave, careful hush. "More when I was younger. So when I listen to female vocalists maybe that's what it seems like. Like they're taking care of me. And they are taking care of me. With their voices. Or maybe I just want to fuck them," Sean giggled. "Can you turn off the tape? I'm going to sleep."

I punched the switch, then climbed over Wayne and through the plastic seams. The moon was high and full and I followed it as far as the stony bank. I stood on a tall boulder and peed a platinum rainbow into the sea. I took off all my clothes and threw them on the rocks, then slipped quietly into the narrows. The cold sleek water swirled over me like a dark cape. I wanted to know why she did it. I had an idea until my teeth started chattering and I had to get out. Back in my shorts on the shore, I felt stupid and lonely and homesick, like a cartoon of a marooned sailor washed ashore on a desert island. But the next morning, when Sean unzipped his sleeping bag, a fresh rush of hope surged through me. His favorite boxers were wide-legged, brown paisley, torn cleanly in two places along the side seam. They were enough to get me out of my tent every day.

Farwest's smokestacks were in fact steaming that morning, a Sunday, as part of a dry run. We started work on the last Tuesday in June. Mike, Wayne, and I were assigned "filler" jobs midway down line two. We were given black rubber boots and plastic yellow jackets and pants: slime suits. Our task was to toss salmon parts onto pronged ledges that revolved into the chopper. Farther down the machine, the torn flesh was tamped into tuna-fish-size cans, the likes of which I'd lifted so many times downtown, that descended by conveyor from the can loft. Sean worked down the line on "cutter" duty, snipping the more prominent skeletal remains from the soon-to-be-sealed products. By the time they got to us, the fish had been frozen, beheaded, flayed, and eviscerated; behind us, a tremendous tank collected the fish from the eviscerators ("gutters"). Sliding the tank's door two inches or so would guarantee a steady influx of oily pink meat; opening it four inches or more sent fish flying all over the floor. Therefore, one rear filler gauged the vertically sliding door and set fish in rows; the two frontliners flipped these fish two-by-two on the rotating ledge, trying to keep up with the whirling prongs.

From the start we worked six days a week, fourteen hours a day. There's nothing to describe but several million cold slick pink salmon cuts wiggling their way through my hands, squirting their blood into my eyes. The joints in my fingers were achy and numb every morning and rarely thawed out before lunchtime. We talked and sang songs but I can only remember how much I had to pee and the long lines for the bathroom and the difficulty of taking down my yellow pants with frozen fingers. They gave us fifteen-minute breaks every three hours and a half-hour break for lunch. The only time we really got to relax was when someone's arm went through the works and they'd have to close down for an hour. We looked forward, perversely, to these surprise respites. They reminded me of snow days. Wayne's back was killing him from stooping to the steel tray where we lined up the fish, but he kept on. I'd watch Sean's netted head bob with the girls down the line and see his scissors flash.

To make up for the lost income of the June strike, Sean and I joined the cleanup crew for four hours each night. We'd hose down the walls and floors and then I'd clean my machine. I got to know every piece of the chopper: the steady prongs, the whirling set of circular razors underneath, the metal rails regulating the cans. A migrant Filipino mechanic who spoke no English taught me how to send the works forward and backward and then left me alone. One evening, about three weeks into my sleep deprivation (by this time, I was averaging twenty hours of work a day), a white girl from Quality Control asked me to try a new cleaner. She said it would be better than using just water. I wondered what difference it made but gave in. I set the machine on three-quarters speed and sprayed the foam on the prongs.

"Is it cleaner?" she asked excitedly, standing back so as not to get sprayed. She was wearing crimson lipstick, a gelled pageboy cut, a clean gray set of cotton overalls, and canvas sneakers, not exactly dressed for the weather in here.

"How should I know?" I asked. I hosed the prongs. "Should I feel it to see if it squeaks?"

"I guess," she said, flicking her hand to show her indifference. But her face was impatient and expectant, like some major revelation was coming if I would just get on with things.

I felt a prong quickly with my fingers but it slid under me, as oily as ever. I looked back at her and shrugged. "Who knows," I said. "It's always slippery as hell." Just then, I felt a claw pull my left hand. As if in slow motion, I looked back down and told my brain to remove my hand, but it was too late: the machine had taken it. My wrist slammed against a metal bar and I was sure I was about to join the Amputee of the Month Club. Then with tremendous, unrelenting force, my wrist bone suddenly caught between a prong and bar, just before the circling knives. I knew if my wrist broke I was fucked. My arm would get sucked right through.

"Fuck!" I yelled. "I'm in the fucking machine!" Quality Control girl's face turned as gray as her uniform, and she backed away. I decided I better be really polite and calm, otherwise she'd run off. "Hey," I said. "Listen. Please. Could you please *turn the fucking machine off*?" Her eyes filled with tears and she put her hands over her gaping maw. Her backwards pace quickened. "I can show you how," I yelled through my teeth. The pain was intense and I shut my eyes against it. "It's really easy, you just press that button near . . . ." When I opened my lids she was running away to the heart of the factory. "Quality Control, my ass."

She returned with a mechanic who promptly hit the power button. The whirring razor wheels slowly ceased hissing. Great news, but I was still caught in the vise.

"Now what the fuck do I do?" he asked her. She was blank as a chalkboard on the last day of school.

"There's a crank," I said. "If you turn it I can get my fucking hand out."

He jumped at the sound of my voice, having already given me up as another Farwest casualty. In his surprise, he turned the manual wheel forward, putting even more pressure on my ulna.

"You're turning it the wrong way!" I screamed. "Turn it the *other* fucking way!" He did; the prong released, and I lifted my wrist out of line two. Looking down, I stared at the dime-sized hole all the way to the bone. With my left wrist crooked into my right arm, I wandered back to find Sean. He was walking toward me.

"I heard," he said.

He looked at my eyes, not my wrist.

"Look, Sean, you can see the bone."

I took a deep breath and held my deformity away from me, as if giving him a present offhandedly, trying hard not to show my affection. It was the only time all summer he looked at me like he cared, but maybe he just felt faint.

"I think we should call an ambulance," he said, and sat with me until it came. My heart swelled up with my hand. The paramedics gave me oxygen and told me I was in shock.

A night doctor stitched me up and gave me ibuprofen, but it only dulled the pain. I got back at five in the morning. Everybody else was asleep. It had started to pour when I was getting stitched up, and rain smacked our shanty like bullets. As I tried to get comfortable, the tarp above my tent collapsed under water pressure; then my tent collapsed onto me. Sean gave me the couch and slept on the floor. "When it rains it pours," he slurred quietly. Two hours later I reported for work. They sent me to the can loft, where I was supposed to watch a conveyor belt for dented empty cans. I liked it up there. It was hypnotic and warm and the sun bathed the red wooden floor in dusty morning light. During shutdowns we'd sleep like cats in the sunshafts. I had a new game of waving at people using only my left hand, which was three times its normal size.

At lunch I sprinted to the park on Deer Mountain's lowlands and called my parents from a pay phone. I used their calling card; I knew they were at my grandparents' house in Maine. My grandmother answered and said they were out.

"How are you?" she asked. I hoped she wasn't mad I hadn't come.

"Well, I just got my hand caught in a machine and my house fell on me last night, but otherwise things are great!" Sarcasm was lost on my grandmother, though, who was, anyway, a bit deaf. There was a long silence. "It smells like Maine here," I said.

"That certainly does sound exciting, dear. But your parents are out for the afternoon. I don't want you to waste your nickel. I'll tell them to call you back later." Before I could remind her that I was nowhere I could be reached, she hung up. I felt hopeless and sure that things couldn't get any worse, until I read the *Ketchikan Daily News* after my afternoon shift and learned that a gay serial killer in Milwaukee had been caught with boys' genitals preserved in his fridge in gefilte fish jars. He'd been picking guys up at bars. I'm not saying the article cheered me up. But it gave me perspective. Who knows what could have happened if I'd stayed home that summer? I would have gone home with anyone and taken anything. I took some ibuprofen and a nap.

Greg came around and took pity on me, offering to put me up in his place that Saturday night. I happily agreed. He bought two tabs of acid from a moon-faced kid named Jeremy, who'd burned his leg badly on Farwest's incinerator. Greg picked me up at Tent City that Saturday morning and we drove to a surpassingly beautiful state park on the tip of Revillagigedo, flanked by the narrows and the Pacific. We climbed and smoked and talked and I don't remember a thing besides the peace of high altitude and moss and sea and company and him watching me piss over a cliff.

"I'm sorry," he said. "I didn't mean to stare."

"I really don't care. We're on acid, who cares what you do?"

Greg showed me his dream journal later that night and talked about mysticism until I couldn't take it anymore and flicked on ESPN (a TV and *cable*! I was in heaven). In the morning, I took a hot shower and came out in the tight but clean pair of underwear Greg had given me. He smiled approvingly.

"They fit you better than Sean," he said. "He's been up here a couple of nights, too. Beats that ripped-up pair of boxers he's been wearing. Sean crawled out of his blankets in some sorry-looking torn-up rags." Unsure how to take this, I quickly dressed in yesterday's clothes and said I was ready to go. We drove back to Tent City and I brought my mildewing bag to the laundry building.

Tent City's bathhouse had a dozen coin-operated washers and dryers in the front and long benches great for whiling away the drizzles with Hopalong Cassidy or *Mustang Man.* Since there were no toilets (that's what outhouses are for), sinks took up the middle portion; showers were in the back, sectioned off by gender. There was a rear entrance, and fishermen selling to the factory would sometimes make use of the bathhouse. Once in June, when trying to find an open shower, I'd walked in on two cabin boys, too beautiful to ever remember—a blonde, a brunette, both slim, smooth, and sleek, gleaming in modular cells. On this Sunday morning in early August, I started a long-overdue load and read Ketchikan summaries, scrawled in magic marker by bored launderers on flip-chart pages taped to the cinderblock walls. Each page started with the phrase "Ketchikan is . . ."

Ketchikan is . . . Alaska's first city.
Ketchikan is . . . beached on Guam by super typhoon Paka.
Ketchikan is . . . built on a trestle over a cliff.
Ketchikan is . . . a breeze.

A Tlingit woman, similarly occupied, struck up a conversation with me. She asked if I wanted to get high and took me to her one-woman tent, closer to the narrows. We smoked from a crushed soda can. She told me she was a lesbian.

"That's why I don't mind stripping," she said. "There's no tension for me. See, I strip down at the Marine bar in the off-season. You should come by in September."

I thanked her and said I probably wouldn't be around anymore. We stumbled back to the laundry. Sean entered just ahead of us, carrying his toiletries and a towel. I moved my clothes to the dryers and checked my face in the mirror, wondering when it was ever going to be time to shave again. I spied Sean's small bag near a sink and had an idea. I slunk to the men's side and called out.

"Sean?" There was no answer. "Yo, Sean, dude."

"What?" he yelled, two cells down. "I'm in the shower."

33

"Yeah, I figured."

Even as I heard the sirens sounding off in my head I walked to him because I knew this was going to be my only chance. Naked, his hair streamed back, dripping, his belly shimmering in rivulets and tributaries and his pubic hair curled over a penis that still seemed to be unfurling, free at last from those exasperating boxers.

"What?" he asked, squinting in the spray. I looked down.

"Just can—can I borrow your razor? I think I want to shave."

"Yeah, go ahead. It's in my bag at one of the sinks. You can just leave it there."

"Okay." I stared at the long brown hairs on his thighs, his small flat ass, committing his body to memory.

"Can you leave me alone? I'm trying to take a shower."

"Oh. Yeah. Sorry."

I tore myself away and down to the dryers, to the next open flip-chart page.

Ketchikan is . . . paying a price for fouling the environment.

Ketchikan is . . . the salmon capital of the world.

Ketchikan is . . . never more than ten blocks wide.

Ketchikan is . . . rain.

Ketchikan is . . . real Alaska.

"Ketchikan is . . . so amazing," I scribbled, but I think I meant Sean. I ran his sharp steel over my cheeks, mingled his dead cells with mine.

The season was coming to a close. Sean moved to a shanty by the shore that someone had forsaken. One day when he was sick with the flu, I visited him and asked whether he wanted a massage. He refused. "It's kind of like how I am with female vocalists," he joked weakly, coughing sharply. He regained his breath and rasped, "I just don't like guys to massage me." He only whispered because he couldn't breathe. He was the first of us to leave. Susie let me borrow her pick-up to drive him to the ferry headed for Bellingham. When he was all packed and saying goodbye to the crew, I rifled through his duffel and took a last reminder.

Sean, from the lock-in in Washington, his dark nipples, torn boxers, his dead mother, our hug at the ferry. Sean: I took your favorite shirt. It was tie-dyed and bears danced through rainbows. It was too

34

small for me but I thought I deserved it. The pits were the only part that smelled like him and not fish juice. They say you can't take it with you but I hoard these memories like bread in lean winters. I collect them like squirrels stow acorns. I fold them like T-shirts in a bureau and pull them out when I need their small comforts.

I left two weeks later with a cashier's check for four thousand bucks. Wayne and Mike were staying on until September, when the fishery closed for the off-season. Greg was leaving in October; he drove me back to Gravina, and we promised to keep in touch but never did. (Later I did hear from Susie and Mike; they had moved in together in San Diego and were talking about marriage.) I slept the whole way back to Wisconsin. It was nice to be back at home for a bit, even though I understood how much I'd outgrown it. I gave my dad $350.00 for plane fare.

Trance and I met at the beach on the shores of Lake Michigan on the last day of summer. It smelled like the factory: rotting fish guts. The lifeguards were taking down their high chairs and the waves crested with a yellow chemical foam. We waded in a ways together in the cold contaminated lake.

"So you went to freaking Alaska." Trance flipped an old blue frisbee.

"The last frontier," I agreed.

"The last frontier," he repeated. "Bet that put some hair on your chest."

I turned toward him so he could see. "Look." I pointed to the three brown hairs curling out of my sternum.

Trance looked uncomfortable. "I didn't mean for real," he said. "Fuck, man. I'm never gonna get any."

I looked at his burnished chest, at his burgeoning beer belly, and into the hot afternoon haze. "Yeah, well. You're Korean."

Tran flicked the frisbee over my head. I grasped for it but caught only air. It soared over the water and landed softly in a school of poisoned alewives washed ashore.

When Will You Be Here Again?

Michael Lowenthal

In Edinburgh last summer, I attended a dance party called Joy at a club called Ego, where for five pounds you could buy a pill to boost both. It was fun enough, but the music and the men and their sweaty machinations were virtually the same as I can find at home in Boston.

The next day I boarded a bus to Perth, where I switched to another for Inverness, where I switched again for the port of Ullapool, where, after a workday's worth of travel, I began the three-hour ferry trip to the Isle of Lewis. The northernmost of the Outer Hebrides, Lewis is a bastion of cultural and religious traditionalism. Just that week, the island's conservatism had proven newsworthy: No transportation to Lewis had ever been available on the Sabbath; when Loganair announced plans for Sunday flights, the Lord's Day Observance Society vigorously protested. (They had balked, too, seven years ago, when swing sets in the island's capital were unchained so that children could play on Sundays.)

Given my sexuality, perhaps I should have worried about traveling to such a place, but in fact I found myself, when the boat's horn blasted, thrilled to be going where gayness would be unspeakable. Not that I believe it should be, nor would I choose to live in such a place, but as much as I want every corner of the earth to be welcoming, sometimes I crave a break from sexual orientation. In the ferry's cafeteria I ordered a plate of haddock, then sat listening to the men around me bantering in Gaelic, with its otherworldly, abracadabric lilt.

In the morning I set out hitchhiking. I headed toward the ancient stone circle of Callanish and a middle-of-nowhere restaurant I'd been told was worth the trek, but distance itself was my true destination. My first ride came from an off-duty "estate watcher," whose job entails hiking rugged coastline, eyes peeled for salmon poachers. We stopped for coffee at a co-worker's home, where we spoke of unpredictable island weather and local bird-hunting rituals. I told them I'm American, and a writer, and that was plenty; our affection was mutual, immediate.

Next I tagged along with a carpenter who drove me considerably out of his way so that I wouldn't have to walk to a hard-to-find museum. My subsequent ride, too, took me more than two miles from his intended route because he wanted to make sure I saw Dalmore, "the prettiest beach on Lewis." When we shook hands, after twenty minutes of intense conversation, I felt we knew some essential truths about each other.

Or did we? Neither my sexual orientation nor his had come up. All the strangers I'd met on Lewis were unfailingly generous—but would they have been so kind if they knew that I'm gay?

I wasn't lying, I told myself, or pretending to be straight. I simply hadn't mentioned my gayness, and in doing so presented a self that, far from being false, seemed more fully authentic than the version of me that many people meet at home, where sexuality often trumps all other traits.

From the beach at Dalmore I hiked two miles along dramatic cliff tops, avoiding boggy patches and sheep carcasses, to the hamlet of Carloway, population 493. I had to thumb it only a minute before a car stopped and its driver, a bald man with a friendly, scrubbed-potato face, waved me in.

"Headed to Callanish, are you?" he asked in rock-a-bye accent.

I told him I was, and that I was also looking for a restaurant I'd heard about, where the chef served wild scallops that her husband harvested.

"Tigh Mealros," he said. "Lovely food, but a touch dear."

"Really? How much?"

He pondered as we paused to let two ewes cross the road. "Twenty-five pounds at least, I'd say."

I explained that that was well out of my budget.

"Ach, well," he said, "there's plenty to see for free," and proceeded to take me on a detour to view a two-thousand-year-old battlement, then past a home where, through the open garage door, we could see a man weaving Harris tweed. The air was peppery with peat smoke.

After showing me the Callanish standing stones—a mystery as old as the Egyptian pyramids—my new friend insisted on driving me to the restaurant. "After all," he said, "when will you be here again?" He spoke with a salty, timeworn authority that reminded me of why I'd made the trip: to get far from my ghettoized life.

Just downhill from the ancient site, he nodded toward a bungalow as we passed—one of perhaps twenty homes that compose the village of Callanish. "That bed and breakfast?" he said. "Run by two men." He raised his eyebrows till his forehead jammed with lines. "There's some on the island say they're gay."

The word was such a shock that I barely recognized it. It might have been a riddle told in Gaelic.

"Terrible, isn't it?" he went on.

No, it wasn't terrible. But I didn't respond; I wanted to know his uncensored thoughts. It had been years since I'd heard how people speak when they think nobody gay is present.

"Well," he said, with a quick glance into the rearview, "I suppose there are some who think that kind of thing's all right. People do it for all sorts of reasons."

Still, I said nothing. I concentrated on the roadside piles of peat.

"Like you, maybe. A hitchhiker on a budget?"

We'd arrived at the restaurant, which I saw was just a private home at the end of a short drive. My ride pulled to the road's shoulder, hazards flashing.

"If I were to give you twenty-five pounds," he whispered, "would you do it?"

At first I wasn't sure if this was idle talk, or an offer. His trembling hand on the gearshift made me certain. I trembled, too; I'd never had sex for money. It would make a great tale to share with all my friends back home. It would pay for my wild-scallop dinner.

He must have interpreted my pause as bargaining. "Thirty pounds, then?"

"No," I said. "I don't think so. Not today." I thanked him for the ride and got out.

As the man sped away, I tried to understand why I'd acted as I did. I wasn't interested in having sex with him—for money or otherwise—but why at least hadn't I told him that I'm gay? I imagined his life in this remote, religious outpost, a life of bleak loneliness and lies. I should have let him know he'd met a kindred spirit.

But maybe he hadn't. Does being gay give me an automatic bond with every sex-hungry stranger? With every sweaty shirtless man in a midnight club? It's more complicated than you think, I might have told him. What you're looking for is what I came here to escape.

Then, ashamed, I knew the truth wasn't all that complicated: It's a luxury to have acceptance to run away from.

I approached the restaurant, only to learn from the cook/owner that she wasn't offering dinner that night. I decided to backtrack the mile or so to the stone circle. I would stand at the center of the ancient monoliths and feel the chastening holy charge of such sites: dwarfing and simultaneously magnifying.

As I turned up the narrow lane to Callanish, I thought guiltily of the man who'd made the pass at me. How desperate he must have been to concoct the story of a gay B&B on this strict, Sabbatarian island—a rash ruse to broach a terrifying subject. I'd employed similar tricks myself as a closeted teenager.

Just then I happened to notice, on a clumsily lettered sign next to a rickety mailbox, a dusty three-by-five decal of a rainbow flag. In Boston's South End, I've mocked gay people for putting stock in similar emblems: community-by-lowest-common-denominator. But this small sticker on a wind-swept shore of Scotland filled me instantly with pride and tribal yearning. Could there really be gay men here?

I marched up to the porch, where a squint-eyed man asked, from around the cigar he was roughly smoking, if there was something he could help me with.

"I don't want to make any assumptions," I said, "but I saw your rainbow-flag sticker, and I've got a story I think you'd find interesting."

Now another man joined him at the door: barefoot, with a gone-to-seed beard and a jolly paunch.

I told them what had happened, and immediately they invited me inside. *What did he look like?* they asked. *What color was his car?* Their eyes gleamed in a way I've witnessed among men in similar conversations the world over: part titillation, part urgent hopefulness. But they honored my decision to keep the man's description vague. "Right, probably safer," said David, the squinty man. "We were just keen to find out, because, as I'm sure you know, there *are* no gays on Lewis." He and the other man laughed heartily.

They were lovers, David explained, and had moved here together after years on an even tinier, remoter island. They hadn't announced their gayness, but they surely hadn't hidden it. They lived quietly among their neighbors, cutting peat and keeping warm like all the rest.

When I told them I'm American, Tom, the barefoot one, said that just that afternoon he'd been watching the American *Queer as Folk,* which they received via satellite on the Sky Channel. "The soundtrack's brilliant," he said. "But altogether I like the British version better."

He poured me a cup of tea and we sat together for nearly an hour, discussing the merits of both shows. We compared notes on clubbing in Glasgow and New York. At times I could hardly understand their porridge-thick accents, but I recognized a familiar sense of humor: a sidewise glance that spots hypocrisy head-on. And, too, there was the foursquare dignity of those who've been called queer and learned to gain strength from it.

Had I fooled myself into thinking there are places beyond gayness? That sexuality is something someone might outrun?

A phone call came from the next-door neighbor, one of whose rams had gotten his horns stuck in a fence. As David pulled on his boots, preparing to lend a hand, I thanked the men and left them to their work. My lodgings were a thirty-mile hitch clear across the island, but I wasn't worried about finding my way back.

 Girona

Colm Tóibín

Girona is two hours' journey north of Barcelona on a slow train. Between the station and the river Onyar the town is dull and grey, a market town built in bits and pieces in the various styles of the last hundred and fifty years. Solid, commercial, a junction for roads that lead elsewhere: the motorway to Barcelona, the motorway to France, the road to the coast.

It is only when you reach the river that you realize that you have arrived in a strange medieval city: the city the Romans called Gerunda. The houses back straight on to the river on both sides. From any of the three footbridges which cross it, you can stand and watch the colors of the houses reflected in the water, each shade looking as though it was baked hard in the sun: the mustard, the light yellow, the light brown, the white, the deep blue. Each building is painted by a different color, and each color is made to seem richer by the matching tones in which the shutters and traditional blinds are painted. They take care of the city now that Franco is gone; they know how important it is.

I went there in the early spring when there was still a strong, cold wind coming down from the mountains. But in the mornings if you sat on the sheltered ledge at the side door of the cathedral, the sun was warm enough to keep the icy wind at bay. The cathedral stands high over the city looking like a great old box. It can be seen from the motorway and the railway, even from the distant foothills of the Pyrenees. There was a Romanesque church on the site in the eleventh century; the Gothic cathedral was begun in the fourteenth century and finished in 1579. The nave, completed in 1417, is the widest of any cathedral in the Gothic world. The façade was built in 1773, and makes the building look like a square iced cake, belying the solemnity and great power of the building inside.

It comes as a shock then to enter the cathedral by the side door. The darkness inside is so rich and palpable that it seems to dazzle as the sun dazzles. There are no side columns, nothing to detract from the sweeping arrangement of stone, except the wash of light coming from one of the side windows. The air is cold. Stone upon stone rises up, each one perfectly cut and in place; this is a world ruled by the geometry of the Middle Ages. All over Europe the architects of the great cathedrals were consulted and submitted their views to the architect of the cathedral of Girona under construction: Would it work? Would the nave stay up without supporting pillars?

The old city is built on a hill and spreads out on both sides of the cathedral. On one side is Carrer de la Força, part of the Call, the old Jewish quarter. Before the Jews were expelled in the fifteenth century, there were four hundred Jews in a city of four thousand people. More and more emphasis is now being placed on the city's Jewish heritage. Typically, the motives are political: to make Catalonia distinct from Spain by emphasizing its non-Arab influences.

Carrer de la Força is narrow and cobbled. At night it is dimly lit; the streets that wind up to the left seem mysterious, as though they were part of a maze leading toward some Jewish heartland of the past. It seems impossible that anyone would live here, in the houses off these steep lanes leading up to the old walls of the city.

The waking dream of being there is broken only by the sound of cars and motorbikes that noisily brave these cobbled hills. All day the abiding sound is of the honking of horns as cars and bikes prepare to turn blind corners at frightening speeds. Yet at the weekend there is nobody around.

At lunchtime on Easter Saturday we wandered through the old city, which was deserted as though a new Black Death had overtaken it: no cars, no people and at each corner a breath-taking view down a side street, a Romanesque church suddenly appearing, or the mountains coming into view in the green distance.

Signs of the slow transformation from the Romanesque to the Gothic are everywhere. The squat shape of the church of Sant Nicolau to the right of the cathedral gives way to the less modest and more towering form of Sant Pere de Galligants just beside it. The starkest version of this shift is in the cathedral itself. In the main building there is no sign anywhere of how it was made; the Gothic construction seems finished, monumental, definitive. The Romanesque cloister, on the other hand, still preserved at the side of the cathedral, is less imposing and more homely. The arches are lower and rougher, seeming to reflect man's humility rather than the greatness of God and the power of His church. The arches in the cathedral are perfect in their symmetry and geometry, deeply sophisticated in their conception and three centuries away from the buildings in the cloister.

The cathedral museum contains old vestments and jewel-studded monstrances and thuribles, all the grandeur and wealth of the Catholic Church. In the back room, behind glass, however, is the Tapestry of the Creation, from the latter half of the eleventh century, one of Catalonia's great treasures and a masterpiece of Romanesque art. In a series of circles and squares woven in muted shades of green and orange, the tapestry tells the story of the Creation. The text that fills the rim of the main and the inner circle is from Genesis, although the visual references in the tapestry are taken from a variety of sources. Christ is in the center and everything seems to radiate from Him. On one side is Adam with the animals; on the other is Eve emerging from one of Adam's ribs; below are the birds of the air and the fish of the sea, each with a different pattern and color. The fish are almost comically two-dimensional.

The other treasure of the cathedral museum is a book called the *Beatus,* dating from 975, which is a commentary on the Apocalypse with 114 miniatures done in sumptuous colors, suggesting nothing of the somber quality of the church beside it: all blue, pink, orange, and yellow, the colors still perfect a thousand years later.

I was staying in the Hostal Bellmirall on the street of the same name, so close to the cathedral that the bells seemed to reverberate in the room. In summer there was a huge bunch of sunflowers on the stairs, and the balconies were laden with plants. Everything had been made comfortable for the visitor without interfering with the medieval atmosphere. Two walls of the bedroom had been stripped of plaster to reveal the old stone.

We ventured one day in to L'Hostalet del Call and had turkey and prunes as a main course for lunch. Catalan cooking, in which roasting fruit and fowl together is an important element, is natural in Girona, part of the everyday fare. Another time, L'Hostalet del Call was full and we wandered down along Carrer de la Força, until we came to another restaurant that advertised black rice on the menu. We had to wait half an hour for the black rice, and when it came it was indeed black. It was in a large shallow dish and looked as though it had been left too long under a grill and the top of the rice had burnt to a cinder; it was black as charcoal. The waiter grinned at us and began to serve it. The black color came from the ink of the squid that had oozed through the rice and hardened very slightly on the top. But the dish, full of shellfish and seafood, was moist and succulent.

One day in Carrer de la Força I found a doorway that led into a bar.

The bar was called Isaac el Sec, after Isaac the Blind, a medieval Jewish scholar, and it was built on the site of the Jewish synagogue. The main bar was a patio in the old building overhung by trees, the stairway was covered in ivy. The tiles on one of the eaves were the same cobalt blue and burnt orange as a page of the tenth century *Beatus* that had been open in the cathedral that day.

In the middle of the day they played Sephardic music; but at night it was jazz, the place was lit by lanterns and spotlights on the soft stone. There were no tourists around; hidden away here, in a small space in the old medieval Jewish quarter of the city, the voices were all Catalan. The bells of midnight rang from the Gothic cathedral while the hushed voices from the tables around the patio continued on into the night.

One day I called the Casa de Cultura on the other side of town to see a local historian. I went around to the back door, as instructed, and through a room of boxes, and then through a room where under a small light a woman was re-assembling the broken pieces of what must have been a large ceramic jug or pot. The historian explained that the pieces were from an underwater excavation recently made in the sea off Cadaqués that had examined a wrecked ship from the first century. Archaeology in general, she explained, only gives you an idea of what remains; finding a ship tells you what was actually there, a minor miracle for an archaeologist. The woman in the outer room continued working on her small ceramic pieces, remnants of a cargo going somewhere in the Mediterranean in the first century.

All around in the towns and villages were similar remnants: bridges, churches, castles, roads. There were festivals as well that dated from medieval times, which were still put on, not for the tourists or for old-times' sake, but for the same reason as always, for entertainment and amusement and to keep evil spirits away.

On Holy Thursday there was a sign up in one of the shops in the village of Verges, north of Girona, which announced that there was

still a need for some Apostles, an Angel of the Orchard, and a number of shield-holders. This was the night of La Dansa de la Mort, the
Dance of Death, and no one knew how old it was, or when it began.
There was evidence that such a festival had taken place in other
towns in Girona, but this was the only one to survive.

The main square was split in two by a stage where, before the
Dance of Death, a Passion play in Catalan rhyming couplets would
take place. The locals were dressing up in one of the houses off the
square: Jesus was smoking a cigarette and a Roman soldier sported
a fat cigar. The Passion began with Palm Sunday, Jesus arriving on a
real live donkey. Suddenly, soldiers arrived from all sides carrying
spears and torches. There were wild cries and drums as the cross
appeared. At times the rhyming couplets took away somewhat from
the gravity of the occasion, but the locals and the participants took it
all very seriously.

There was a clear sky that March night and a full moon. Along
one of the winding narrow streets of Verges snail shells had been
stuck to the walls, filled with oil and a wick placed inside each one,
to light the procession through the town. These hundreds of small
burning wicks, meticulously placed all over the old walls of houses,
were like a sky full of glittering stars. After the Passion play, we
waited for the real ritual, the dance through the town, which had
survived the centuries.

In the town hall overlooking the square through which the
procession would pass, the mayor of Verges (who belonged to
Convergència, the ruling party) had invited the party faithful and
various friends to drink champagne and watch the procession from
the balcony. There were no priests invited to the town hall and there
were none to be seen at the Passion play. Before Franco died, one of
the organizers said, the room would have been full of priests and
church dignitaries, as well as the local police and the local school-
teacher, all representing Franco. The people of Verges would have
stayed out in the cold.

Most of them were still out there now, lining the streets, waiting
for the procession to pass, just as their ancestors had done every
Holy Thursday for as long as anyone could remember, with the
exception of the Civil War years when religious processions had

been stopped by the Anarchists. The new rulers of Verges waited on the balcony, champagne glasses in hand. As it moved toward midnight, the night became colder and the sky clearer.

The procession began typically with the figure of Christ being led through the streets, and scenes from the Passion acted out by citizens of the town. Upstairs in the town hall we watched this in a desultory sort of way, most people moving away from the balcony to talk among themselves; it was only when the drumbeat started that the room became tense and people crowded to the balcony.

The Dance of Death. A number of figures were moving through the streets dressed as skeletons. Their costumes were black and skin-tight, the bones painted white, almost luminous against the black; the bone structure was detailed, down to toes, ankles, shins, knee joints, spine, ribs, and shoulders, all in place, realistic—and grotesque. The dance was to a drumbeat, a jig, a shuffle, a loose jump. One of the figures carried a scythe with the message in Latin that none shall be spared, another a sign in Catalan telling us that time is short. There were also two children, dressed as skeletons too, carrying small containers full of ashes, as well as a skeleton carrying a timepiece.

There was something melancholy and understated in the small leaps and jumps the figures made through the streets, as though this was all that their tired bones could manage. They kept turning toward each other, and then back toward the crowd, as though looking for help or solace. The heads were painted skulls on black, skin-tight material, realistic like their bodies, and expressionless. The skeleton carrying the sign was the center of the dance and the others moved around him in a monotonous and simple set of movements.

The drummer's hands were a skeleton's hands, but he was dressed in a black tunic, and his face was a mask rather than a skull, a mask designed to frighten and terrorize as he moved through the streets establishing the rhythm of the dance with a thick wooden stick and a drum. Around him were four hooded figures carrying torches.

The skeletons' costumes were so well made that as they stopped and did their shuffle it was impossible not to be disturbed by their appearance. It was stark and direct and the sound of the drums was diabolic and mocking in its rhythm. There was an awe in the upstairs rooms as they passed and a stillness down in the square. It was hard, for those few moments, not to feel wonder and fear; the images passing along the street were so powerful, the walking dead, reminding us that to dust we shall all return.

The closer you move to the Pyrenees, the gruffer people become, the more watchful and serious are their expressions, the less they smile unless there is good reason. The town of Berga, in the province of Girona, is two hours' drive northwest of Barcelona, a place where people seem to keep a careful eye on you if you are a stranger coming into their shop, or walking around the narrow winding streets of their town.

It is a Catalan town, as someone pointed out to me almost as soon as I arrived, and the Arabs never set foot in the place. The people of Berga have a particular way of speaking Catalan, keeping the vowel sounds to a minimum, letting the liquid el sounds flow over their speech like molten lava. They frown a lot as they speak; they take things seriously.

In particular, they take their Patum seriously. This is a festival of fire that takes place on the Thursday of Corpus Christi and the following weekend. Like the Dance of Death, La Patum has its origins in the medieval world. Outsiders are not encouraged to come to Berga for La Patum on Corpus; the first night is for the people of the town, who know the dances, the jumps, and the passes, who know how to follow the fire and stay out of trouble at the same time. Visitors can come on Sunday when a special Patum is held for them. The citizens of Berga like to keep things regulated and orderly.

So on the afternoon of Corpus, there was nothing festive about the atmosphere in Berga, no shouting in the streets, no groups of young people singing and dancing. The bars of Berga were, in fact, singularly quiet; the shops were closed.

Later, a few of them would open to sell special hats and scarves and T-shirts to keep the sparks from burning the participants. I was strongly advised to invest in this special gear before setting foot in the square where La Patum would be enacted once more. It was important to be on time, I was told, because as soon as the church in the square rang half past nine, the drummer and the musicians would begin.

The dignitaries and their close friends and relations sat on the balcony of the town hall overlooking the square; the giants, the eagle, and the dwarves were in the town hall awaiting their turn. On a slope above the square, chairs had been provided for those who didn't want to risk getting burned and stamped on during the next few hours of music and fire. Others sat on the steps of the church near the band. The man in charge, the man with the huge drum that sounds *patum, patum,* sat on his own special balcony constructed on the other side of the square. Anyone who lived on the square and owned a balcony had plenty of friends and they all watched and waited for the clock to sound half past nine. Down in the square the crowds were ready, wearing red hats and red scarves and old clothes.

The first to come were the Turks on horseback, moving through the crowd to the beat of the music and the drums. The music was brassy and jolly, but with that odd note of melancholy that characterizes the music of the *sardana,* the Catalan national dance. The crowd's job was to move around the square, following the figures in small or large groups, all the time being pushed, jostled, and shoved. Those who knew the ropes, who had Berga in their blood, could move around the square without hitting into anyone.

After the Turks had done their rounds came Michael the Archangel and the devils, each carrying a sort of tambourine with fireworks attached, which spewed out sparks every time it was shaken. The square was full now, you could barely move, and the organizers worked hard pushing the crowds back, protecting the figures, directing thousands of people who were moving at considerable speed, following the fire.

It was becoming more dangerous. Now it was the monster, four or five strong men held up his back, and one took control of his long neck that led to a ferocious head with long sticks of fireworks attached. The crowd ran after him and he ran after the crowd. He took particular interest in anyone standing at the edges of the square, anyone protected by a wall, or anyone who carried an umbrella to protect himself from the sparks. The fire coming out of his mouth seemed to go on and on as the ferocious music played.

The eagle that came next was almost as big as the monster. It wore a crown, and its long tail became a lethal weapon when it twirled. The music changed its measure, became solemn and ceremonious, stately and somewhat sad as the eagle careered around the square. The frenetic tone was gone, there was no shouting, no tumult, just this strange bird and the people, openmouthed. Suddenly, the music changed, everybody waited for it, the moment at which the slow music would give way to a beat that was sudden, loud, and clear. The eagle began to move faster, faster as the music speeded up. Everybody jumped up and down to the beat. All the sadness was just a preparation for this. In the last moments the eagle turned and turned, and anyone close by lay on the ground to avoid a smack from its long tail. Legend says that its tail had once killed a soldier. Then the eagle was led, victorious, back into the town hall.

The giants who came next were placid and regal. They were followed by the dwarves whose heads were far too large for their bodies. They danced together in the middle of the square.

One by one, men with their heads and shoulders covered in grass, with fireworks coming out of the grass, began to appear in the square. They mingled with the crowd. The balconies were now full, the square was packed, there was a sense of anticipation, as though the real Patum were only now about to take place. I had booked a spot at a second-floor window overlooking the square, and I now moved there, as the dance of the dwarves was coming to an end. The figures covered in grass had fanned out to all parts of the square, there were more than seventy of them.

When the dwarves had finished, the square became tense and crowded as more people wearing headgear to protect themselves tried to move toward the center. Then the lights went out, all the shops and houses and the two bars in the square turned off their lights as the music started. The square was in darkness, the drumbeat was more concentrated, *patum, patum,* the drum beat out the sound as the grass-men lit their fireworks. I could see the swirl of people down below, moving round and round the square, as though pursued. Soon the smell of sulfur from the fireworks was overwhelming, it filled the square and the only light was the light from fire sticks, which was all sparks and was soon clouded in smoke. Soon, you could see nothing except smoke rising and a vast soup of human figures doing an infernal dance, like water bubbling. The music was loud and fast and had a demonic edge to it, a sort of mocking gaiety, and it was clear as the smoke and the smell of the sulfur rose, and the crowd below seemed to suffer, desperately moving and pushing among swirls of spark and smoke, it was clear that this was a vision of hell, with all the medieval imaginings of fire and brimstone, darkness and pain. This was the devil's cauldron, the place to which you could go for all eternity, being acted out on the feast of Corpus Christi.

When it was over and I went back down to the square, everyone was exhausted. Soon, the whole thing would start again: the monsters, giants, eagles, dwarves, and then the great smoke. In the meantime, the bars were serving a cocktail called *mau-mau* in big *porron*s, which had a spout from which large numbers could drink each in his or her turn as it was passed from hand to hand. It was nearly over, someone said to me, it would be done again on Sunday night, but it was never the same, as it wasn't for the people of Berga. On Friday afternoon there would be a smaller Patum, with all the same ingredients, for children, so the next generation could come to know their heritage: when to jump, when to follow the giants, and what to do when the fire began.

Everywhere

J. S. Marcus

The day the English archaeologist arrived at my hotel he asked me where he could swim in the ocean. I described the island's circumference for him, starting with the natural harbor: the natural harbor, the public beaches, the topless beach, the nude beach, the nude singles beach, the nude family beach, the deserted nude beach, a stretch of shoreline not acknowledged as beach, the resorts' walled-in beaches, the gay beach, the nude gay beach, more resorts, the airport, the inactive volcano, the excavation site, a long stretch of nothing, slums, the man-made harbor, the telephone exchange, warehouses, the natural harbor. He asked about the deserted nude beach. I described the black volcanic sand and the hollowed-out cliffs behind, the nationalities of people I had seen, the only restaurant, which was Chinese and which I said I couldn't recommend. He told me I was wrong about the cliffs. Morphologically speaking, he said, this was a typical island, and hollowed-out cliffs wouldn't occur because for some time—since its birth, he had learned before leaving England—the island had been sinking. I am not a geologist, of course, and not an archaeologist (I went to the island on a whim), and after our meeting I couldn't walk under the cliffs at the deserted nude beach as if they were hallucinations, but he was probably right about the island. Everything was in dispute there, as if people were pushing it into the sea.

The disputes were various—economic, political, logistical, anthropological, comic, violent—but always seemed connected to the fact of the excavation. Some disputes had been caused by the excavation, some predated the excavation but had been aggravated by it, some concerned the excavation site and nothing else; there were petty disputes, discussed by everyone then promptly forgotten; there were abstract disputes that could have shaken up someone who hadn't heard about the excavation and knew nothing about the island. For instance, because of the decade-long influx of tourists and, more recently, of journalists, archaeologists, and tourists interested in the excavation site, the garbage was increasing exponentially, and no one would agree where to put the new garbage dump. There were illegal currency exchanges in the hotel lobbies. The airport's new runway was too short. There was ethnic violence between Hindus and Muslims and economic violence between the Chinese and the

Vietnamese. An Italian photographer, in need of a white coral brick wall for a fashion shoot, wanted to sandblast a hundred-year-old façade off a block of former slave quarters. Since its independence the island and another island across the channel had been fighting a cold war over fishing rights. The team of Belgian archaeologists presiding over the excavation had arbitrary rules for deciding who could visit the site, how long they could stay, and what they could see while they were there. And results of radiocarbon tests seemed to suggest that someone might have to rewrite the history of the island, the history of the archipelago, the history of the oceans, and the history of the peopling of the earth's land masses.

The English archaeologist liked keeping track of events, and one evening he listed the island's disputes for his wife in what sounded like a prearranged sequence. I happened to be part of the conversation and asked him about it afterward: Why, for instance, had he begun with fishing rights and stopped with the peopling of the earth's land masses? He said he hadn't considered the order beforehand, but, when he thought about it, he had to admit that he didn't really care for fish, and that he truly believed a tree hadn't fallen—and for that matter, he added, an island couldn't sink—unless someone was there to know it.

I came to the island knowing nothing, on a whim, although for funding purposes I had to disguise the whim as someone else's. After reading about the excavation in the newspapers, I asked a friend at a foundation about the possibility of a grant. I hadn't seen her in months and was just making conversation, but the prospect excited her, and the next day she came to my apartment to tell me that I would have a better chance if she proposed the idea as hers and then proposed a list of recipients with me at the top of the men's list; as a formality, she explained, the foundation would first have to offer the grant to a woman, and she asked for names of unqualified women, or women who I knew wouldn't be interested. She always called me after committee meetings, and I knew that I had been chosen weeks in advance, but it was easy acting surprised with the president of the foundation. He awarded me the wrong grant over lunch, and then, after realizing who I was, told me that he himself had suggested my name. "I have a special interest in your work," he said.

My work before the trip had consisted of unpublished travel books and eight-millimeter documentaries, but the money officially came from the foundation's mixed-media fund, so I could have done anything I wanted. Originally—when I knew nothing—I had ambitions: I decided to bring along a sixteen-millimeter camera, an eight-millimeter camera, a video camera, a regular camera, dozens of lenses, and a tape recorder; I brought volumes of an empty journal, a table-top computer, an archaeologist's handbook, an atlas, and an extra passport. During my first week I developed a routine. Each morning I would carry equipment down to the harbor, stand on the pier behind the Sinhalese slum, and wait to buy a hydrofoil ticket. (The only way to the excavation site was by hydrofoil.) In line, I would pick out a stranger, or a group of strangers, befriend them, photograph them, tape them, follow them to the excavation site, write down what I thought about them, and spend the evening in my room hoping for an idea. Eventually, though, I stopped using the cameras, and then the tape recorder; I set aside my journal; I rarely went to the excavation site. I could feel my ambitions narrow and spent most of the time talking to people at my hotel.

Everyone at the hotel was part of a family-like cluster. The English archaeologist had a wife, who was also an English archaeologist. There was a young lesbian from Seattle and her girlfriend, who was middle-aged and Dutch. There was a Canadian woman of French, African, and Malay ancestry, born on the island, and staying—discreetly, she said, because she was at the hotel and not at her brother's house—with a French journalist, there to write about the excavation, and his son from an unhappy marriage. There were three Swiss college students, two men and a woman, planning a trip to Fiji, and a waiter from the Upper West Side of Manhattan who wanted to be a novelist and often paid for the students' dinners. The man who owned the hotel was from Athens, and each morning he brought a new young man unselfconsciously to breakfast. And there was myself and the man from Montgomery, Alabama. He arrived as I did, knowing nothing, but eventually came up with conspiracy theories about the excavation; we would stay up late on the terrace alone with his evidence, until the teenager from Australia, who slept on the terrace and thought no one noticed, returned from wherever and took off his T-shirt to use as a pillow.

People at the hotel, after my ambitions narrowed, tried to find new uses for my time. One of the Swiss students began needing help with his camera. On the terrace after dinner, the Canadian woman, who came out to the terrace to despise East Indians, would try to interest me in island politics or in also despising East Indians; "They beat their wives the way other people beat their children," she would say. The owner of the hotel decided I should read Greek poetry and gave me an English translation of Cavafy with little circles next to poems about young boys having sex with each other. The waiter from New York was always reading—Freud by the swimming pool, Kafka at the beach, T. S. Eliot in the Polynesian restaurant—and found the Cavafy poems on a table where I had left them. He became interested in a poem called "The City," which didn't sound like it had a circle on its page. The poem, he said, perfectly described his mood on the island, and he thought it should also describe my mood after he found out that I also lived in New York. "You will find no new lands," he would repeat to me. "You will find no other seas. The city will follow you." The woman from Seattle and her Dutch girlfriend, who were listening one morning, told him not to bother with Cavafy or Greeks in general, or Freud, or Eliot—they couldn't get their minds off the fashion shoot. The Dutch woman took the opportunity to ask why I didn't seem to have strong feelings: "You're an artist," she said to me. When she and the woman from Seattle were talking about the fashion shoot they liked to use the word "desecration," which made me think of the excavation site.

There were a series of incidents during my stay on the island—mutilations, or desecrations, really, under the circumstances. Someone was going over to the excavation site while the archaeologists were asleep and doing things to the artifacts: Amulet-like objects were being smashed; a wooden thing, relatively intact for something twenty thousand years old, was also smashed and its pieces left in the tidewater; bones were reburied.

The archaeologist in charge of the excavation site didn't like discussing the mutilations. In his photographs (the well-known one showed him holding tiny skulls in both hands), he looked like an explorer from the last century, but in person, invoking various rules he had established, or dodging questions about the most recent mutilation, he resembled a very contemporary bureaucrat. The reason he refused to answer questions about the amulet-like objects, and the bones, and the wooden thing, is probably because neither he nor any of the other Belgians knew anything about them, except their age, which had been calculated in a laboratory back in Louvain. The official pamphlet about the excavation, authored by special copywriters from London and doubling as a multilingual advertisement for the Belgian brewery that paid for the printing costs, claimed that 2 percent of the findings had been classified as "sacred," 1 percent as "nonsacred," and 97 percent had yet to be classified. "Unknowable" was the word one of the Belgians used; he was supposed to spend his evenings in the archaeologists' pavilion going over that day's discoveries, but he developed a fondness for the discotheque and the impromptu international dinners in the restaurants. At sunset, from my hotel-room window, I could see him arriving in the motorboat he had privately leased from the Belgian consulate. He had a weakness for champagne, which people bought for him by the bottle after finding out who he was, and he never returned until morning. He always left behind his key in the ignition.

A discussion about the mutilations led to controversy at my hotel. The Canadian woman, who had gone to school in Paris, told us that Belgians were notoriously clumsy and insisted the archaeologists themselves had dropped the artifacts, or stepped on them. The English archaeologist's wife blamed a visiting group of other, unnamed archaeologists who were known for resolutely opposing new versions of the archaeological record. "Stubbornness," she said, "often leads to sabotage." Gossip about the mutilations, argued the waiter, was the climax of everybody's day. The man from Alabama said he knew a publicity stunt when he saw one. The lesbian and her girlfriend didn't care about the excavation site, and neither, though for different reasons, did the owner of the hotel. No one paid attention to anyone else, not even after the screaming started.

I could never make up my mind. Sometimes the desecrations

seemed like accidents, sometimes obstinacies, sometimes culmina-
tions; sometimes they seemed part of another, more important lie;
sometimes they seemed never to have happened at all. But whatever
I was believing at a particular moment, I knew that . . . well, that
wooden thing for instance. Put it together with the other things that
had been dug up and it suggested something, but on its own it
meant nothing at all, until it was found hacked to pieces.

After the argument, the larger family-like cluster of everyone at
the hotel began coming apart. The Swiss students left for Fiji the
next day, and the waiter joined them a few days after that. The teenager from Australia left for another island farther up the archipelago,
where he said the women were better looking and the police would
let him sleep on the beach. The English archaeologist's wife went
back to England. The Canadian woman broke down, and she, the
French journalist, and the French journalist's son moved to her
brother's house in the hills above the town.

"It is entirely possible," I confessed to the man from Alabama the
day before he left, although I didn't suppose he was listening, "that I
know everything there is to know about these desecrations."

I knew who was going over to the excavation site, how he went
there, where he stood, and how he hid himself from his own noise. I
knew all about it: How could I not have known?

My apartment in New York, the taxicab, the airport . . . the airport, the taxicab, my apartment in New York. I always felt on the
island that I had already left it, or that I hadn't yet arrived. Always
at the very ends of the trip, but in truth, of course, I was everywhere,
with my body and with my life. Everywhere, like someone watching
his own soul.

I finally had a sense of it—this everywhereness—the night before
my plane took off. The people remaining at the hotel were treating
each other as strangers, and I decided to take a walk, as I had often
done, by the dock where the Belgian always left his boat. I walked by
a small restaurant and saw a woman I had never seen before, although she had the confused accent and skin color of people native
to the island, so I had probably seen her several times; I had probably always seen her. She spoke in French, asked me to sit down, to

drink with her, and jokingly asked to be taken away—into the water, I thought she said. It reminded me of the Cavafy poem about the ancient town waiting to be sacked by barbarians. The townspeople wait until they realize the barbarians will never show up, because there aren't any barbarians left; everyone—everywhere—is waiting. I was more tired than drunk, but jumped over the thin rope that separated the restaurant from the street. I sat down, and I brought her back to my hotel, I did everything, though of course I was waiting for someone of my own.

Mohammad and The Island in Syria

Robert Tewdwr Moss

The train journey from Aleppo to Lattakia is probably the most beautiful you can make in Syria. Having missed the early morning express, I caught the slow train, which left shortly afterwards. It was packed with students and took simply hours. The views from the window were charming. We passed over valleys studded with fields and orchards, with lone cypress trees standing sentinel near by; we wound around mountains with little terrace farms and olive trees hugging their sides, and occasionally disappeared into long dark tunnels beneath them. The landscape was rich in cultivation. I saw a farmer in a baggy *shalwaar* driving a plough pulled by two brown cattle with long horns between twisted olive trees, while his wife, dressed in bright blue with a pink headscarf, stooped, planting the furrows.

To my surprise, I had renewed my visa without any problems, although the process had been baroque, to put it mildly. I was now free to travel for a further two months. The students and I started talking. They said that the mountains were mainly populated by Christians and Alouites. By tradition it was the Alouites who occupied the upper slopes, while the Christians occupied the lower parts. The Alouites, they said, always liked to be high up, as was evidenced by their white-domed shrines, which could be seen on top of most of the peaks.

One student, Mohammad, was a dashing young man with dark brown wavy hair, long at the front and short at the back. He had a fine, long olive-skinned face with high cheekbones and brown eyes flecked with amber. He wore beautifully tailored navy blue slacks and a shell-pink shirt and dark blue cravat. He looked like a young Spanish aristocrat. He was studying English and his friends—among them another two Mohammads—law. They were returning home after exams. Like many students, they lived and studied at home, coming into town for a few days a week for tutorials and exams and staying in local hotels. I asked them for the address of a cheap but clean hotel, and when we arrived Mohammad took me to a taxi, gave orders to the driver, and said he would meet me at the hotel, the Badia, that evening at seven o'clock.

The taxi drove through the wide streets. Nearly all Syrians love Lattakia, and all Lattakians believe they are a cut above most other

Syrians. This is partly because it is the town nearest the president's village, Qadaha, but mainly because, as a port facing Europe, it has a peculiarly Mediterranean air. Strangely, the center—still laid out on the Roman plan—is the densest, most cramped, most ramshackle and most unglamorous part of the town.

Lattakia began life as a Phoenician fishing village around 1000 B.C., and in succession was taken by the Assyrians, the Persians, and then the Greeks under Alexander. In about 311 B.C. the Seleucid Greeks named it Loadicea (hence the present name) after the mother of the Byzantine emperor Seleucus I. Mark Antony, during his shuttles to and from Egypt to see Cleopatra, granted it autonomy and reduced its taxes. It is mentioned in the New Testament, and St. Peter passed through with his retinue. Around the time of the second century A.D., the Byzantine emperor made it the capital of Syria. Subsequently, the Byzantines lost it to the Arabs, who lost it to the Turks, who lost it to the Crusaders. In 1188 Saladin took it, and the Moslems held it until the Mongol invasion of 1260, as a result of which it was transferred back to the Christian prince of Antioch. Worn out with history, under the Ottomans it shriveled into a ruin with a silted-up harbor. Only when the French arrived in the 1920s did it receive a revivifying facelift.

Given this constant battering by invaders, it is not entirely surprising that Lattakia presents a thoroughly modern appearance in which hardly anything of the past is still standing, although there is much to be found underground. On my first evening's stroll, I saw a pair of Roman columns being heaved out of the ground as a result of roadworks. The legacy of all this upheaval is a town with a special talent for adapting and using what has come its somewhat promiscuous way. Today, with its long boulevards lined with modern blocks of flats sporting large balconies, built by the French, it could be any contemporary Mediterranean town, peppered as it is by numerous boutiques, cafés, and brasseries, which the Lattakians love to frequent.

Lattakian women are famously beautiful and dress extravagantly, as close to the Parisian model—whether classical or trendy—as they can. They have wonderful cascades of thick dark hair, pale skin, a taste for dramatic colors in lipstick, and fantastic costume jewelry. Lattakia was the only place in Syria where I saw women wearing miniskirts.

The town boasts two corniches, and I always confused them. The modern one was wide and long and sweeping, crowded every evening with the young and beautiful, and the young and beautifuls' mothers. Men would stroll along arm in arm, ogling the girls. Rupert had told me that at night parts of the corniche were littered with young men hungrily seeking each other's company. To find myself in Lattakia was suddenly to find myself in a more relaxing environment where pleasure was sought and found, and where it was a feature of the local economy to provide it.

The Hotel Badia was located on the third floor of a block in a square opposite the Ugarit cinema. It was so primitive it did not even possess a sign in English. I asked the taxi driver to wait and raced up the stairs to inspect it. I needed only a peek in reception to realize that it would lack even the most Spartan comforts. The taxi driver said he knew a nice hotel on the corniche that was very reasonable. It was called the Safwan and overlooked the town hall, whose garden was dotted with the Roman statues that were unearthed every time the road was dug up. For only five pounds a night I got a room for three with a balcony and an *en suite* bathroom of a standard noticeably higher than that at the Rose of Aleppo—but then I was paying all of two pounds a night extra. I returned to the Badia at the appointed hour but Mohammad failed to show up. I left a note for him with my new address on it.

The next morning there was a knock on my door at about eight o'clock. I opened it to find standing before me a tall, well-built, prematurely graying man in his mid-thirties with striking green eyes. "Good morning," he said. "My name is Mohammad and I have received your note from the Hotel Badia."

"There must have been some mistake," I replied.

"Yes. So I see. I was expecting you to be my friend Robert from Oxford, who is professor of Akkadian languages."

The confusion had arisen because the dim hotel concierge had given my note to a Mohammad who lived in a flat in the same block. This Mohammad clearly did have a friend called Robert, whom he presumed had arrived unannounced. He politely apologized, then suggested that we go out for breakfast.

We found a pleasant café on the corniche overlooking the sea and sat outside. All around us, well-dressed Syrian families were having breakfast before going off to work or school. Mohammad, it turned out, was now an architect, but in the past had worked extensively on various archaeological digs at Ras Shamra (the local name for Ugarit) and the Roman amphitheatre at Jebleh, just down the coast, as well as in the east of the country. He told me that it was well worth visiting Ugarit, the Phoenician town where the European alphabet had been invented, which as a journalist, I felt I ought to do.

By Bronze Age standards, the remains at Ugarit are quite extensive. Most of them date from the fourteenth century B.C. and are remarkable for their construction in stone, whereas the contemporary cities of Mari and Ebla, having been built of mud brick, have not survived in anything like the same condition. Among the ruins was an acropolis with temples to Dagon and Baal—the Canaanite god— and a labyrinthine sequence of rooms belonging to the royal palace. One of these had yielded a great treasure trove of tablets inscribed mainly with the Ugaritic alphabet consisting of thirty cuneiform symbols, the first to equate a sound with a single sign. This was a great improvement on the previous system of depicting words by means of picture-based images, and its ease of expression led to its being taken up by the Greeks, who were trading partners, and thus it was handed down to us. The picture of life that emerged from these tablets helped to provide historians with considerable insights into the Canaanite world, which several centuries later was to be colonized by the Israelites and make biblical history.

Like so many early Syrian archaeological sites, Ugarit could not be described as imposing, but it was in a peaceful rural setting surrounded by orange groves and with commanding views over to the sea and the long-defunct harbor, once the link between Babylon and the eastern Mediterranean. The remains of those houses still standing often had burial vaults beneath them, and the streets were characterized by stone channels that had once conducted water around the city. I was struck by the narrowness of the streets as compared with the grandeur of Hellenistic and Roman remains. Today I was the only person picking my way around the sleepy ruins, deserted save for the presence of a flock of long-eared goats that sent the stones rattling from the walls as they scrambled over them.

I took a taxi from Ugarit and rather extravagantly asked the driver to take me to Saladin's castle in the mountains outside the town.

Of all countries, Syria has the right to the title Land of Castles. There are castles from every period and every tradition, wonderful jewels in its architectural heritage. There are Crusader castles, Arab castles, Byzantine castles, Assassin castles, desert castles, mountain castles, some extraordinarily well preserved, some romantically desolate. Saladin's castle, described by Lawrence as "the most sensational thing in castle building I have seen," is one of the latter. It is one of the most beautiful sights in Syria, built on a great tongue of rock between two green ravines with views beyond the mountain pass over the plain of Lattakia and as far as the sparkling Mediterranean. Today the spot is utterly deserted, the town that nestled in its enclosure for protection having long since disappeared. There is a spectacular road that winds up around the rock on which the castle sits, dreamily surveying its lonely rural domain. As the road nears the lower reaches of the building, it is cleft in two by a huge jagged lance of rock standing like a broken tooth, which eight hundred years ago used to support the drawbridge that passed over the sheer drop to the ravine below.

As I wandered through the keep, the donjons, the stables, and the great halls, I noticed some tall, blond Europeans striding manfully over the ruins. They looked rather at home. The party consisted of an American, a Dutch student, and two Australians who were kayaking their way along the world's great rivers and hoping to write a book about it. I found the idea of kayaking down the Euphrates an alarming one. What if you didn't realize you'd been swept over the border into Iraq? How do you even know if you're approaching a border when you're bobbing about in a kayak? It all sounded very risky.

Later that afternoon Mohammad II took me to the museum he used to work in. It was near the port and had once been a khan before becoming the house of the governor of the Alouite State during the Mandate. There were some beautiful girls—real girls with thick chestnut hair, long painted nails, long eyelashes, honey-colored eyes and glamorous clothes—floating around. One of them actually had a rose in her hair. They were so different from the dreary brides of art who habituate English art establishments. As we left, Mohammad said to me, "Let me know if there is a girl you like. I can arrange something for you. The girls here are very free."

That evening, after dinner with Mohammad and his wife, I traced my steps back along the corniche. It was getting late. I noticed a few lone figures dotted about on the benches in the park opposite the museum, and a constant drift of single men up and down the corniche. A young soldier in fatigues was lounging with a gun outside the police station.

A car drew up beside me and the window was wound down. "Good evening," said a fruity Syrian voice in English. "How are you? You speak English?" A round face with bulging eyes was protruding out of the window. On the other side, behind the wheel, was a moody-looking man of about thirty with an open shirt and a very hairy chest. I confirmed that, being English, I could indeed speak English.

"You want come back with me and my friend? He want to give you coffee."

They must think I'm a pushover, I thought.

The goitre-eyed passenger looked up at me coyly. "You want threesome?"

"Certainly not," I said in my primmest tones.

I walked down to the gardens where the cafés were and sat on a seat facing the sea to recover my composure. A tall youth in tight jeans and a leather jacket slouched past. He hesitated by a bench at the end of the path on which a lone figure sat, and then moved to a bench directly opposite. After a while he stood up, crossed the path and sat down next to the figure. Cigarettes were lit, a conversation started. A few minutes later the two men got up and strolled toward my seat in the shadows. The second youth was wearing smart navy blue slacks and a dark cravat. As they approached, he was talking to the leather-clad youth in a low voice, their heads close together, and a splash of lamplight fell across his handsome face. He looked like a young Spanish aristocrat.

The next morning I embarked on a full day of touring. As I left the hotel, the owner handed me a note that had been left the night before. "I am Mohammad," it read. "I come to the Hotel Badia. They tell me you are in Hotel Safwan. I come at II P.M. and I wait for thirty minutes. Tomorrow I come again to see you." That explains a lot, I reflected, perhaps a little sourly.

I sat on a bus to Tartus, waiting for it to fill up, getting more and more irritated the longer it took. The sweet lost-child's voice of Fairuz stole over the airwaves from the radio to soothe me. Now in her fifties, Fairuz still carries in her voice that unique freshness, that questing innocence which suits the Syrian mornings, before the afternoon heat blasts away the soft coolness. She is a goddess throughout the Arab world, quite simply adored by everyone, man, woman, and child, in the Middle East. There is no equivalent in Western culture, where singers are divided by class or age. Fairuz unites the whole Arab-speaking world.

The bus ride was distinctly uncomfortable and cramped, not to mention painfully slow as we passed through Jebleh and the industrial town of Baniyas, bypassing one of Syria's most somber and brooding castles, Qalaat Marqab, built of black stone and situated high on a rock keeping watch over the Mediterranean.

The old town of Tartus—or Tortosa, to use its Crusader name—is a wonderful crumbling rabbit warren of a place standing within the confines of the fortress. Its city walls, hugging it protectively against encroaching modernity, now seem maternal rather than defensive. Even the sea out of which they once loomed has retreated several yards down the beach. Today you can still find a tiny mosque built in what was one of the guard's rooms overlooking the sea, but most vestiges of the old fortress have long since been built over, on, or around.

The lanes and alleys are so narrow, low, and dense that it is impossible for an *ajnabee* (Westerner) not to stick out like a sore thumb. Housewives chatting with their neighbors and old men playing draughts in the cafés would stop whatever they were doing and stare at me slack-jawed. At one point I encountered a group of schoolchildren in their dark green quasi-military uniforms brushing the streets with red-bristled brooms. (On Fridays many children have to carry out community work such as this.) The children surged round me with cries of excitement and bore their find off in triumph to their teacher, who looked horrified that his charges should be consorting with such decadent company. One little girl publicly decorated me with a gold pin of the president's head. "This is our president and we love him," she cried. I thanked her for the gift and took a photograph of the group. As I raised my camera, I noticed that all the girls hung back while the boys thrust themselves forward, in line with Islamic principles decreeing that women should not be photographed. One large-limbed hobbledehoy cried out, "Tell them in England the truth about our country. In Europe they say very bad things about our country and our president. Tell them it is not true. That we are good people." In his own way he had a perfectly valid point. If we had the opportunity to stand in the Syrians' shoes we would understand more about the choices they have had to make.

Across the sea from Tartus is Syria's only island, now called Arwad, to which, in Phoenician, Roman, and Greek times, the town always played second fiddle. The name Tartus in fact derives from this second-string status, being a corruption of the Roman Anti-Aradus, meaning the town opposite Aradus.

The ancient cathedral of Our Lady of Tortosa is one of the earliest known shrines to the Virgin, possibly established by St. Peter himself as he passed through into Turkey. Today the building still impresses the visitor with its dreadful austerity. After fluctuating fortunes that have seen it used as a mosque and a barracks, it has, since independence, become a museum, and contains a veritable treasurehouse of unlabeled antiquities lying around in the gloom.

Today you can feel the fist of modern development battering against the frail walls of old Tartus with its inescapable series of ring roads, roundabouts, and industrial buildings. It seems scarcely believable that this little town was the very last bastion of the mainland to be yielded up to the Moslems by the Crusaders. After two hundred years of war in the Latin Orient, or Outremer (the land beyond the sea), as the Crusaders themselves rather poetically called it, the knights quietly disappeared from Tartus over the waters to Arwad, taking the famous icon of Our Lady with them. For another ten years they harassed the Moslems from the tiny island, eventually, when all hope of reestablishing themselves was exhausted, withdrawing to Cyprus.

After my stroll through the town I took a boat across a choppy sea to Arwad, home to four thousand people. It is still crowned by a Crusader fortress and in the harbor the remains of the ancient Phoenician walls are still standing. Most of the time they are submerged beneath the waves, but when the sea is low it reveals a great lacy curtain of rocks, thousands of years of erosion having given them the texture of birds' bones, the huge slabs tessellated with a filigree of hollowed-out holes. Scattered along the promenade, lying on sheets on the ground, were crude souvenirs made by the locals. They were garish and tacky—wooden ships, fish, and stars encrusted with shells and pebbles painted bright pink, yellow, and blue.

After visiting the castle, I went back to the waterfront, found a café and sat down. I noticed a small boy staggering into the kitchen behind me, carrying a heavy bucket that he dropped with a thud onto the floor. Inside was a clod of hummus. Next to it stood another bucket of hummus, which was nearly empty. The boy stuck his hand into the sand-colored goo and extracted a lump of it, flicking it into the first bucket and shaking his hand to dislodge as much as possible. Then he inverted the bucket and started scraping the remains out with his fingernails. I could hear it landing in the bucket with a splat. It turned my stomach. That was that. I could never eat hummus again. The choice of food in Syria is already palate-jadingly limited (unless you dine in a private middle- or upper-class residence), and to have to cross a staple element of the diet off one's list was galling. What was left? Falafels? Chicken on the spit?

The waiter arrived. I ordered a glass of tea. He enquired whether I would be requiring anything to eat. I replied that I would not be eating, thank you.

Two youths strolled along the promenade and sat opposite me. One, who had prominent spots, said he was a university student visiting his uncle. It was Friday, and the mosque was broadcasting its sermon across the island. It sounded like quite a rant. After it ended, the boy, who was called Samir, pointed out a squat, bearded man with red hair in the middle of the crowd emerging from the mosque. "That is the village sheikh," he said. "He is twenty-eight and he studied law at Damascus." The man was wearing a long white *djella-bah* and a white skullcap. It was he who had given the sermon. "That man is very important on the island," said Samir. "If there is anyone who has done something bad, this man can shame him in the mosque and then everyone on the island will scorn him."

I did not fancy the idea of my misdeeds being trumpeted around the island through the mosque's loudspeakers, and the information rather blighted my appreciation of this picturesque spot. I imagined a straitened life in a little house at the end of one of the narrow, twisting alleyways, a life of Lorcaesque exposure to the pervasive inquisitiveness and need for conformity of one's small-minded neighbors. How many times a week were you sleeping with your wife? Why had she not conceived a child? Why were you arguing night in, night out?

Samir said he had been lucky as he had an Italian girlfriend and she had invited him to Naples for a holiday. For many Arabs the word girlfriend seems to imply almost any woman outside the family with whom they have a nodding social acquaintance. He must have been very well connected, I reflected, to have secured a tourist visa to Europe. His trip had made a tremendous impression on him. He seemed to regard Islam as a retrograde influence, holding his country back from developing into a modem state. The particular novelty of Italy was that "you could utter your opinion and no one would arrest you." He longed to live in Europe, he said, where he was sure he would do well.

Then came the inevitable girlfriend question. How many did I have? he asked, as if every *ajnabee* ran an unofficial harem with a selection of types to satisfy every whim. It was impossible to have sexual relations with a girl anywhere in Syria, he continued, unless you belonged to the class of rich internationalists, in which case you could do anything you wanted, including having your hymen replaced in Harley Street. It was particularly difficult on the island. "You can have a girlfriend, but by girlfriend we do not mean the same as you in Europe. I have a friend. He is very handsome and rich. He is an engineer. He earns three hundred dollars a month. It is a lot in Syria. He tells me he has many girlfriends. Sometimes he has sex. Well, in a manner of speaking. You can only go so far. You see, you can never have penetration.

"If a girl is discovered not to be a virgin on marriage," I asked, "what will happen to her?"

"She will die."

"At whose hand?"

"At her father's. Her husband's. Her brother's. It does not really matter which. But she will die at any rate." He laughed uneasily.

"So how do you satisfy your sexual feelings if you are a young professional man in Syria and you don't have enough money to get married?"

"It is simple. We cannot."

"Is there any homosexuality on the island?"

"Yes. There are many such men on the island. But I, I am not interested in such activity. And in fact I scorn such men. I scorn them. Besides, for this there is the death penalty. This crime is even worse than to take the virginity of a girl to whom you are not married."

In fact the legal punishment for homosexuality was nothing like this extreme. Nevertheless, it all sounded pretty dire, and I was beginning to long for the next boat back. The sky had turned dark and stormy, the sea a steely grey. In the distance the ferry chugged into view. Samir walked me to the jetty where there was a rowdy gang of people who jostled each other and leapt on the boat before it had docked while others leapt off. It took a further three boats before I could embark, and by this time the sea was very rough.

"Goodbye, Mr. Robert," said Samir sweetly. "Please write to me. Maybe we can meet in England."

"Or maybe Italy," I said jokingly.

"Yes. Both would be nice," Samir replied solemnly. "OK. So long. *Ciao*."

The crossing back was nerve-racking. The boat was positively weighed down with people and luggage. Some were sitting— somewhat unenviably—on the roof. The man standing next to me had been a sailor, and was teaching me how to stand with my knees slightly bent to resist the buffeting of the shiny black waves. I was relieved to regain the mainland.

Reading
the Body

Boyer Rickel

Across from me sits a dark-haired young man, perhaps seventeen, whose plain round face is marked by a mild outbreak of acne. His eyes, large and brown, pass over me easily, then out the train window, as I settle into my seat. His clothes strike me as charmingly typical for his age: stone-washed jeans, a dark blue T-shirt emblazoned with a KISS EUROTOUR logo beneath an unzipped, eye-stopping windbreaker—a patchwork of neon-bright chartreuse and pink and orange. On one knee rests his daypack, well worn at the seams.

I can't help cataloging his every ordinary detail—and smiling at the lesson in his plainness. I realize I'd fantasized, like a dreamy adolescent, that the men on this trip would approximate the beautiful Italian characters I've seen so often in movies—the self-absorbed Gino, for example, in the recent *Where Angels Fear to Tread,* his nose and cheeks and chin as finely chiseled as a fifth-century sculpture; his chest, in billowy, unbuttoned satin shirts or shirtless altogether, a flawless mahogany.

My partner and I, a painter and a poet, Arizona natives, are remarkably untraveled, given our love of art and our ages. At forty, I've visited exactly three cities beyond the U.S. borders: Nogales, Mexico, sixty-five miles south of Tucson, where we live; Toronto; and Montreal. Gary, who is forty-five, traveled twenty years ago in Mexico.

This June day, however, we are on a train running southeast through the Po Valley from Milan to Bologna. For what seems an eternity, we have been in planes, on shuttle buses, in air and train terminals, and finally in this second-class train car. We've folded ourselves into the cramped seats of public conveyances (or waited to fold ourselves into them) for over eighteen hours; we've been awake for more than twenty. Yet now, at least for me, everything delights—the pimply young man, the four-year-old boy next to him who tugs with his teeth at the ham in his hard-roll sandwich, the mother who seated the boy there, who eyes him solicitously from across the aisle, giving little hand signals to direct his lunch excavations—everything delights, now that I am in Italy.

Gary stares out the train window, his face relaxed, at the moment unreadable. I would guess he's struck by the greens that stretch in endless variety to the horizon—crops, fields of corn and grape arbors for miles, with here and there patches, like lovely rashes, of wild red poppies. Six-foot-two, with square, wide shoulders and narrow hips, he is ropy and dust dry. From long hours outdoors—a love of solitary work in the garden and solitary hiking—his skin is cooked dark; his face, when he laughs, crinkles endlessly. This face I have learned to study to consider what he might be thinking; he says little, and dislikes, especially, me speaking for him.

As for myself, I can hardly sit still for the thrum of adrenaline. In this mood, not unlike the cell-to-cell heightening of sensation I used to experience in the early days of a new sexual love, every image seems to bear special significance.

Now the young man seated across from me turns to the boy, then winks and chucks the boy's chin, tousling his hair. I'm momentarily startled. The boy kicks both his legs joyfully and grins all round. Heads pop out across the aisle, the mother and passengers in our area a fleet of smiles. To touch a stranger's child—as an American, I'm trained against such familiarity; as a homosexual, I find the injunction raised to the level of taboo.

The tableau evaporates quickly as we settle into our separateness, the boy having at his sandwich, the young man gazing out the window again, his knees, spread wide apart, bobbing at intervals with the train's motion. I cross my legs, for some reason feeling a need to cover myself. Gary shifts—he never quite fits in train or plane seats, his shoulders too wide, legs too long; he opens the guidebook on his lap. And then I think I see the young man massaging his crotch, stroking himself up and down with the fingers of his right hand, slowly, giving at last a little squeeze.

Amused, not quite believing, I watch this from the edge of my vision while smiling toward the child. Next the youth absentmindedly tugs at the daypack drawstring draped over his thigh, pulling it taut between his legs. With his left hand, he runs the button on this string rhythmically, faster and faster, up and down its length, five or six inches.

§

Bologna, famous for its centuries-old university, is renowned as well for the two medieval towers still standing side by side in the city's old quarter. We know this not only from reading our guidebook but from comments by the couple who will be our hosts in Italy. Michelle, for many years one of Gary's closest Tucson friends, and her fiancé, Riccardo, a native Bolognan who visits us often, have frequently mentioned the visual drama and delight of Le Due Torre.

So it comes as no surprise, shortly after we drop our luggage in the foyer of our friends' apartment, when they urge an evening stroll before dinner to the towers, Garisenda and Asinelli. From there, Riccardo assures us, it's just a short walk to the Piazza Maggiore, Bologna's central square—where, if we're not too tired, we might stop for a drink at one of the bar-cafés.

Though Gary and I have been up now for more than a day, our friends' enthusiasm and the cool evening air, sweeping through the third-floor apartment from balcony doors off the kitchen, give us new life. Besides, we both feel a powerful need to stretch our legs after the long confinement of travel.

Garisenda and Asinelli pop into view in just a few short blocks— as soon as we step from the covered sidewalk. Instantly Riccardo slips into a more confident, almost textbook prose. (At other times, he hesitates, groping for the right word, having spoken English for only three years; perhaps he's practiced these phrases with other Tucson travelers—we're the third set to visit him in the last six months.)

"In the Middle Ages, there were towers like these all over Italy," he begins, the fingers of his right hand uncoiling to emphasize the point. "But ours are in especially good condition." By his tone, one can tell he has sincere affection for the landmarks.

Michelle, who holds on to Riccardo's arm up near the shoulder, points out her favorite architectural details as we walk: frescoed ceilings of upper apartments, glimpsed through windows whose shutters have been thrown open to the night; ornate marble inlays in building foyers; tall carved entry doors with brass door-knockers cast as small lions' heads or small hands. Since May, she and Riccardo have strolled this way almost every evening, she says.

The stark, four-sided towers, meanwhile, rise ever higher, like cubist missiles, as we draw nearer. At more than three hundred feet, Asinelli is particularly commanding; Garisenda, half as tall, tilts drunkenly to one side.

"Wealthy families were always at war with each other; the towers were their forts," Riccardo explains.

Mixing my centuries, I immediately imagine the nobles I've seen in Renaissance paintings—the gentlemen in their velvet garments and embroidered tunics, the bejeweled ladies in puffy satin gowns—huffing up narrow, twisting staircases at a moment's notice. "At one time we had over two hundred towers." Riccardo sweeps his hand toward the night sky proudly. "All over Europe, Bologna was known as Turrita, City of Towers."

It occurs to me that, here in the presence of only two, their singularity, their unique scale, lends them majesty now—if not a touch of phallic absurdity.

"And the bigger the better," Riccardo adds. "Every man wanted a bigger one than his neighbors."

"Some things never change," Michelle intones, as if reading my mind, her voice low in mock seriousness.

"What?" Riccardo eyes us.

"Every man wanted a bigger one. . . ," she repeats.

"Sure!" Riccardo's face lights in a broad smile. "That too!" Even his forehead plays a role, the brow wrinkling as his eyebrows jump. Gary just shakes his head.

A block further on, the Piazza Maggiore opens out before us. Its sudden airy volume, after the mile of narrow streets we've wandered, is stunning. I take in a deep, involuntary breath. And then I see why the piazza's expanse is so striking. Light from strategically placed floodlights splashes the façades of grand Gothic and Renaissance buildings on all four sides, up massive stone columns, across bas-relief figures and patterned, ornamental shapes. Opposite from where we stand, the never-completed Basilica di San Petronio is particularly impressive for its contrasts: on the lower half, horizontal bands of red and white marble, richly carved; above, rising a hundred feet, nothing but plain, raw brickwork, looking much like the exposed adobe of Spanish missions in the Sonoran Desert. The whole piazza, lit at its edges, glows with an exquisite unreality, reminding me of so many Fellini night scenes.

When I am able to look ground-level, I see small groups of people sitting in broken rows along the basilica steps and strollers crossing this way and that at angles, one couple walking arm in arm, a giant schnauzer at their side. My insides hum with the thrill of it all, yet I experience no urge to rush my step. The rhythm of the piazza is obviously leisurely, a rhythm I fall into gratefully.

We stumble in one direction, then another. We want to see everything, from the high, ornamented arches of second-story windows along the east side (Renaissance apartments for university faculty), to Giambologna's three-tiered, sixteenth-century fountain of Neptune, who towers above the level of the piazza at the northwest entrance.

We spend a long time gathering in all the details, all the nuance, of this fountain. Though a bundle of muscle, Neptune strikes me as more a welcoming figure than a fearful one. His posture is soft, almost sensual, his right knee bent, the foot resting on a dolphin in sinuous motion. As in most Neptune sculptures, his right hand supports the trident; but in this one he grasps it low on the pole behind his shoulder, his arm swung back at a gentle angle like a relay runner reaching for a baton. His left leg, bearing the weight of the body, tilts slightly, pushing the hip forward. And his left arm he extends toward the square as a balance to the right while gazing over his left shoulder.

One perspective we most certainly would have missed had not Riccardo, grinning slyly, nudged us into the perfect spot to appreciate the sculptor's humor. Guiding each of us in turn by the shoulders, he has us stand just back of Neptune's right hip. All we can see, looking up, of the god's extended left arm, which is shielded by his torso, is the tip of his thumb—like the head of a dauntingly long and erect penis.

Seated, finally, at an outdoor café table directly across the piazza from the Basilica di San Petronio, whose lighted upper expanse stretches, flat and broad—as if an enormous human brow towers opposite us—I have to give up on the conversation running among Michelle, Gary, and Riccardo. The mix of exhilaration, fatigue, and pleasant alienation I feel in this new time and place, thirty hours from another life, one I can hardly seem to remember, leaves me numb.

Michelle and Gary talk excitedly about possibilities for tomorrow. I love seeing him so voluble. Michelle, whom he cares for deeply (a psychic once told him she'd been his sister in a former life), can draw him out like nobody else. She throws her long black hair back from her shoulder, laughing at something he has said. Then Riccardo points to something in the middle of the piazza.

I stare blankly at our drinks. I think I have never seen a more beautiful green than the green of the mysterious aperitif Riccardo has ordered for us; standing in four tall, narrow, inverted glass bells on stems, they glow as if lit from within on the perfectly white tablecloth.

§

I've not trusted my own eyes ever since the youth on the Po Valley train. Gary also noticed him, I discover when I bring up the subject late that night (as we fit sheets to the foldaway bed in Riccardo and Michelle's living room); he too thought the young man's actions oddly, if unconsciously, sexual. But I've not had the nerve to mention that I think I notice men everywhere touching themselves in public. The whole thing seems a little silly. I can't stop myself, however, from keeping count.

In Florence, our third day in Italy, we visit the Uffizi, the museum housing the Medici art collection. I stand in tears before the Botticelli *Annunciation*. Something in the purity of Mary's isolation, the indeterminacy of her gaze—if she looks anywhere, it must be inward. Each object in the narrative is rendered with a radiant precision, the artist's care a form of love, from Gabriel's transparent outer garment to the pale gray-and-green-checkered marble floor tiles beneath Mary's feet. The exquisite stillness of the moment I find wrenchingly beautiful. Botticelli seems unconcerned with showing the world what he can do with paint; rather, he draws all attention to the nature of the moment; he embodies, and the viewer experiences, the poignancy of Mary's fate.

After four hours in the museum, we stroll across the Ponte Vecchio, the bridge where Dante first caught sight of Beatrice, through the courtyard of the Pitti Palace to the grounds of the Boboli Gardens, the gardens of the Medicis. Dazed by so many medieval and Renaissance masterpieces, I'm grateful for this resting place, the acres of cool tree-lined paths, the grace of fountains, the views of Florence from hilltop lookouts. A more extraordinary day is unimaginable.

Yet on the train from Bologna to Florence, in walks from the

Duomo to the Uffizi, from the Uffizi across the Ponte Vecchio to the gardens and back, and on the train home to Bologna again, I cannot stop myself from registering eleven touches. And on our second evening walk to the Piazza Maggiore, five more. And on the day we stand speechless inside the Scrovegni Chapel in Padua, a day-trip by train—Giotto's frescoes, the modeling of human features and swirls of grieving angels a mystery of beauty I fumble to express in my journal, the pages an abstract expressionist tangle of scrawled phrases and blacked-out words, the frescoes, I decide, a mystery of beauty no prose can embody—nine more touches.

"Michelle," I say our fourth day at breakfast, a roll and *caffe con latte* with two spoons of sugar—I'm hooked, me, who for years insisted self-righteously it's not coffee if you put something in it—"do men here. . . ." I lose my nerve. Then find it again: "Do men here . . . touch themselves in public?"

"Yeeeeees," she yowls, stretching the word interminably, her pitch ascending. "Riccardo, did you hear that?"

He smiles weakly. Down. At his roll.

"They do it all the time! Anywhere!" Syllable by syllable, her pitch streaks up and down. "On all his jeans, he's got this little worn spot," she says, staring at Riccardo, who won't meet her eyes. "It drives me crazy when I do the laundry."

We have been in Italy less than a week, yet a curious—and wholly unanticipated—theme has crept into my journal. I determine to discuss it with Gary as I sit alone on the steps of the Duomo in Florence at the end of our second day-trip here, a day we devote primarily to the art in churches.

Dusk, the square between the Duomo and the Baptistry is a great outdoor theater with many stages, small dramas taking place everywhere. A group of sailors dressed in identical white uniforms, topped by white berets with black tassels, stand side by side, arms looped shoulder over shoulder, a chorus line. In their vertical regularity they remind me of the folds of an accordion. They've asked a young woman in red Lycra pants and halter top, her dark hair hanging to her waist, to take eight snapshots, one for each of them. Behind these sailors, groups gather and disperse at intervals before the magnificent Ghiberti bronze door of the Baptistry, which depicts Old Testament stories: a tall, middle-aged woman in a severe blue suit addresses a dozen schoolgirls who listen with admirable concentration as she gestures from one narrative panel to the next; then a young woman in leopard-patterned miniskirt and black high heels poses, one foot perched on the second bar of the protective railing, while her female companion snaps photos from a variety of angles; next, seven elderly couples, all wearing sneakers, approach.

What draws my attention from them—and convinces me to discuss with Gary my journal observations—are the antics of four teenagers, two boys and two girls, not twenty feet in front of the step on which I sit. The two boys seem to be flirting with the girls by being sexual with one another. They wrap their arms around each other's waists; one lays his head on his friend's shoulder. The girls burst into laughter. The boys draw apart, pretending their feelings are hurt. Then one gives the other a kiss on the cheek. The girls double over, jerk up, briefly turn their backs, swing around, their hands at their mouths, a twist of giggles. Now the boys are laughing, their pose exposed. Then the taller wraps himself around his shorter friend from behind, resting his chin on the boy's shoulder.

This goes on and on, the boys doing anything they can to keep the girls entertained, riding piggyback, holding hands, blowing in each other's ears. Their play is a dance, spontaneous and graceful, not the least like the boyish roughhousing I remember from my youth—also performed at times in front of girls to impress. These boys do know how to touch each other's bodies.

I'm fascinated, and frustrated Gary has been gone the whole time, circling the Duomo for twilight photos. During the thirty minutes he's been away, the square has vibrated with youthful energy, not only the four I've been watching closely, but two boys and a girl on scooters playing tag, zagging this way and that, half a dozen dark-haired young men dressed like *New York Magazine* models, pleated pants and bright, billowy shirts with slicked hair, who stride off and onto the square (though where they go off to I can't tell), as well as an indeterminate number of young people in groups and solo on the steps around me and in the open area that I don't bother to follow, not wanting to miss the next move by the flirting boys.

Shortly after Gary rejoins me, as I'm trying to fill him in on the various scenes, two motorcycle officers zip to a halt at the edge of the square. Instantly the hum and weave of youths evaporates. The space stands two-thirds empty, stripped to those of us who are middle-aged or older and one young woman with a baby in a stroller.

I have a memory that is kin to this feeling, this undercurrent I've been experiencing. As an adolescent twenty-five years ago, confused by my sexual fantasies about other boys, I was moved inexplicably by certain stories. I especially remember reading Thomas Mann's *Death in Venice* with a fascination that entered my body as a physical sensation. This was something other, something beyond the usual pleasure of entering the lives of compelling fictional characters. A part of me was being addressed that I didn't yet know myself how to contact.

> [T]he boy was absolutely beautiful. His face, pale and reserved, framed with honey-colored hair, the straight sloping nose, the lovely mouth, the expression of sweet and godlike seriousness, recalled Greek sculpture of the noblest period; and the complete purity of the forms was accompanied by such a rare personal charm that, as [Aschenbach] watched, he felt that he had never met with anything equally felicitous in nature or the plastic arts.

I'd read nothing quite like this open adoration of a boy's features. At this point Aschenbach tells himself his interest in Tadzio is aesthetic; by mid story an element of eroticism infuses his descriptions:

> His honey-colored hair clung in rings about his neck and temples. The sun made the down on his back glitter; the fine etching of the ribs, the symmetry of the chest, were emphasized by the tightness of the suit across the buttocks.

On the steps of the Florence Duomo, I confess to Gary having experienced Tadzios everywhere, not just boys but men and girls and women so striking that in their form and motion I think I see a synthesis of the aesthetic and the sensual. At the Uffizi two days earlier, in the Botticelli Room, as I leaned to note the delicacy of detail in the flowers at the lower left corner of *Primavera,* I caught sight of an extraordinary family standing to my side—two boys, a girl, their mother, all with wavy golden hair, satin skin, perfect oval faces, and oversized soft eyes. They might have stepped from a Botticelli canvas. That day they seemed to follow us—to the Boboli Gardens, then the Masaccio frescoes, and finally the train station.

But it wasn't just their physical beauty that moved me. I was transfixed by their ongoing physical relation to one another, the way the siblings and mother brushed or leaned unconsciously on each other's bodies, holding hands loosely, sometimes by one or two fingers, releasing their contact and then reconnecting as easily as breathing. These touches were not claims, not the nudges, the protective, confining embraces that tell a child or sibling that somebody else is in charge. The family, rather, seemed wrapped in an invisible, blanketing dance of comfort.

As my emotion grows in the telling, Gary simply nods in acknowledgment. I am always more excitable, more effusive, than he is. I'm relieved he at least remembers the family.

The men and boys are what most amaze me, I confide, given the taboo I grew up with against men touching. I find my days here infused—I'm almost ashamed to say it—with a heightened sensuality. (What I don't say—it's the kind of thing we don't know how to discuss, and who wants to break the spell?—what I don't say is that I sense in our lovemaking, since we got to Italy, a new intensity.)

I recount how often I've seen men in unselfconscious contact with each other's bodies. In the central shopping district of Bologna, how often pairs, many of whom I take to be fathers and sons, walk arm in arm. One twosome wore similar dark suits and ties, their resemblance startling, the round faces, slightly downturned noses, and small, close-set dark eyes; the father a shrunken, silver-haired version of the black-haired, thirtyish man attached to his side.

And on the train back from Padua, how the schoolboys stood in bunches, draped on one another, at times virtually entwined for balance in the aisles, joking and singing songs, bursting with adrenaline, unable to remain seated. At train stations their voices soared as they hung out the car windows. At one stop, a boy standing next to my seat raced to the end of the car. I watched as he threw his arms around a young man who had just climbed aboard. Startled at first, the new passenger, recognizing his assailant, embraced him tightly, face flushed. They kissed, pulled back, embraced again and kissed again, speaking both at once and rapidly. And then they separated, heading in opposite directions.

Almost daily in Italy, in the presence of certain works by Giotto, Fra Angelico, Masaccio, Filippino Lippi, Botticelli, Piero della Francesca, I have been deeply stirred as I am each time I hear the simple, haunting theme and harmonic progression underlying the Allegretto of Beethoven's Symphony No.7; as I am each time I watch, in the closing moments of the film *Babbette's Feast,* the old worshipers joining hands round the wishing well, following their transforming encounter with sensuality, with God's healing grace.

I can't help fumbling to name these sensations, these moments of body knowledge; Gary can't help remaining silent, at home in color and line and volume as means of conveying the unutterable.

The body knowledge we experience through art, we *do* work in our own ways to negotiate; body knowledge of the erotic or sexual in our daily lives, on the other hand, we are spectacularly incapable of articulating. In these matters our understanding accrues through action over the years. We dare not speak of what we feel, let alone talk about what we do—as though mysteries of the flesh are too powerful, too interior, to enter into through language. My small confession on the steps of the Florence Duomo is as close as I can usually come to discussion of such subjects.

This time it is enough. On the train back to Bologna, a young man in our compartment lounges, half asleep, head resting on a male friend's shoulder, their inside arms loosely entwined—a detail Gary and I register simultaneously, an ether of intimacy encircling us like an embrace.

No guidebook, nor even personal testimony, can prepare one for the glad shock. A friend said simply he wished he could be there to catch me as I fell in a dead faint.

As the train slows to a halt, out the windows I see the standard parallel tracks, the standard chains of orange-red train cars at rest; a faded green one is pulling out. In the last mile, we have crossed water, which speeds my heart.

Yet out the windows, the unremarkable, unimaginative architecture of yet another train stop, this one half a century old, with massive sweeps of fascist concrete. We know we will be staying here four days, so we sit—on the outside calm, as if above the bustle, or as if we are old hands at this. Let the others gather their things in a frenzy and bump through the aisles and out the doors. This refusal to rush is Gary's influence, the rhythm of a painter who can spend months on a single twelve-by-fourteen-inch canvas.

At last our footsteps clack in the suddenly empty train car. Down the metal stair to the landing, then along the walkway as we shoulder our travel bags into the enormous hollow of the station proper. Glassed-in gift shops, snack counters, and currency exchange offices have taken bites from the open rectangle.

Today is mild. A low, woolly cloud mass, softening the edges of things, has hovered since we stepped from the apartment door in Bologna. Yet now, through the floor-to-ceiling windows and glass doors of the far wall, something about the light signals a change, a silvery cast, a burnish that draws us forward. We ignore an old man who thrusts small hotel ads into our hands; we stride toward the light, which leads to the broad stone terrace and stairs cascading to the Grand Canal of fifteenth-century Venice.

—the glow of not-quite-ochre walls, the glow of not-quite-peach; a row of four-story Renaissance houses, carved white wooden balcony posts, the crackling fragments of light along the water's surface, the quiet—Gary smiles and points toward both his ears; inside my head a refrain, *no cars, no cars*

—the drapery of three young men sprawled on the station stairs in bright white T-shirts and denim cutoffs, legs wide apart, the genitals of one peeking out; their heads thrown back and resting on their palms, staring at the clouds, all three with curly hair (one light, two dark) and features not yet edged by age, their loose-tied backpacks scattered on the steps—Gary nods; in my head, *the Graces, three Tadzios*

—the chug of the vaporetto motor in ripples up our legs, on our waterbus a density of bodies not stiff as in New York subway cars but a matter-of-fact, alongside-the-body community; heads turn this way and that, arms point—the radiance of church domes, the up-sweep of palace balconies, and then on a crumbling dock, a couple necking; he sits, legs dangling above the water; she's on his lap, her legs looped around his back, her yellow skirt hiked up, a bottle of wine to their side on the weathered deck; on the vaporetto, a community of knowing, nodding heads

Sometimes naming the magic does not destroy it; sometimes naming calls the magic more directly forth. As we pull into the dock at the Piazza San Marco, I'm struck by the row of marble nudes arrayed atop the length of the Libreria Vecchia, their postures a compendium: adorations of the human form.

Climbing from the bobbing vaporetto to the landing, I stumble—but don't. Gary, stepping up at my side, gazing toward the buzzing piazza, has looped his arm securely through mine.

ENVOI

We must make choices in Rome. Having spent our time awash in the iconography of religious paintings and frescoes from the Gothic period and the Renaissance, having spent our days in still, sometimes dark, places—the interiors of the churches and museums of Florence and Bologna and Venice—we decide on a change. We are ready for open space and the relative austerity of antiquity. If we haven't time for the Sistine Chapel and Vatican Museums, so be it.

Our first priority is the Roman Forum. As it happens, our hotel, chosen from a guidebook and secured by phone, is close to the Vatican. It's no trouble at all to pass through St. Peter's Square on our way to the ruins. The square, a great bowl formed by two semicircular colonnades, like arms extending from either side of the church, is so large, all that's human shrinks to unreality. Tourist buses, permitted to pull up on the edge of the square's cobbled skirt, look like Matchbox toys.

As Gary prepares to take a photo, three cardinals pop out from among the columns to our right. In their floor-length black robes, dusting the cobblestones, they seem like men on a conveyor belt, gliding, or men without bodies—only their heads and hands peek out from the heavy drapery, which swallows their trunks and limbs.

The cardinals aren't without color, however. Long tassels hang from brilliant pink sashes tied at their waists, and two wear skullcaps of the same neon color. This pink I think of as gay-pink, a shade several of my out-of-the-closet students wear proudly. One is never without some bit of the color, whether it be a large triangle silk-screened on a black T-shirt, or socks strobing from atop his Reeboks. Inspired by him, I purchased a bright pink visored cap for this trip—a perfect match for these men of the cloth.

With a flick of my hand, I signal to Gary I'm about to slip in with the clerics for a photo. My task is complicated, unfortunately, by the six carbine-toting guards who fan twenty feet back in a protective semicircle. I make my move (not too close), am not fired upon; Gary gets a snapshot; and we chuckle at this bit of Catholic color-irony—the church that would just as soon treat our kind like those bothersome Renaissance rationalists, some of whom were burned at the stake.

Even from a several-block distance, we can see we've made the right decision—the Roman Forum is a landscape of essentials, the ruins like giant bones scattered in an enormous garden. Behind the three forty-foot, fluted columns remaining of the Temple of the Castors, nothing but sky, an open and endless blue. The scale here is represented by implication: for the volume of a massive, stadium-size basilica, two and one-half arches of a single side wall; for a temple, a row of white marble nubs spaced five feet apart, like tooth stumps, where pillars once rose.

I must restrain myself from holding my arms outstretched, or from simply running. I welcome such openness, and the simplification of color: red (earth) and blue (sky) and white (marble) and brown (brick) and green (trees, grass). In the late June warmth, the urge is strong to simplify on bodily terms, to strip off our shirts and feel the sun on our skin as we walk our whole first day, and the morning of the second, in the Forum and on the hill above, the Palatine, the ruins of the rulers' palaces.

When the second afternoon turns cloudy, we head for the museums nearby to spend the last of our sight-seeing hours among the pre-Christian marble and bronze sculptures. In one room, nothing but heads, the busts of emperors and poets lined up on stepped rows. All particulars—an oblong skull, foreshortened brow, or twist of nose—faithfully conveyed: these are portraits. Elsewhere, along the walls and on pedestals in the rooms' centers, idealized studies of the human form, primarily male, figures from myth and pre-Christian religion: on Hercules and the Dying Gaul and Neptune, perfectly symmetrical pectorals, a precise line descending from the neck along the sternum, then branching in an arc to either side below the breasts and up to the smooth, hollowed pits of the arms; a fine crease running up the inside of each full thigh to the upper hip; calves and shoulders muscled, but modestly so, in balance; buttocks rounded and firm.

By accident, yet as if to focus our attention on the male body, we visit last the courtyard of the Palazzo dei Conservatori Museum. I grab hold of Gary's arm, gasping in amazed delight at sight of what is propped along the courtyard walls: enormous body parts. Something about the exaggeration makes me want to laugh. The scale is parody. Here, on a pedestal, a hand standing on its wrist, the forefinger pointing toward the sky, the whole of it six feet, end to end; nearby, an upper arm, perhaps ten feet long; at the back right corner, a head and neck the size of a tiny European sedan. These and the other fragments—feet, one elbow joint, a kneecap, a chunk of torso, and so on—were once unified in a towering statue of Constantine.

The clouds having lifted some, we decide we have just enough energy for a small detour on our walk to the hotel; we'll visit the Piazza Navona to see Bernini's Fountain of the Four Rivers. There are, in fact, three fountains on the square, each peopled by figures with rippling musculature—they've spent too long in the gym, by Golden Age standards. In something of a sight-seeing stupor, we have difficulty figuring which fountain is which. The one of Neptune, trident upraised, body twisted in combat with an octopus, is recognizable enough. But we must poke our noses into the guidebook's brief description twice to know which of the other two represents the rivers at the Earth's four corners.

A man approaches, shirt trailing from a back pocket, skin deeply tanned, a map of Rome in hand; we are kin, tourists in small ways lost. He asks directions to the Pantheon. Gary finds us on the map and helps the man, from England, chart a course. Off he heads. Briefly we turn to the fountains.

Breaking from the piazza's edge, we see the Brit two blocks ahead, crossing an empty street. His skin glows in the failing light—the ancients would approve, I think, of his balanced proportions. A sudden *bleat bleat* interrupts my thoughts; two tiny blue-and-white police cars, like mechanical bugs, skid to a halt, wedging our tourist brother in the street's painted median.

We quicken our step, close enough now to see a hand dart in and out of a police car window. A finger points to the shirt dangling from the man's butt, then to his chest. His brow crinkles in confusion, smooths—he tugs the shirt hastily over his head.

As the cops pull away, we lope to his side. "Don't go walking about without your top," he laughs. "I gather that in Rome, a shirt-less man is something of an affront!"

A few blocks on, the sky, which seemed only moments before to have cleared, explodes. All along the street, pedestrians scurry to shelter under doorways. Under ours, a scooped, shell-shaped canvas awning, two young female shop clerks edge out to observe the spontaneous river rising toward the curb. People in clusters, who moments before idly window-shopped, or walked purposefully, as did we, toward their destinations, hug themselves against the surprising chill in the air. I see my face in theirs—I'm annoyed, I'm tired and cold, hands jammed in my pockets, rocking on the balls of my feet, eager for the comfort of our hotel room. Gary, who embraces rain anytime at our desert home for the sake of his garden vegetables and flowers, couldn't be more radiant.

And then we hear angels—four sweet, high voices, singing. I laugh, my body relaxes. Four teenage Gypsy girls skip down the middle of the river, holding hands in a line, kicking the water. Their long skirts fly, their dark hair shakes. In thin, short-sleeve cotton blouses, drenched to transparency, they light the street.

Destino

Rigoberto González

My father holds a peculiar fascination for extraterrestrial life. For years he subscribed to the Spanish version of *UFO—OVNI: Objetos Voladores No Identificados*—which came packed with firsthand narrative accounts of close encounters with space aliens. That magazine was fully illustrated with amateur drawings depicting these intriguing and evasive creatures. He even confessed to me one night, as we were looking up at the stars and he pointed out Polaris yet again, that one of his fantasies was to be abducted by a UFO.

"For what?" I asked, shuddering at the idea of space travel. At the time, our favorite show was *Battlestar Galactica;* our favorite reruns, *Star Trek* and the black-and-white *Twilight Zone* and *Outer Limits*. But I suspected that the imaginative special effects and costume artistry did not begin to address the disconcerting reality of what was out there.

"Just," he responded quizzically. "Just to know."

Just to know. I never asked what it was exactly he wanted to know. I simply gazed up at the stars with him and tried to imagine the extraterrestrial forces that had mesmerized my father to the point of wanting to become a part of unraveling the intergalactic mysteries that had puzzled humanity and charmed Hollywood. Perhaps his desire is not unlike my own appetite to be somewhere else, hoping to stumble upon a place for reflection about who I am, where I stand, and how far I can go.

In Spanish, the word for "destiny" and "destination" is the same: *destino*. The word suggests that to travel to a place is to complete an expectation, fulfilling an unstoppable course of direction. The word *destino* also implies that travel occurs less out of choice than out of need, which for my family has been the case. My father doesn't believe in travel for leisure. Like his father before him, he travels only when there's a purpose—a trip to the good swap meet in the neighboring town, a commute to a well-paying job, an overdue visit to family living just south of the border or farther south in Michoacán.

Always the journey is on a road that my father has driven before. Or, if it's on a new road, the journey usually marks the first of many, so he invests time in learning the street names, the gas station locations, and the key symbols—buildings and billboards—that will guide his path from then on. Traveling means moving through familiar grounds, coming across the same places, and meeting up with the same people. The well known translates into safety and practicality. To my father's thinking nothing is more pointless than wasting costly gas on unnecessary excursions. And nothing is more dangerous than straying into the strange, unknown terrains of faraway neighborhoods, cities, or lands. My father is no tourist.

Much of my father's thinking is affected by class. Being a tourist denotes a certain level of privilege and disposable income. I grew up in a migrant-farming family that labors hard for low wages, income supplemented by government assistance—everything from food stamps to unemployment insurance. Any money saved up is spent in the lean months. In the migrant farmworker calendar, there are many such months.

Like many families, mine learned to travel through television. This kept us from remaining ignorant to the notion of a world. Channel 4 gave us Africa via Marlon Perkins and Mutual of Omaha—*animalandria,* my grandfather christened it. Channel 6 gave us New York, Los Angeles, and New Orleans. In the late 1970s, the local stations gave us a bit of bilingual programming on Sunday mornings via Carmen Zapata in *Villa Alegre* and *The Val de la O Show.* When my family invested in cable in the 1980s, we gained access to the informative international travelogues of the Spanish station variety shows, such as Florida's *Sábado Gigante* and Mexico's *Siempre en Domingo.* As part of their regular weekend itinerary, hosts Don Francisco and Raúl Velasco introduced the Latin American community to each other: Caracas met Mexico City; San Juan met Valparaíso; Rio de Janeiro met Acapulco, and so on. Couch tourism compensated for the lack of time and money necessary to make those visits in real life.

Exploring vicariously through television remains satisfactory to most members of my family. Of course, this doesn't guarantee an advanced level of geographical knowledge. For years as I was growing up in Mexico, I had heard people refer to the United States simply as *el norte*—the north—because that's the direction one travels to seek work. Conversely, after my family had migrated to *el norte,* when they talked about Michoacán or Mexico, they spoke generally, referring to these places as *el sur*—the south. So when television hosts discuss notable cities, my family understands them as places somewhere else, to the south of south, or to the north of north. To unfold a map is useless since distances between two points is also vaguely understood as "far" or "really far."

So it was with some hesitation that I began to share my traveling experiences and this exotic act of climbing into an airplane to get places. My father, grandmother, and brother have only flown once in their lives—none of them aspire to do so again. They marvel at the fact that for years now I have been flying on average twice a month.

In my immediate family I am the only one who has moved away—really far—from home. I left Michoacán with my family to go to *el norte,* and then I left them behind, moving out on my own at age seventeen. I moved from southern California to northern California; to Phoenix, Arizona; to Albuquerque, New Mexico; to New York City; to Seattle, Washington; and most recently back to the East Coast, to Brooklyn.

After I visited my first U.S. city outside California, Chicago, in the summer of 1991, I bragged to my family about it.

My cousin inquired, "Is that far north?"

I said, "Closer to Canada than to Mexico."

My aunt, wanting to show she appreciated this feat, added with an air of authority, "Almost near Sacramento, then."

Over the years I've kept in touch from all of my homes and on all of my wanderings by sending my family postcards, sometimes wondering where on the abstract map of destinations they are placing me. To keep my peripatetic existence somewhat comprehensible, I never reveal that I sometimes visit places just for fun. Always, I explain I am going to certain cities for work. Since my family knows about my skills as an educator and translator, they assume it's for one of these reasons. No one asks for further clarification and none is offered.

I will on occasion be asked a curious question about what I have seen and what I have done, and my replies are brief and accessible. I like to give historical discourses such as the ones on *Sábado Gigante.* The few times I attempted to do this, the conversation was quickly sidelined by more pressing concerns—a pot left boiling on the stove, children fighting, the telephone. The topic was tabled indefinitely.

At first I was a little hurt by my family's lack of interest and short-lived curiosity. Since I move and travel so often, it has become a joke among relatives to ask me as soon as I walk in through the door: "So where do you live now?" When I call: "So where are you calling from now?" Half guessing game, the exchange is brief, focusing eventually on what we have in common: them. I recognize that I am not meant to educate my own family about the places I've seen. Mine is a more serious role.

My brother and my first cousins settled into family life at an early age. With marriage came children, and with children came the responsibility of providing for them. This was no different from the generations before us. And for years I was always reproached for my choices, which were not theirs: I stayed in school, I moved away, I didn't settle down. I have never made an official announcement to my family that I'm gay and therefore will never marry. As I near my mid-thirties, making such an announcement would be stating the obvious. But out of politeness, people assume I'm not settled down because of my itinerant jobs.

I am surprised, then, when I hear my cousins point me out to their young children as a role model—as concrete evidence of what they could do and achieve if they study, earn good grades, work hard. For us, settling down has always been a sign of growing up, maturing. Refusing to establish roots is seen as an act of defiance, immaturity. But that notion is slowly changing because I have demonstrated that I can be financially independent, and that I can afford to travel and move ahead and explore on my own terms. Mine is a lifestyle never seen before in the family and though they don't understand it completely they acknowledge one important fact: that it's a life possible even for one of their own. I had grown up in Mexico just as they had, I had worked in the agricultural fields just like they did, and here I am now, booking flights, making hotel-room reservations, and renewing my passport.

Even my father and grandfather, ever the staunch traditionalists, have begun to show a level of appreciation. For years they worried that no one was around to look after me or take care of my domestic needs. They also felt disconnected because they didn't know how to reach me. More recently their apprehension has been shifting toward acceptance. As proof of this, my brother reported a certain family exchange to me over one of our weekly phone conversations:

"He sure does get around," my father had said to my brother. As usual, the men had gathered on the porch in the afternoon to drink beer and swat mosquitoes.

"He must make good money," my grandfather added.

"Does he have to travel so often?" my father asked.

"He likes it," my brother said.

"Well, if he likes to travel and he's making good money, he must be really happy," my grandfather concluded.

"I guess that's fine," my father said. End of topic.

My brother did pursue the matter, however, by confronting me with the essential question: "But, hey, don't you feel lonely being away and alone all the time?"

I think about it carefully, rummaging through the complex itinerary of memories in my head. I have to confess that I'm frequently alone and that I hate being lonely, but mine is a solitary profession. But sometimes I wonder if I chose the field to make sure I'd have to leave my family, and if my decision to live independently of my family was informed by the fear of remaining closeted. In any case, being a writer and a traveler has brought me to this, a solitary life. I read and I write, by myself. Single and unattached, I leave my computer and seek social interaction, on my own. And because I relocate frequently, I leave friendships behind and succumb to a sense of perpetual adjustment.

Yet while traveling, I arrive at a city and look forward to becoming engulfed immediately by the street signs and pedestrian traffic, by its social and cultural offerings. There is something invigorating about this energy, and the challenge of keeping up with the flow of motion is exciting. In rare instances, however, I do feel displaced and invisible: I get lost, I roam through a city simply observing and not communicating with another human being, I walk into a place where people are socializing comfortably because they did not come in solo and for the first time like I did. I feel then that I have not escaped the solitude of my relationship to my work, and that I am still in exile, excluded from the everyday din of life. I long for a familiar voice at that moment and I resist the urge to rush back to my hotel room to make a phone call. I cannot be afraid or defeated. I owe it to my family who lives unable to venture into the unknown without having a proper purpose. I owe it to the younger generation who must know the beauty of travel and the satisfaction of opportunity, advantage, and adventure. Above all I owe it to myself to reap the rewards for the sacrifice of moving on without family or friends.

"Yes," I admit to my brother. "I get lonely."

My reply is honest. Judging by the silence that follows on the other end of the line, I suspect that my answer has startled my brother. Suddenly I feel as if I have betrayed myself.

For years I tried to convince my brother to travel. Now he has the excuse that he works a full-time job to support his family, but before that he had no excuse I would accept.

"What for?" he would ask. This was a short but complicated question, and I didn't have a brief answer for it.

I'm reminded of my father's alien abduction fantasy: his is a dream that will never come true; he will never embark on mind-twisting expeditions to other worlds or dimensions. Our destinies are as different as our destinations. But the spirit of the migrant worker is what connects us. My father's wishful leaving and my insistence to stay away from but always connected to home prove to both of us that, at the end of the day, we're simply living out the restlessness of the migrant soul.

My father is now retired and settled back in Michoacán with no plans to go anywhere "except six feet into the ground." And as I ride the subway into Manhattan in search of a sturdier suitcase to replace the nearly defeated Samsonite in my closet at home, I suspect that my father keeps his fantasy of alien abduction alive after all these years, even if he now sits tucked safely in his house, catching a glimpse at the evening sky from his living room or the kitchen as the day comes to a close and his mind escapes, however briefly, from the day-to-day turmoil of worries and responsibilities. My father, the former migrant farm worker and would-be cosmonaut, still envisions himself floating out into space with his back turned to the world, his face looking fearlessly into the great abyss of things mysterious, unknown, and new.

In attempting to reconcile my privilege, I reach for a fantasy of my own, that my wanderlust blossomed within me in the womb, just like my sexuality.

As my father tells it, he and my mother were following the grape route north. My mother was pregnant. They were driving along the back roads because the highways and the speeding cars frightened my mother. They came across a fork.

"Which way should we go?" my father asked my mother.

My mother contemplated the two paths before them for a few seconds. My father remembers that the roads were dark and neither gave any hint about where it was heading. My mother said that it really didn't matter. Both roads were going north. Since she was pregnant and an undocumented alien, she only wanted to make sure that her child was born a U.S. citizen. To secure him or her a future with prospects and opportunities, any city would do.

"Which way then?" my father pressed on.

"Go right," my mother said, pointing. And right they turned, arriving at Bakersfield, California, where I was born, as was, a year and a half later, my brother.

I don't have any early memories of Bakersfield because my family returned to Mexico when I was two. And I was not to know the city until I visited some cousins there in 1993, when I was twenty-two. But I had passed the town a year before. My father and brother were driving me to my new home in Davis, California, where I was going to be attending graduate school. As with any road trip, my father's strategy was to get there quickly so that he could quickly turn back and get home. At about three in the morning, we had been on the road for five hours. My father preferred to travel by night to avoid the traffic and to be on virtually empty roads in case the car broke down. We had taken off from the Mexican border, where my family was currently living. Suddenly, once we passed a dark canyon, we came across an off-ramp with a sign just before it that read: BAKERSFIELD. I turned to my brother and pointed out, "Look! That's where we were born!"

I didn't feel any sentimentality or longing for the place of my birth. Bakersfield was just another place for all of us to pass through.

Tea with
Paul Bowles

From a Tangier Diary, 1991

Edward Field

The Moroccan taxi driver knew the Villa Itesa, where Paul Bowles lives, and drove me there, even though I gave him the wrong address. It was a plain block of flats standing alone in a quiet middle-class residential area of Tangier, well beyond the bustle of the center of town. Across the road is the walled compound of the Voice of America and the American consulate, with armed soldiers patrolling the sidewalk around it. How can he live here? I thought. Then, immediately, But of course, where else would Paul live? In spite of his reputation for daring the Unknown, he had found a safe, ultra-respectable neighborhood.

It was spring. Instead of plunging from winter into summer like New York does, Tangier was enjoying week after week of cool, changeable weather—clouds alternating with sun, breezy days, rainy spells, chilly evenings. Though when the sun came out it blazed with an African fierceness.

The knowing taxi driver drove right around the building to the entrance at the rear. Passing a watchful concierge, I took the elevator to the top floor. The building was in much better condition than the rundown, once-pretentious apartment house where my friend Neil Derrick and I were living for the several weeks we planned to spend in Tangier. Paul's neighborhood, the Marshan, home to the Moroccan middle-class and foreign residents, was respectable compared to ours, with its downtown raffish mix of classes, and where I hardly saw a foreigner, much less an American, and you really knew you were in Morocco.

Paul Bowles has lived in the same building since 1957. His wife, Jane, who died in 1973, had a flat a few floors below him, which was now owned by the painter Buffy Johnson. I had met Buffy in Paris in 1949 with Gordon Sager, a novelist, both friends of the Bowleses. They were just back from Tangier, sunburned and sleazily dressed, part of a scene that seemed terribly decadent to me—the word "decadent" had a pejorative meaning for me then. They lived hard, drank heavily, were into drugs, and positively reveled in what seemed to me a sordid sex scene involving orgies and hustlers. That was a different era—the war just over, the DP camps still full, and I was a communist, or practically. But just the same, what a little prig I was, judging these two. What financed their gypsyish life-style, I wondered?

Private incomes? Allowances from families? Being kept? I vaguely disapproved of their pleasure-seeking lives, though, bohemian as I was, I also disapproved of those who took the conventional route of security. A few years later, I saw an abstract mural by Buffy Johnson in the old Astor Theatre in Times Square. So she got commissions. But at that time we called doing such commercial art "selling out."

Paul Bowles, brilliant writer though he was (my generation was in thrall of him for his story "Pages from Cold Point"), seemed to be one of that "decadent" crowd and, like them, able to live, mysteriously, without an obvious source of income—my friend, the late American writer Alfred Chester spoke darkly of "Paul and Jane's millionaires," who gave them handouts. Virgil Thompson bitchily claimed that after getting all the grants as a composer, Paul Bowles turned to writing and got them all again as a writer—though with the recent movie of his novel *The Sheltering Sky,* all his works in print, and a major Paul Bowles revival underway from New York to Paris to Tokyo, there is no doubt where the money is coming from now.

I had mailed a note to Paul a few days before, asking if I could see him, and it seemed that in no time Neil and I had come home from the covered market at the Socco Grande, loaded with shopping bags, to find a friendly note under the door inviting me to tea. As I stepped out of the rickety elevator of the Villa Itesa and rang his doorbell, I was cursing myself for not bringing a gift, even some pastry.

A dark, slender, saturnine Moroccan let me in, barely mumbling a word. I could not tell if he was a servant or friend or if I should shake his hand. He did not welcome me in any way, simply held aside a heavy drape over a doorway for me to enter the living room, without coming in with me. This, I learned later, was Mohammed Mrabet, Paul Bowles's companion, helper, and bodyguard, who was considered dangerous, in what way I was not told. From his manner and looks I was prepared to believe it.

It was stiflingly hot inside the living room. Paul, considerably aged from twenty-five years before when I had first met him, was reclining on cushions on the floor, and half rose to greet me, looking surprised, as if I were the last person in the world he was expecting to see. His face was that of a superannuated boy scout with a false upper plate and a fixed, pert expression, and his body, though still agile, was shrunken and had lost its articulation. His torso seemed to be of one piece, without chest and hips or waist between, as if it had consolidated. But he did have all his hair.

With us in the room was Rodrigo Rey Rosa, a darkly handsome young Central American writer, whom I had met in New York at the Moondance Diner in Soho. He had been a student of Paul's, and Paul has since translated his stories. Also there was Walter Clemmons, a journalist who had flown in from New York specially to interview Paul about Gore Vidal, whose biography Clemmons was writing.

Paul's act of surprise at seeing me, as if I had unexpectedly dropped in, aroused my suspicion that he had invited me to prevent Clemmons from quizzing him about Vidal. A paranoid atmosphere, which makes you suspicious of everything about him, surrounds Paul, especially since he is known to set up iffy situations in which he can sit back and watch how they turn out. Or perhaps it is something in me that is susceptible to him in that way. But I was reassured by the undeniable fact that he did have his chauffeur drive him into town to deliver the note under my door.

Faced with this awkward situation, I found myself blabbing out of self-consciousness, and saying all kinds of outrageous things. I couldn't stop myself, and even bad-mouthed a mutual friend, at which Paul turned to his protégé, Rodrigo Rey Rosa, to protest, "Oh, but we like him, he's a friend of ours!" I was irritated because of course I also liked him, and felt it was Paul who made me say stupid things.

His power is such a controlling one and he is so reserved, I tried to lessen the awkwardness paralyzing the room and loosen things up by talking scandalously. I shouldn't have but dropped the alarming news of a mutual friend being HIV-positive to try and get some kind of response. Nothing. Then, going further, I brought up an old friend of Paul's, Maurice Grosser, who had still been sexually active into his eighties and had recently died of ARC, perhaps the oldest AIDS-related death in the country. This evoked the stern comment, whether true or not, I don't know, that anyone discovered to have AIDS in Morocco was quietly put to death by the authorities.

Trying another tack, I told Paul how much I enjoyed reading the recently published biography of him by Christopher Sawyer-Lauçanno. Another mistake. He scornfully dismissed the book as being mostly material supplied by Virgil Thompson and full of errors. I argued that a biography being interesting had nothing to do with it being factually correct. I said no interview with me had ever been accurate, which might offend me, but readers couldn't care less, if it made a good story. Walter Clemmons joined in to agree with me. I was beginning to sympathize with Clemmons in his task of worming anything out of Paul. Paul claimed not to have cooperated with Sawyer-Lauçanno on the biography, though Sawyer-Lauçanno told me that Paul had talked with him extensively about his life during numerous visits to him at the Villa Itesa. The bone of contention clearly was that the book had not been submitted to Paul before publication for approval, and deletions, as had been the French biography by Robert Briatte, which does not violate Paul's discretion about personal matters.

In the suffocating atmosphere, I kept bringing up people that Paul and I had in common and mentioned another author, Michelle Green, who had spent a lot of time in Tangier recently, doing research for a book on the expatriate colony since the war (later published as *The Dream at the End of the World* [HarperCollins]). Paul dismissed her by saying that all she was interested in was who had slept with whom and suchlike and, with a triumphant expression on his face, claimed that none of the old residents on the Mountain whom she had interviewed had told her anything but had maintained a clubby solidarity. I knew differently, but kept quiet.

The Mountain is an outer neighborhood of Tangier where the wealthier expatriates live, people such as the Honorable David Herbert—though the richest of them all, Barbara Hutton, lived in the old town, combining a group of houses into one. She had claimed to live in the Casbah, the ancient walled fortress, but actually her house was just below, in the lowlier-sounding Medina, overlooked by the Casbah. Jane Bowles used to socialize with this set, for whom the Moroccans were merely picturesque natives and purchasable sex partners. Jane's ladies, as Alfred Chester used to call them, met for tea at an elegant patisserie named Porte's, now closed. With evident enjoyment, Paul launched into a witty account of Mme. Porte, the proprietor of the teashop, who had a shady past as a Nazi sympathizer during the war.

Paul himself has picked up the upper-class manner, dry and reserved, of a retired British colonial. All he lacks is the accent. In the tone of the rich complaining about the servants, he denounced the Moroccan post office for holding back some of his mail—the book *Satanic Verses,* for example, or tapes of his own songs. I've noticed in correspondence with him that he is always dubious about the post office, though everything I've sent him has gotten through. Then, he went on to tell about a building that collapsed just as it was completed, proving the incompetence of the "natives" to do anything right. I could imagine his friends on the Mountain laughing at just such a story. They come here because it's primitive, are irritated when that interferes with their civilized comforts, then are critical when it becomes less primitive.

I seemed to be starting off all wrong, so what did I have to lose? I brought up the subject of drugs—back in the sixties when I last saw him, Paul was always stoned—by asking if I could still go into one of the native tea shops and buy a branch of kif as I used to do (kif in the raw state, so to speak). Alarmed, Paul said it was much better to get a Moroccan to buy it for you. That seems to be how he experiences Morocco now, for it is his servants who deal with Morocco for him, for safety perhaps, as the location of the building he lives in seems to indicate. But it is this self-protectiveness that has enabled him to survive, while Jane Bowles and my old friend Alfred Chester did not. At any rate, I sensed that drugs was a subject he didn't care to discuss anymore, or perhaps, as a supposed expert, he is questioned about it so often that he is bored with it.

At this point, Mohammed Mrabet came into the room and sat a while darkly, before walking out again. Perhaps he was checking to see that Paul was all right. A pretty, young maidservant came through laughing, and her laughter was heard from another room, at which Paul gave a desiccated boyish grin of pleasure and said how lively the servants were together, and how much he enjoyed them. I sensed that they are his Morocco nowadays.

For the West, Paul Bowles is the landmark in Tangier, and for some years taught a writing workshop that attracted students from all over, one of them the young Central American in the room. Paul told us that he had had Salman Rushdie's wife as a student, but early in the course, after he had refused to confirm her own high opinion of her talent, she had quit in a huff. Paul's books, in English, Spanish, and French, fill the window of the bookshop on the Boulevard Pasteur. He was almost bragging, I was surprised to see, as he talked of how much interest there was in him in Europe (at the same time dismissing America, where unacceptable books about him, like Sawyer-Lauçanno's, were being published), even getting in a mention of Bertolucci and the film project. He reminded me of the late Kimon Friar in Athens, who brought out his scrapbooks to show me photos of himself with the Kennedys and incessantly insisted on his uniqueness as a translator of Greek authors. Sixty-five myself, I am starting to understand this syndrome: It is just the loneliness of old age, when the emptiness from the departure of sex has to be filled with something, and fame is one of the possible consolations. We should all be so lucky as Paul.

Another old-timer trait was Paul's reiteration that we couldn't possibly experience the real Morocco like he has, and that everything has gotten worse. His touchstone, of course, was the Tangier of the old International Zone, before it was reunited with Morocco. But I felt comfortable in the city, in fact I am often taken for Moroccan, and I protested that I found Tangier quite livable now, with the city visibly more prosperous. My God, I even rented a typewriter, just like in the "real" world!

Of course, it always was a comfortable city, partly because of the French colonial inheritance—sidewalk cafés, French bread, apartments with balconies, wine—mitigating some of the harshness of the sun, the landscape, the poverty. Now the avenues have splendid, even glittering, new cafés and tea shops, full of middle-class Moroccan men (though still no women), where once there would mostly have been foreigners, the only Moroccans the hustlers and shoeshine boys. But Paul would see this as Morocco becoming Europeanized, less Moroccan. It is true that the kif culture has receded, with its irrationality, magic, paranoia, and acceptance of poverty. I didn't see people smoking kif on the street, as before, but did come upon them indoors with their pipes. Paul said that bars even tolerated Moroccans coming in to drink, if they were wearing a shirt and tie. The bars are occasionally raided, but the middle-class Moroccans laugh off the mild penalties.

Most people, of all classes, still wear the native robe, the djellaba, and many women are veiled, giving the city, with its date palms and whitewashed houses, a biblical look. And things are hardly too modern to complain about. The tourists in the big hotels on the beach who come for package holidays of sea, sun, sand, and local color, might get more than they bargained for walking along the beach on the sweep of harbor, past the pale, happy northerners in their bathing suits, to whom the water seems idyllically blue and clean, but one hundred yards further on, just beyond where the local people are swimming, the sewers empty in a foul black stream that spreads out into the blue waters of the almost enclosed harbor. The stench there is almost unbearable. So perhaps, except for the surface, not much has changed.

The contrasts in the Muslim world are sharper than in ours, not only between rich and poor, but also between ancient and modern. On the road back from the beach Neil and I passed a tiny man, in djellaba and turban, on an appropriately tiny donkey coming into town, with his farm produce in two huge baskets slung across the animal's back. The meeting of two thousand years, Neil said to me, as we in our western garb passed him. We speculated about his traditional life in a rural village, bereft of modern conveniences, and without getting romantic over it, surely preferable to the way the poor live in our slums, many of whom have VCRs and cars.

In the brief moment I could exchange a few words with Walter Clemmons, I could tell that he assumed I was a longtime resident of Morocco, though in fact this was the first time I had rented a flat and spent a period of weeks. I had been told by a genuine, old Moroccan hand that renting a furnished apartment in Tangier was impossible, and anyway it would be too noisy to bear because of the large families packed into apartments around you. But Neil and I had already rented flats in London, Berlin, and Rome, and rather than go on living in a hotel, comfortable and cheap as it was, and having to eat in restaurants, we decided to try.

When I first went to Tangier in the sixties, everybody spoke Spanish, but nowadays they speak French, and fortunately my French, though barely adequate in Paris, is perfectly serviceable in the Arab world. Still, the real-estate agent we approached spoke nothing but Arabic, and his assistant had to translate for us. The agent was a pleasant, dark, little man, younger than his serious demeanor and mustache made him seem, and was not at all dis-couraging about finding us a place to live. From my experience in the Muslim world, I have learned you can trust business people there much more than in the West.

After showing us a gloomy, hideously furnished apartment, wrecked by years of sub-tenants, our agent led us rapidly through the warren of streets of the neighborhood into an old apartment house, built by the French and bourgeois-respectable once but now fallen into disrepair—the elevator was permanently out of order, so we marched up a flight of stairs. We waited outside a door in the unlit hallway while he went in and talked voluminously in Maghrebi with the occupants. He returned shortly to announce that the family would move out and let us rent their flat, if we liked it.

Inside, we found an attractive, high-ceilinged, well-proportioned living room with low couches around the walls, Arab-style. We had disturbed the family at breakfast, for the low table held a coffeepot, cups, and bread. A child's toys were scattered about the floor, but no wife and child were visible. The husband, a pleasant man in his thir-ties spoke excellent French. I told him that I felt uncomfortable about displacing a whole family at a moment's notice, but he said that many people he knew were taking advantage of the opportunity to make some money by renting their apartments to tourists. He had been unemployed since the police had raided his brother's bar, he said, and it would be no hardship to move in with his wife's family in Fez.

We examined the rest of the flat—entrance hall, bathroom with a big old-fashioned tub, and bedroom with a king-size bed, uphol-stered whorishly in zebra plush, and a poster of a naked woman on the wall. When I asked to see the kitchen, the husband told me with a sheepish smile that his wife and child were in there. Modern as he appeared, he would not let strangers look at his wife.

My friend and I decided to take a chance and rent the apartment, and though the kitchen sink had no hot water, as it turned out, and the plush-upholstered bed felt buggy, we got used to the place. It was an adventure being the only foreigners in the building, and indeed the neighborhood. The balcony door gave the living room its light and looked out over a courtyard with a warren of hovels where the poor lived. I never got tired of watching them from the balcony—the women bending over and wiping with rags the stony earth of the alley; in the morning, a schoolboy, spic and span in shirt and slacks, emerging from one of the hovels with his books and setting out for school; much washing of clothes in tubs, filled by hand with buckets of water brought from a single water tap that serviced the whole community; chickens pecking at the dirt, and children playing. I saw two "armies" of children, with garbage-pail lids for shields and wooden swords made from crates, shrieking as they battled each other like soldiers of Saladin. The girls, in a foretaste of their position in society as women, were pushed aside by the greater ferocity of the boys, though they attempted to get into the fray, too. Finally, all collapsed on the ground, breaking their swords into pieces and tossing them around in a frenzy.

I quickly located the neighborhood bakery, where I went out in the morning for a freshly baked baguette, passing on a street corner a crazy boy who was as filthy as the heap of rags he lived on. In spite of his state, he was handsome, with shaggy black hair and beard, and people apparently brought him food and water. I had the impression that he had simply given up the struggle.

I always seemed to be the only customer in the bakery at eight in the morning. Astonishing was the fact that Tangerinos didn't get up early, and equally surprising, though gratifying, was the fact that television sets and radios were turned off early as people went to bed, so the nights were almost silent, except for the crowing of cocks at all hours, or the barking of dogs, which one hears everywhere in the Muslim world, either guarding property like the two curs in the courtyard of our apartment house, or roaming the streets in packs, devouring garbage. I can't imagine anyone being disturbed by the (recorded) calling of the muezzin to prayer as it rings out over the rooftops just before dawn. I always woke to listen.

One can live better in Tangier on a modest amount of money than anywhere else I know, even as a tourist. There are small but comfortable hotels, and the restaurants have improved tremendously from when Neil and I first went there in the mid-sixties. If you cook for yourself, you can find cheap food in the markets, and the covered market at the Socco Grande is a wonder of the world. Paul Bowles, famous as he is, still lives simply; even his three servants don't cost a great deal. In his modest flat he chooses to live without a television set or telephone (while Jane was alive, she had the phone in her apartment and screened his calls). I did see a radio in his living room, the kind with shortwave bands for listening to the BBC World Service, I imagine, if he's anything like Neil and me, but also, since he's polylingual, for French and Spanish radio.

In Tangier, you can get the BBC from Gibraltar, and radio stations from Spain directly across the Straits. (It was startling on Radio Dos, the Spanish classical music station, to hear Mozart referred to as "un hombre," and Bach called "Juan Sebastian Bach.") In our rented flat there was an old television set that brought in only one Moroccan station. This showed mostly government speeches, dubbed movies, Arabic music concerts, news in both French and Maghrebi. Most unusual, though, was a cooking program, on which the chef instructed how to prepare the dishes, but instead of demonstrating himself, like our own Julia Child, he had a silent woman, a servant if not a slave, doing all the work, following his commands. Perhaps this was considered more suitable for a culture in which women still wear veils, though they're often slipping below the nose nowadays and binding the mouth.

The whole week prior to my visit with Paul, however, the small screen fare had been preempted for a conference in Casablanca, first showing all the Arab leaders arriving and being greeted by King Hassan II in an identical ceremony, which included the formal eating of a date and sipping camel's milk as each got off his plane. The conference consisted of long speeches, during which the camera panned the room, often catching the leaders dozing off. The king's eyelids, droopy anyway, frequently drooped further, and he often hid his nodding head behind papers he was supposedly studying, much like the bums in the automats that I remember from the thirties. Arafat, I'm sorry to say, produced the most snores, and the more he ranted and waved his arms about, the less attention anyone paid. On the other hand, later, the cameras showed a cuddly, lovable Arafat in private conversation with other leaders.

After a week of this programming, grateful as I was for the opportunity to see the faces of these exotic rulers, I called in a local repairman to see if the set could be adjusted to bring in Spanish and Gibraltarian TV, but it turned out that a special aerial on the roof was required, and it wasn't worth the investment for only a few weeks.

Even if the Moroccan quality of life has been diluted, as Paul Bowles claims, there's nothing to make you feel more like you're in a Muslim country than arriving in the middle of Ramadan, as Neil and I did. During Ramadan, the month in the Muslim calendar when everything is turned topsy-turvy—no eating from sunup to sundown—there is very little allowance for foreigners who might not want to follow this schedule. In Casablanca, where our plane from New York landed, we found a restaurant open for dinner but were not so lucky for breakfast. With the hotel dining room closed for the month, the manager shrugged and pointed vaguely down the street, implying there would be someplace in that direction that could serve us. Not so. We ended up the only customers in the vast, bleak dining room of a glitzy luxury hotel, where for the equivalent of ten dollars an elaborate but stale breakfast was served, with waiters and waitresses in folkloric costume standing idly around.

Then, during the bus ride to Tangier, no food at all was available at the various stops along the way, where usually there are vendors selling nuts, fruit, pizza-like breads, and kabobs. All gone because of Ramadan. Larache, half-way to Tangier, where in the past one could eat royally, was equally observant of the holiday; the best restaurant in town had closed for the month. At sundown, the streets were suddenly deserted as the crowds rushed into the restaurants to devour the delicious harira soup, the traditional break to the day's fast or raced home for it, except for three small boys, sitting on the curb with big wooden bowls of harira soup on their knees, spoons poised in the air, waiting for the muezzin call that would allow them to eat. We smiled at them and they grinned back at us, waving us over and making room for us to sit down with them and share their soup. Everywhere, people were delighted when we ordered the soup of Ramadan, though often there was none left by the time we arrived.

In Tangier, though, enough restaurants were open for tourists and the foreign colony that eating was no problem. Still, passing Moroccans made us uncomfortable as they stared in wonder through the open doors of the almost empty hotel restaurant at people actually dining during the daylight hours of Ramadan.

Paul Bowles, continuing his argument about how much the "new" Morocco had changed, and for the worse, brought up the rash of recent muggings. A friend staying in Jane's old apartment, below his, walking home after eating out in a restaurant, was followed by a couple of thugs. In front of the building they seized him, but he was able to wriggle out of his jacket, leaving it in their hands, and run across the road to the guards in front of the Voice of America building. Further, Paul said that Bertolucci, in Morocco to make the movie of *The Sheltering Sky*, was mugged right outside the Minzah, the most elegant hotel in Tangier, situated on a busy thoroughfare, where he was staying.

Mugging, in the context of Morocco, seemed to me as a hardened New Yorker one of the few devices the poor have to even the score a little. Hustling the tourists is another, supplying them with anything they want from drugs to boys. Luckily both are in great supply and cheap. For as improved as things seemed to be, poverty is still everywhere. Neil and I were bedeviled by a youth we couldn't get rid of. One day, he came toward us on Boulevard Pasteur, greeting us with open arms as if we had met before, and since he seemed pleasant enough and spoke excellent English, we stopped to chat. A European would have understood from the beginning. Class difference would have protected him—even if he took the youth home for sex and paid him off, there would be no further involvement. Americans, though, are open to everyone, curious about their lives, getting trapped. And sure enough, from then on, whenever we walked on the boulevard, sat at a café, or went to the post office, there was no avoiding him. As if he were plotting our movements, he was there with his desperate smile, waiting for us at key spots. His clothes got shabbier and shabbier by the day, and he looked as if he was going downhill fast—he certainly looked hungry. His story was that he had studied at the American School, which explained his fluent English at least, but that since his mother had died, his luck had run out. Now he lived with his father in a nearby village and somehow managed to get into Tangier every day.

I would ask him in a paternal fashion if he had eaten anything, and give him a little money for food, just to get rid of him. But I don't think he spent it on food but for a coffee at a sidewalk café. His greater hunger, clearly, was to be part of the glamorous world of the Boulevard Pasteur, with its middle-class people, both foreigners and Moroccans. And he was begging us to include him in our lives— invite him to sit with us at cafés, come to our apartment, teach us Maghrebi—perhaps, with the ultimate hope that we would take him away with us when we left Morocco. But though we felt sorry for him, there was no way we could save him.

To avoid him, we started using the back streets, which resulted in our adopting a quite interesting café called the Atlantic, somewhat off the main drag, where a collection of old English queens, long-time residents of Tangier, usually gathered around a table in the corner of the *terrasse*—I'm trying not to think what they thought about us, for Neil and I were not much younger. Still, there we could sit in peace with a glass of freshly squeezed orange juice under the trees that shaded the busy rue de Fez, free from our pest. Unfortunately, he seemed to have become dependent on our handouts, and though we succeeded in keeping him from discovering our café and where we lived, he dogged our trail for the rest of our stay, sometimes cursing us loudly when he spotted us fleeing him down the street.

At our "tea," I had actually hoped to talk with Paul Bowles about my friend, the writer Alfred Chester, who had lived for several years in Tangier in the early sixties until he went mad, became difficult, and was expelled by the government. But their relationship had been a mysterious and complex one that Paul seemed skittish about going into. I raised the subject with him by saying I had just been to look at the building Alfred had lived in; whereupon Paul, sticking to the safest aspect of the subject, launched into a little history of the building, the changes of ownership, and how notorious its reputation had become after Alfred's residence there.

Sidi Bujari 28, where Alfred Chester lived from the autumn of 1963 to the winter of 1965, lies well outside the downtown, and I had had a little trouble finding it, since the tourist map of Tangier ends short of that residential neighborhood. Tangier is built over a lot of hills, valleys, and gullies, making it hard to keep track of directions, but this street is roughly between the Marshan, which is called the European quarter, and the aristocratic Mountain. Neil and I had visited Alfred there in 1965, but things looked quite different now, surprisingly modern, in fact, though even here, as if left over from an earlier time, there is a little shack of a tea shop across from a neat, triangular park with benches where mothers were watching their children playing, and men were talking quietly over glasses of mint tea.

Number 28 is a handsome old mansion divided into flats. I remember that Alfred's apartment on the middle floor had a terrace at the back with a wonderful view over the hills. Almost derelict now, the dilapidated building stands out like a sore thumb on the street of small, well-kept, middle-class, Mediterranean-style villas, with polished cars in the driveways. But at number 28, roots of overgrown eucalyptus trees in the unkempt front yard have cracked through the cement walk, and the steps up to the front entrance are crumbling away. Small windows under the roof are broken, and you would think no one lived there anymore, except for a motorbike parked to one side, and a hand-painted "28" on a rusty chicken-wire fence erected around the house, with a mail box and a crudely painted arrow indicating a side entrance. Even the sky here seems gloomier than over the rest of the block, as if the pretty villas bloomed in the sun with tropical flowers and geraniums around them, while over the mansion dark clouds hung morbidly. Paul spoke of drug dealing, knife fights and a murder, and more recently a fire occurring as the building declined.

The abandoned disreputable look of the place seems a fitting memorial to Alfred. It felt to me as if his combative spirit had returned to haunt it, keeping it as freakish in the respectable neighborhood as Alfred had felt during his life. It was as if he were saying that he would not vacate for the sake of the landlord or to please the neighbors and, even as a ghost, would fight on not to be evicted, as he had so often done in his lifetime. He made life for all his landlords pure hell. I would hate to have been Alfred's landlord.

Paul Bowles looked bemused when I said how important he had been in Alfred's life, as if he couldn't imagine anyone thinking he had been connected to such a dubious character. In fact, Paul made it sound as if, really, Alfred Chester had been Jane's friend, as Robert Briatte's "acceptable" biography claims, though, in reality, it had been Paul who was so taken with Alfred in New York in the winter of '62-'63 that he kept urging him to come to Morocco. So to defuse a dangerous subject, or so it appeared to me, at least, he began talking in an amusing way about Alfred as one more eccentric member of the Tangier scene.

Paul told a story of Alfred inviting him and Jane to lunch, after Alfred's wig, which he had worn from childhood when he lost his hair through an illness, accidentally burned up. Paul claimed he hadn't noticed the wig anyway and so said nothing about its absence. But it turned out that Alfred had invited them specially to show himself wigless and bald for the first time, and was disappointed by the lack of response. "But then," Paul said in his opaque manner, "I never look at people."

Paul gave his own version of an episode surrounding a now famous letter in which he had threatened to have a troublesome Alfred "rubbed out." Alfred had panicked and had reported it to the American consul, and Paul had been called in for questioning. By exaggerating the language of the letter, Paul made it seem inconceivable that anyone could have taken it seriously. But in fact, as Alfred told me at the time, Paul had bragged to him that in Morocco one could have anyone "disposed of" without any problems with the authorities. And Paul had two close friends, William Burroughs and Libby Holman, who, though ruled in court as accidental, had actually shot and killed their mates. After a ludicrous blackmail attempt on Paul and Jane, Alfred had suddenly panicked, realizing that he was surrounded by murderers or potential murderers. The letter incident, coupled with anxiety over the imminent appearance of his book of stories, *Behold Goliath,* triggered Alfred's first crack-up in Tangier, when he cabled me in New York to come and bring him home.

Paul's role in the sad fate of both Jane Bowles and Alfred Chester, the two of them charming, eccentric, hyper, and doomed, is still to be explored. Perhaps, like the relationship of Ted Hughes to Sylvia Plath's suicide, it will always remain open to question. Though nowadays Paul denies his "dark" side, cleaning up his image, as it were, for posterity, there used to be a strongly satanic aspect to him, as if an amoral child, still fascinated by the gorier aspects of Poe, lay behind the composition of the more lurid and horrifying stories. Alfred portrayed this very well in his short story "Safari," in which Paul is called Gerald and has the powers of a wizard.

The similarities between Jane and Alfred are startling: Both were Jewish, gay, spoiled by parents, and with a physical defect from childhood (her gimpy leg, his loss of hair) that made them feel like freaks. Both were made too much of as brilliant little eccentrics. And both fell under Paul's spell and were fascinated, even while expressing reservations about him, by how nervous he made them. Jane hated to be alone with him, she said, and Alfred complained that he spoke in sub-text. It was Paul who, like the Pied Piper, led them both to Morocco, where they plunged into Moroccan life in a way Paul never risked doing himself—though unlike Alfred, who was a confirmed bohemian, Jane was torn between being a lady like the aristocrats on the Mountain and, like the heroine of *The Sheltering Sky,* letting herself be blotted out by the native world. Both insane, and exiled from Morocco, they died about a year apart, Jane in a convent asylum in Spain, Alfred, the better Jew, in Jerusalem.

Alfred claimed he had Paul to thank for both Morocco and kif, though I believe he would have gone into the drug scene on his own, for he was not in the least self-protective, and he never hesitated to pop pills of any kind, but especially dexamils. Perhaps, simply, or not so simply, with their weaknesses and strengths, Jane and Alfred were Paul's natural victims. They had the human qualities, the "juice," he lacked, and like a spider, Paul squatted in his web, where they were trapped, observed their struggles, and fed off them. Jane even signed some of her letters "The Spider's Wife."

Perhaps Paul mistook Jane and Alfred for fictional characters who fell, like those in his stories, into risky situations, while he sat watching as their quasi-fictional fates unrolled. Actually, Paul was not always an innocent bystander in this and admits that he arranged for a Moroccan youth, whom he considered dangerous, to come on to Alfred when he arrived from America—for the simple reason, he says, ingenuously, that he was curious about what would happen. Ironically this man became the love of Alfred's life.

Reading Millicent Dillon's biography of Jane, *A Little Original Sin,* I thought the saddest thing about the relationship between the Bowleses, speculated about so often, wasn't whether or not they'd ever had sex but the money problem; Jane felt so guilty about taking any money from him, living off him. When crazy, she gave his money away wildly. By doing this, she was obviously making a long-withheld protest not only against his tightness but also against a prime condition for being his wife, that is, she had no right to his support and was expected to provide for herself. Though Alfred wrote me, after knowing them for some time, that he had finally concluded that Paul and Jane were one person.

In his letters from Morocco, full of observations of Tangier life, and especially of the Bowleses, besides referring to Paul's supposed use of unsettling sub-text in their conversations, Alfred wrote of Paul behaving in ways, such as throwing tantrums and smashing things, that do not gibe with any other report, for Paul is always portrayed as dry, reserved, and controlled. It might have been that Alfred had the capacity to drive Paul to extreme behavior, or possibly that Paul, in a dry period of his creative life, was learning from Alfred to let go a little, trying out what he imagined was Alfred-like behavior. Jane always had to go wildly crazy to disturb Paul's aplomb, or his writing schedule (like all great artists, he was monumentally selfish about this), but she (also an artist and equally selfish) did succeed. He must have suffered horribly throughout the years from her uncontrollable, but somehow willed, disintegration.

Alfred's behavior in Morocco also caused a certain amount of trouble for Paul, though Jane always stayed loyal to Alfred. She kept cautioning him that it wasn't done to let the outside world know of their doings (as in the case of the "rub out" letter). Alfred was always threatening to "expose" them, but Paul pleaded ignorance, asking me, ingenuously, in a letter, "Expose what?" for his generation was deeply in the closet, in spite of it being no secret anymore that the whole Tangier colony, like Bloomsbury, was rife with homosexuality and that Paul and Jane were both gay, but their marriage gave them a cover he clung to, even when it was no longer necessary. And as we talked of Alfred's era in Morocco, Paul seemed to be shying away from any mention, much less discussion, of such a sensitive subject, which was perhaps the reason, I thought to myself, that he was not giving Walter Clemmons the least chance to get onto the subject of Gore Vidal.

However, to be fair, Paul might also have been observing the custom of the country, since homosexuality in the Arab world, though traditional, is not something you need to proclaim—it's no big deal, you are simply free to engage in homosexual activity, whatever the law might say. No need for gay lib here. Paul's circumspection on this matter suits Morocco. And presenting a respectable front—he is a WASP, after all—is important to him. I could not help but think, sitting on a cushion in that airless living room, that this man had had one handsome Moroccan lover after another through the years and had managed his life brilliantly.

Paul emphasized to me, referring to Alfred's letters from Morocco that I was editing, that he didn't want Alfred's versions of events of the period to be published, when they were untrue, since in print they would gain credibility. He pooh-poohed Alfred's belief that he spoke in sub-text. Even I thought that this belief was undoubtedly linked to Alfred's paranoid delusions, but faced with this subtle manipulator I had to allow that it may also have been a kif-lingo that Paul had used during those druggy years, if no longer.

Whether Paul had any role in having Alfred expelled from Morocco, I do not know. But apparently Bowles couldn't, or didn't, do anything to prevent it. He only told me at our "tea" that Alfred's landlord, a Dutchman, who lived across the hall from him, had announced triumphantly one day that he had finally managed to get Alfred deported. If Alfred had heard of the apartment through Paul in the first place, as is probable, Paul would have felt guilty toward his landlord neighbor for foisting on him such a difficult tenant. Moreover, Alfred in exile always saw Paul as powerful enough to get him back into Morocco if he so chose, and pleaded with him in letter after letter. "The omnipotent Paul" was clearly a fantasy, but it had some truth at its core, for Paul was the presiding genius over Alfred Chester's Moroccan period.

But it was not Paul who precipitated the final breakdown from which Alfred never recovered. It was the visit of Susan Sontag, the beautiful, world-famous (and therefore more powerful) "Mary Monday," as he called her in his novel *The Foot,* in which fragments of her brief stay in Morocco are recorded. As much as I can make out from the somewhat obscure and garbled text, Alfred was convinced that his Moroccan boyfriend would be fascinated by Susan and she would seduce him, which was as delusional as the fear he had previously had in New York of another lover's betrayal, which had also sent him into a tailspin at the time.

I finally couldn't have been more pleased, to be fair to Paul, when for a moment Paul dropped his defensive mask and said about Alfred with a grin, "Oh, but he was a wonderfully entertaining person to talk to."

I was feeling uncomfortable as hell. Paul and I were too much at odds in our opinions, and I didn't want to keep arguing with him in front of the others, though if we had been alone rather than in a public audience, I think we could have talked more frankly and enjoyed our differences. Anyway, I wasn't sure how long I should stay on, especially since no tea was, or seemed likely to be, served. So I got up. Paul, too, got to his feet, and when I stammered something about seeing him again, he looked blankly at me. (I remember that Jane also had a quality of making me feel clumsy.) I foolishly blundered on and, knowing that he used to go to the Café de Paris on the Place de France, suggested that perhaps we could meet there. This evoked an incomprehensible denial that he ever went to cafés. I was ready to protest that he did have his chauffeur drive him into the city and that it was not such a preposterous suggestion, but I was somehow violating a code of behavior—perhaps by trying to pin him down—and felt a wall erected between us. So I finally had the good sense to shut up and leave.

After this "audience" (that seemed the only word for it), I walked back to my rented slummy flat with a mixture of admiration and envy for the way Paul Bowles had set himself up for old age. It took an iron will to do it, as those around him destroyed themselves. I was reminded of a single woman I know in Oregon, a Gurdjieffian guru, surrounded by a community of disciples who will obey her for as long as she can give orders and will look after her to the end. Like her, Paul has managed his life very well. Most of his old friends are dead now, but though I know it is never the same, he is surrounded by new ones, and his last years will not be solitary.

Paul Bowles doesn't leave Tangier anymore, though lured by the promise of medical attention, he did fly to Paris for one night to appear on the literary interview program *Apostrophe*—and reported the city as beautiful as he remembered it but had no desire to stay. He's obviously prepared to die in his adopted country and be buried, I imagine, in the English Cemetery, attached to St. Andrew's Church, of the Diocese of Gibraltar in Europe. Neil and I visited it the day after my visit to Paul and walked under shady trees by the graves of members of the foreign colony, largely British colonials, but also with more dubious residents mixed in. Ella St. John, 1889–1975, was buried together with Dora Thompson, 1883–1975, ancient ones, perhaps lovers, who were lucky enough to die in the same year, if not together. Another headstone read, "Walter Burton Harris, Born August 29th, 1866. He came to Tangier in 1886 and was associated with the *Times* as correspondent in Morocco and elsewhere from 1887 till his death, April 4th, 1933. He loved the Moorish people and was their friend." So Harris came to Morocco at twenty, and managed to live his whole life away from the puritanism of Victorian England. Almost like Paul Bowles escaping puritan America. Then, we came upon: "In loving memory of Jay Haselwood, 1914–1966." Jay had been a close friend of Paul and Jane's, who had run the most popular bar for the foreign colony, mostly gay, in Tangier.

Like Genet's grave in Larache, forty miles away, Paul Bowles's grave will be a place of pilgrimage for the restless, rebellious young. But like so many others in this benign climate, he looks like he will live to an ancient age, a living monument. Already, it is *de rigueur* to visit him on a trip to Tangier. And he is clearly enjoying his new-found world celebrity, as documentaries of him are being made almost monthly, part of a Bowles industry of formidable size.

Since I never received another invitation "to tea," I didn't go back and, without Paul having a phone, there was no way to call and say goodbye when Neil and I left Tangier several weeks later—I still hadn't caught on that people just dropped in on him in the afternoon, and you were either admitted or not admitted. But back in the States, I received another note from him, saying he was sorry he hadn't seen me again, and to drop in the next time I was in Morocco, so friendly that it gave me the odd feeling that I must have dreamed the awkward visit to him, and nothing real had taken place at all.

Postscript: Ironically, after his death, the body of Paul Bowles was returned to the cemetery in upstate New York to be interred next to his parents.

An Untropical Island

Bruce Shenitz

When Dutch friends of mine announced they'd be getting married—ten years and two children into their relationship—I suspected that the wedding would not be a typical white-veil-and-morning-coat affair. I'd often joked with them that I would actually make a special trip to the Netherlands if they ever took this seemingly unlikely step, but as soon as they told me they would be getting married on Texel, a Dutch island in the North Sea, I told them I'd be there. I had been hearing about my friends' holiday and weekend trips to the island for years, and based on their accounts and some photographs, I'd already imagined Texel into some Old World version of Cape Cod, though perhaps with a bit more rain, clouds, and comfortably autumnal melancholy. But my friends were worried I'd be disappointed in "their little island." What allure, they might have wondered, could this small North Sea destination hold for someone whose sense of seashore and beaches was more likely to run along the lines of *Baywatch* or Jones Beach. They also worried that Texel might not be an interesting place for someone who, by his own admission, is emphatically not the outdoorsy type.

Much as I wanted to be at the wedding of these friends, I have to admit that I was happy to have any excuse to make a trip to the Netherlands. It's occupied a special place in my personal geography. Amsterdam was the first place I ever visited in Europe, on a memorable trip I made in my early thirties. If I were the type of person who said things like "I must have lived there in a previous life," I would have said it about Amsterdam. And not just because it's a welcoming place for gay people, though that certainly hasn't hurt. Perhaps it's because knowing some German and being a native speaker of English, I walk around feeling as if I can almost understand what's being said all around me—if only I could flip some invisible switch inside my brain. In her poem "Amsterdam Letter," Jean Garrigue refers to "A fitness of things," which captures my feelings as well as anything I've ever read.

In fact, Texel turned out to be a way to sample Dutch life and landscape in a way that I never could during my many visits to the country's more cosmopolitan cities. Within its small area, the island contains some of the major environmental and historical influences that have shaped the Netherlands: a dike-protected coastline, vast tracts of polder that stretch to the horizon, and, as residents and visitors repeatedly told me, "always wind." (As I rode my bike into a relentless headwind one day, I had one of those moments when something very obvious becomes viscerally understood: so *this* is why they had windmills everywhere!) There are also remnants of two critical chapters in the country's history: the East India company trade of the seventeenth century and the Nazi occupation of the twentieth.

Texel is the southernmost of the West Frisian Islands, located in the North Sea just off the Dutch coast. The islands of the Wadden Sea ("wad" is Dutch for "mud flat") stretch along the coasts of the Netherlands, Germany, and Denmark, and comprise the largest unbroken nature reserve in western Europe. Texel is the largest of the five Dutch islands and the most readily accessible from Amsterdam (a bit over two hours by train and ferry); that may explain why it's the most developed island and the only one that allows non-residents to bring cars. It's roughly the size and shape of a squashed-down Manhattan, about fifteen miles long and six miles wide. There are thirteen thousand year-round residents, but it can accommodate forty-seven thousand visitors, most of whom come in the summer. Most tourists come from the Netherlands, with Germans accounting for the bulk of the non-Dutch visitors. The island also has some eleven thousand cows and fifteen thousand sheep, and more than eighteen thousand lambs are born each year. "More sheep than people," you will often hear from Texelaars, which refers to both the human and ovine residents of the island.

When we arrived on the island, on a Friday afternoon, about thirty people were already at the large "group house" where the wedding guests would be spending the weekend. Guests were matter-of-factly enlisted to help out with some small tasks—moving tables and chairs, affixing name tags to the small platoon of bicycles that had been rented. It had been a long time since my partner and I had done anything so communal, and despite some initial doubts, we relaxed into the spirit of the weekend. There was a wonderful moment on Saturday morning, as everyone got on their bicycles so we could ride into town where the marriage would be performed. The bride and groom led the way ringing their bells and we were off.

Weddings are often difficult for gay people (the truth is they're hardest on single people, gay or straight), but I didn't anticipate any problem at this one, since I knew most of the guests were friends or relatives from Amsterdam, and I'd come to expect a matter-of-fact attitude toward gayness as the norm. That was indeed the case, even though my partner Stan and I were the only gay couple there (though not the only gay people). The entire weekend has come to occupy a special place for me; it had been a long time since I'd taken time out to spend with friends for such an extended period.

Although we had bicycled some before the wedding celebration, I was eager to explore a bit more of the island on foot on Sunday morning as the festivities were winding down. Unfortunately, it had rained overnight, and we woke up to threatening skies. June is normally a fairly dry month, I'd read, but I apparently had come to northern Europe during an unusually wet period. But even the government tourist brochure warns, "Although Texel has significantly more hours of sun than the Dutch average, let's be honest about it: cloud masses drift by here as well." I soon learned that the only way to approach uncooperative weather was to ignore it. To do otherwise might mean that you'd never even go outside. As Stan and I set off for an easy walk to the nearby forested area called "De Dennen" ("the pines"), gray skies produced first drizzle, then rain. Since we kept seeing cyclists and other hikers on the road, including other wedding guests, we realized that we were expected to take the authentic Netherlandish weather in stride. People on the island seemed to regard the weather in about the same way as many New Yorkers look at their city: a source of ritual grumbling combined with a get-on-with-it-already attitude.

After most of the guests had departed late Sunday afternoon, our host dropped us off at a hotel in Den Burg, the island's largest town. Small as the island is, it apparently is popular enough on the tourist circuit that the young woman working the desk took it in stride when we told her that one double bed would be just fine.

(We'd actually had a more puzzled reaction a few days earlier at a hotel in Paris, of all places.) We dried off and warmed up in our room, and by evening the skies had cleared. We took advantage of the late summer sun—it remains light until well past 10 P.M. in June—and had a stroll before dinner. The town's shopping district looked much like the pedestrian-only shopping areas of many a Dutch city, but almost as soon as we entered a side street, we found ourselves in front of a cobblestone courtyard shared by five houses. Its hushed stillness suggested the quiet interiors that lie behind public faces of these beautifully preserved brick homes, many dating back to the eighteenth and seventeenth centuries.

The weather was gray and drizzly the next morning, and after our drenching the day before, we decided to try some indoor activities. We started the day out at EcoMare, a natural history museum and aquarium focused on the island's ecology. After the morning seal-feeding, we went off for an easy walk in Dune Park, which contains beach and dune trails. We could smell and feel the chill ocean winds, and caught sight of an occasional sea bird flying over the sparse vegetation. As in other parts of Texel, the ocean is often hidden from view by dunes or dikes, even though it is the major shaper of the island's landscape and weather. The trail led to the top of a dune, where we caught a glimpse of the water before heading back to the museum.

In the afternoon, we took a look through the Oudheidkamer or House of Antiquities, in Den Burg. This small museum, which is located in a sixteenth-century house, showcases everyday household objects from the past, and was a delightful surprise, even for the antiques-impaired. Each room contains a jumble of items from different time periods: the bedroom features an eighteenth-century bed alongside turn-of-the-century photos on the dresser. In the back of the house is what the museum calls "the smallest herb garden in the Netherlands open to the public." As I stood next to a water pump in the rear of the garden and looked back up at the museum's shuttered windows, it took only a small leap of imagination to envision it as part of a scene by an artist from the Golden Age of Dutch painting. I took a few pictures, which failed completely to capture that feeling. It occurs to me that while it may be the ideal to enter into a travel experience as a blank screen on which to register impressions, the reality for me is that I walk into many situations with that screen already filled in—in this case, with the hushed quiet of a Vermeer or de Hooch domestic interior. Perhaps it's simply a different kind of discovery to see the correspondences between one's mental picture and the external world.

In early evening, we moved to a quiet hotel near the east coast of the island in order to try out a more rural setting. After settling in, we set off for a walk along the road paralleling the Lancasterdijk. As we headed south, sheep were grazing along the leeward slope of the dike at the edge of the road. There is a Dutch expression that is literally translated as "having your sheep upon dry land" (that is, enjoying the fruits of your labor after working hard and setting something aside). With unperturbed sheep just yards from the threatening ocean below, the expression came alive. This was not spectacular terrain in variety or color, but there was a comfortable solidity about the scene. We eventually came upon a group of noisy youngsters who had just finished exploring marine life at low tide. As the winds and clouds whipped up again, they scampered to put on long pants and rain gear, which seemed like a good cue to start back to the hotel.

For my final day on Texel, I used the public bus system to hop around the island and sample some of the twenty-four walking routes on my map. I started out on a walk that took me to the Georgian cemetery, which contains the remains of some five hundred soldiers from Georgia, the former Soviet republic. They were interned as P.O.W.'s on the island during World War II, and the cemetery commemorates the unsuccessful April 1945 uprising in which they died; there is also a memorial honoring a local resident who hid soldiers and supplied them with food. Next to the Georgian cemetery is a local burial ground with an ominous inscription over the gate: "I await you too."

The sun was finally making an appearance, so I decided to catch the bus to De Muy, another nature reserve on the west coast. By the time I got there, the weather was still mild, but the bright morning sunshine was gone. And yet, it seemed exactly the right weather to visit the heath, along with a few other walkers and their dogs. By the time I crossed over to the beach, it had become chilly and gray again, and the appearance of a group of children who carried beach pails and wore both bathing suits and ear warmers did not seem at all out of place.

I decided to catch a 6 P.M. ferry and cut short my beach excursion. My major regret was having to miss one more late-evening walk along the Lancasterdijk. A day earlier, when I had been taking a walk there at 10 P.M., a solitary gull had silently coasted by. The white trim of its wings had caught the fading rays of the summer sun and suddenly flashed against the darkening sky, as if they'd been dipped into fluorescent paint. Perhaps I'd traveled a terribly long distance just to watch a drifting gull, but the peace of that summer night and the shifting balance of light, water, and land are the memories of Texel that will stay with me the longest.

Faux Amis

Brian Bouldrey

Apéritif

That night, I preferred standing around out in the farm-yard in spite of the heat and manure. The sky was cloudless, except in the far west where some cirrus clouds might have been skywriting, formerly, blown askew, all the signs, like these, rendered inscrutable. This was south-west France: I'd always wanted to wallow in it. By now, however, Jean-Marie had shown me enough, and I wanted to get out, go to Spain.

Pierrette, the new mistress of the house, had washed our hiking clothes in some kind of deluxe machine that cycled through an alarmingly two full hours, and I had been afraid they would never dry in time for us to continue our walking the next morning. But the stones of the old rugged sprawling farmhouse that Michel called "Chateau La Rignalle" still held the heat of the day, and, when I grasped my T-shirt on the line, I thought that at least I had one less thing to fret about.

Jean-Marie stepped out and spoke to me in an inhale, two whole sentences, only possible in his language, "There you are! I have come to tell you a little secret."

This pleased me; in the past few days, he'd been distant, I thought, as if he'd had enough of me. "Oh?"

"Yes, it is about my uncle, Michel. Pierrette has told me that his health is quite bad, and he is limited to the number of glasses of wine he may have, and also, he may have no dessert."

What did this have to do with me? How would this secret make the two of us closer? He adored his Uncle Michel. "*J'adore,*" he'd said (and I thought he was gushing a bit too much—adore!) and would never do anything to hurt him. But from the looks of Michel, he'd done enough to hurt himself, enjoyed the farm's fatted ducks, for-bidden Armagnac, and unlicensed tobacco all too much. Jean-Marie said, "So we must not make any yum-yum sounds when we enjoy the dessert my new aunt has made us."

This, I could do. I thought Jean-Marie might forbid me the wine, which I needed more and more at these nightly *chambre d'hôte* pit stops, where Jean-Marie spent the night jabbering away with the hosts while I sat trying to figure out how to eat tiny birds and complicated shellfish—or worse, finished my food long before anybody else had and stared at my empty plate while the rest ate like human beings.

"Oh-oh," said Jean-Marie before walking back into the house. "Here is Coco. Don't get Coco excited." Coco was an emotionally damaged German Shepard–Great Pyrenees mix, and in the three short hours since we'd arrived at La Rigalle, Coco had made it clear she did not like me.

Get her excited? Why was this screwed-up dog my fault? Dogs usually like me. Women usually like me. Men usually like me. Here, Jean-Marie seemed to be avoiding me. Pierrette, the hostess, was terrified of me. And Michel did not seem to like me—why had he left his *chien bizarre* unattended?

Coco came near me and barked without making me feel specially singled out for hatred. It felt like a household hatred. But Michel and Pierrette Daccord (Daccord! The name smacked of welcome!) ran a *chambre d'hôte* and Jean-Marie and I were sleeping in a big ancient room with big ancient (and separate) beds that had for mattresses layers and layers of cotton batting, which shifted like a regular bed but then did not shift back: initially comfortable until you rolled around (for sex, for instance, but that was only theoretical) and it didn't spring back into shape.

I found the bed a problem because I had been restless. Early on in our twenty-five-kilometer hikes, I'd drop quickly into a sleep of recovery, but by now I'd grown stronger, and I would toss and turn, so that in the last four places where we'd stayed, I'd wake up and find Jean-Marie had removed himself from the room to sleep well, and still, alone. The tossing and turning I blamed on being in a strange place, over stimulated and over tired. Did Jean-Marie seem to be chilling toward me because he knew that my thoughts of France continued to smolder at the corner of my consciousness like an unattended tire fire at the dump? Or was I snoring?

Nobody was looking, so I kicked Coco away. She yipped and fled in the direction of sunset. The sun stayed up later here. It was nearly nine o'clock. During the day, when we were walking the Vézelay road on our way to the pilgrim city of Santiago in Spain, I made myself think of songs I knew and the names of plants and animals I recognized and, okay, God. At night, I wrote long passages in my journal about How to Handle the French, which I wasn't doing, not at all.

All of the men in France were not my type, either: skinny, emaciated even, no power in their hands, all in their mouthy mouth, with all those puissant frontal labials. And their names! Yves! Jean! Michel! What kind of name is Marie for a man?

The heretofore timid Pierrette came out and poured me more of the Ricard, and dropped a second ice cube in. I stared at the caramel-colored cloud. Pierrette stared with me. Michel had taken Pierrette as his second wife less than six months ago, and I had figured she must be nearly half Michel's age; she could have been my wife in a very other life.

"Un peu plus composé, Brian?" She ran her hand through my freshly washed hair. Where had she gathered such boldness all of a sudden? Drink? I did feel a little more composed after a shower. I loved the feel of the bumpy bath mat on my sore feet after our long walks. Pierrette was trying so hard to make sure Jean-Marie liked her. Pierrette didn't want her new nephew to think she was a gold digger, I guessed, and so there was a lot of that business of kissing each other's cheeks, and Jean-Marie didn't care, never discussed it with me. I tried not to create dramas where there weren't any, but it was difficult when I didn't speak the language—or rather, knew enough of the language to get myself into trouble.

"Oui," I tried, *"Je suis peu plus composé."* I felt a sense of accomplishment when she nodded.

Jean-Marie stepped up behind Pierrette. "Dinner is almost ready, Brian," he said. Was I crazy to think that there was a real cooling, that I was nothing more to him now that he was close to his family? He had introduced me as *"mon ami,"* which sounded like lover to me.

"I have a favorite restaurant here in Pamplona," he had said the first time we'd met nearly six years ago, "and nobody to enjoy it with." I appreciated Jean-Marie's stocky good looks (he was Swiss French, not skinny French), but took the invite as one pilgrim asking another, no more. We were on our first journey to Santiago, and he'd walked from his home, and that impressed me. I did let myself, even in my scruffy, smelly state, enjoy his strong neck, absurdly tiny ears, gleaming black eyes.

The Pamplona restaurant turned out to be run by a chef from his small town near Bern, and he gave the two of us a table near the kitchen. I was complaining about a French colleague back home, with whom I'd been quarreling about cigarettes (she was pro, I contra), American temperament (I pro, she contra), and uncooked spinach (I pro, she horrified). We were in the same department, and had to work together. "If a person demands that you avoid them because they are at an impasse, what would you do?" I quizzed Jean-Marie—extracting free advice on How to Handle the French. His English was perfect, from a year as a student abroad. He had picked up and retained a Cleveland accent.

He said, "The word 'demand' means something different *en français*," rather than answering my question. "They are *faux amis,* false friends, *demander* and *demand*. Deman*der* means simply to ask. Impasse is a *cul-de-sac* to us. If somebody demands something and there is an impasse, I would get back into my car and back out, go somewhere else. The person would be disappointed, but life will go on."

We shared a *salade* Landais, with duck *confit,* tomatoes, lardons; the wine was simple and cool, the cheese afterward strong. We tried to speak of pilgrims and maps, but we shared and discussed a love of woodworking, strong beer, and, most amazing of all, these long hiking trips that lasted weeks and months. At this point, I said, "Michael, my partner, doesn't like to go outdoors much like that. None of my boyfriends have liked to strap on a backpack."

Jean-Marie had smiled, batted his eyes as if something merely small had been caught in them, rather than the sand and smoke I'd blown. "Send them to me," he said, a little deviously, "I'll train them."

And, disarmed, we continued to enjoy the meal, and as it progressed, I got the feeling we were ships passing in the night, or some cliché like that, and I let my heart be another cliché and throb. In the end, I admitted my weakness to him: "Resolving things with my French colleague may be beyond my expertise," I said. "It could cost me my job."

"What you need is a proper translator," he said. "Somebody who knows the nuances of words, the *bon mots*." He gave me his address. When I returned to the States, he did save me, and my reputation. We continued to have phone conversations to the bitter end, and when it was over, I wished I'd had some excuse to contact Jean-Marie, beyond the usual Christmas card.

A year after that, Jean-Marie called me: would I like to do the pilgrimage again, this time from Vézelay, in central France? "Before I say yes," I said, "My French is *merde*." He laughed, but we were excited.

Now, Jean-Marie said, as we went into the chateau for the dining room, "Pierrette has made a simple meal, but make sure you do not look like you are enjoying it."

Amuse Bouche

Michel was already on his throne, paring his nails with a Laguiole knife. He was nearly eighty, his hands massive and once roughed up like quarried marble; now even that quality had been smoothed from the wearing down of age. The nails he cut at seemed made of goat horn, like the clasp of his knife. Besides the knife, before him he had his own special plate, and a tarnished silver napkin ring that held a dirty handkerchief. Often, when he talked, bits of spittle would form in the corners of his mouth, and he would have to wipe it off.

He was built like a king, or a big butane tank. His head was fleshy but small, and yet his knuckles were as knobby as the knees of a newborn colt. He made me examine my own hands there under the table, hands that always fascinate people because they are smooth, the palms of a blue blood. Here in France, with my walking stick, I had managed to build up the first calluses I'd had in years, and even a small, curious, painless blister at the tip of my index finger.

Michel had already given up trying to talk to me. What few words I could say in French made no sense to Michel, and because I made no sense, Michel apparently decided that he himself made no sense to me, either. *"Un Américain,"* he said, and blew out his horsey lips.

In truth, mostly I didn't understand. Sitting night after night with other guests in these inns was like getting clues to a mystery. One person would say, "*Moo moo moo moo* cheese *moo moo* at the market *moo moo moo moo* strong *moo moo* bad (evil?) *moo* down there." And another would respond, "*Moo moo moo* Roquefort *moo* cloud." Now, entering the dining room, I heard Michel say to Jean-Marie, "*Moo moo Américain* Type," Type pronounced "teep," as he tossed back a whole glass of something gold from his own private unmarked bottle. When he lifted his hand, I noticed that half of the man's pinky was missing.

Jean-Marie said, "*Moo moo moo moo?*"

Michel answered, "*Moo Américain* Teep!: My country, my family, my religion. Is it true for this *Américain* too, *moo?*"

Jean-Marie turned to me. "Is it true?"

Pierrette burst from the kitchen with a plateful of tartines *de foie gras:* thin, toasted bread with powerful, simple diabolical medallions of rich meat. "I am sorry," she sang in the upper register in which so much of French needed to be spoken, and "*Moo moo moo,*" which I figured meant, "for keeping you waiting," but may as well have been, "But I had to slaughter the ducks myself and extract their livers."

She placed a tartine in front of me first, tiny but potent, an amusement for the mouth, foreplay, and I waited as she gave one to Jean-Marie, and finally one to herself. On Michel's plate, she set a crusty baguette for him to slice. No treat for Michel, but a task. I put my tartine completely into my mouth and experienced the thick salty star-matter of flavor, and almost forgot my promise to Jean-Marie. As if she knew I was about to show some sign of pleasure, Pierrette reached my hand and gripped as her aged husband cut circles of bread, which he did in the way he might cut up an animal, a thing he'd done all his life. It seemed a crime to use such a fine knife for this trifling job. But bread could be a cruel business: I would trudge into towns at the ends of these walking days exhausted, footsore, and see the word *"pain"* over one of a dozen bakeries, and I'd think the word for bread was a secret torture for an English speaker.

Michel continued to talk to Jean-Marie as if the other two of us were not in the room. Pierrette whispered to me, and I understood all the words, not a *moo* in the mix: "Don't you think my husband is a little crazy?" But she said *"bizarre"* and the word sounded more like an appellation for ghouls. I didn't know how to respond; I was a guest of both husband and wife. I would rather think about the tartine's taste, the thick pasty quality meat could have. I wanted more. Now I was done and the first course seemed hours away, and I could not speak and I could not move my food around on my plate. Where were my elbows? Was that an itch? Should I drink all my wine?

Michel said, "Pierrette, the *moo* potage, for God's sake."

The Soup

Pierrette was up at once. When she opened the kitchen door, I could just see in. It was lit only by dusk, and a picturesque mess: cartons of eggs from the henhouse, too many tomatoes from the garden, a half-chopped onion, three melons, various limp and perked lettuces. It smelled like all of Gascony—like a used wet chamomile teabag. I'd noticed that the outdoor and indoor worlds of rural France sometimes switched places, ferociously ordered in nature (all those trimmed hedges!), gone back to the wild in the house. Chateau La Rigalle, a house built for some sprawling extended family and its servants, was now occupied by an aging farmer and his eager young wife and the occasional agritourist. Pierrette, obviously, had done her best to keep up a number of the rooms (I'd snooped around earlier) but simply given up on others. Under the stairway, a complete chaos of dusty garden implements, buckets, and various leather and rusted metal implements for inexplicable tasks. The dog, too, was feral, didn't even respond to civilized bribery.

On the Chemin Ste. Jacques, the road to Santiago, however, I'd seen just the opposite. I was walking just that morning through a forest of perfectly aligned trees that had been planted under Napoleon. The weeds and wildflowers looked like houseplants released back into the wild with their spotted fronds and symmetrical leaf arrangements; the cows looked mascaraed and coiffed. Now and then, deer would spring out on the trail and walk right by, fatted and tame. It made me say, "Let's have an expensive meal in town tonight."

Jean-Marie apologized. "We have to eat with my uncle tonight; he will make us an expensive meal, but it will be free."

"Then how can I pay you for all the help you gave me with my colleague last summer? I have to do something to show my appreciation."

He laughed. "Do you remember what I said when you first asked what my fee was for the dealings of that negotiation?"

He had said it was free: *"C'est libre."* I told him so.

He laughed again. *"'C'est libre'* doesn't mean it is free, actually. It means that you are free to give what you can give."

I felt a hole in my stomach open, then shrink too rapidly. He laughed and laughed and laughed, so I must have been blushing. *"Pas de problème,"* he said, and pushed me off balance with my top-heavy backpack. I fell on my back like a turtle. Overhead, two swallows cavorted, as merry and reckless and harmless as blunted art scissors. He was laughing even harder, and from this angle, despite so many weeks spent together, I noticed for the first time that a light shone through a place between his nostrils—he'd had it pierced at some point. For the rest of the afternoon, I insisted that I write Jean-Marie a check, give him a generous fee, but he wouldn't listen.

Pierrette bounded through now with a baroque tureen full of *potage de*-what? It was orange. I'm not a picky eater, but orange food sometimes spooks me.

She ladled soup into our shallow bistro bowls and she gave me my portion first again, so that I had to sit, fidgeting, while everybody else waited in silence. *"Bon,* Brian," Michel must have realized that he had only been talking to his nephew the entire meal and made an awful effort to engage me. I wished he had not. The only thing worse than not being talked to is being talked to. *"Moo moo* where in the United States do you live and *moo?"*

"Chicago," I said. I was using my tight professional smile, and that made me mad, because I was on vacation, after all.

"Ah," said Michel expansively, and then, as Pierrette spooned for him not potage but a thin broth from a special gilded bowl (a handful of sliced carrots floated in it, a mockery of hearty fare), he said, *"Moo,* Chicago, Illinois." I nodded. "But you know," Michel leaned closer, "we call it here in France, Illy-NWAH, *moo."*

Before I could unscramble and feel offended by this, Coco bounded in, and sat at her master's chair. Michel gave her bread. She loved the bread. If only this dog would stop hating me. Then she'd get something good to eat.

The potage steamed but it did not burn my mouth. This seemed a miracle, because soup, like donut-shop coffee, usually seared and scalded rather than tasted. When soup could be tasted, it was mostly salt. But this was herbal, even though it was made of carrots and squash. Somehow they were root vegetables without the rooty taste—she must have used tiny sweet carrots and acorn squash no larger than acorns. It was a candy version of soup, the texture of oiled silk, I thought, and distracted thus, I realized that, in my bowl, it was gone.

I ran my spoon frantically along the bottom, and what that did was make me aware that I was probably being rude. Did people scrape their plates in France? Did they sop with bread? Michel was still yammering about what he did and did not know about Chicago.

"Tell your uncle that Illinois is actually the bad pronunciation of the name the Native Americans of my region called the land. It would be like me calling him Franchise."

Jean-Marie was silent for a moment, sipped his soup, then said, "*Comment?* I mean, what?"

This was the other problem with the language gap—I had only baby talk to convey complex ideas. If they were *moo*ing, I was *goo*ing. I really wanted to get up and go to the bathroom, but I could just do that once, realistically, during a meal, already dallying with the rude, without seeming ill. But the air was thick at that moment and the soup, dammit, was gone.

"*Excusez-moi,*" I hit upon it—"But I must wash my hands because Coco licked them." Both Michel and Jean-Marie looked at me doubtfully. Coco growled when I stood, that bitch.

Still, I fled. The bathroom was in an unlikely place, built off the kitchen. I closed the door to the bathroom. It had been all girlied up by Pierrette with certain odd concessions to her tough old farmer husband. A tiny cigar box made of Lalique glass and framed pictures of hunters matted with exposed cardboard corrugation. And potpourri, even it was woodsy potpourri. The bathroom was old and damp and windowless. Pierrette probably had to scrub it each day to keep it from going back to the wild.

I looked at my face in the mirror, then held my hands up to it, as if I couldn't see properly unless mediated by reflection. I'd read in some men's health magazine that one should sing "Happy Birthday" to oneself two complete times while washing one's hands. I turned off the water reluctantly after the third refrain, and dried my hands. In the hallway, I ran into Pierrette. She pressed me against the hallway wall with an imploring look I had no time to register. "Brian," she said, "you must help me, I cannot be around that man another day." What was strange: she said it in an almost unaccented English.

Before I could respond, we heard Michel shout, "Pierrette! *Salade!*"

The Salad

Pierrette stopped her intense pressure and slipped into her kitchen. I realized she'd been clutching my shirt at an awkward place where a button was, and I had to tuck myself in again. This felt like a racy thing to do. I stepped back into the dining room. Jean-Marie hardly acknowledged my return, for he was in deep, serious conversation with his uncle about—me? He was saying, "*Moo moo* depart from him/it *moo moo moo* early in the morning *moo moo* when we are not seeing each other." What? What? Had I heard correctly? Was he plotting secretly to ditch me along the trail soon? And was this how I was to find out? He says it right in front of my face?

"*Ah, quelle déception!*" Michel laughed ruefully.

"Deception?" I blurted.

"Brian!" Jean-Marie seemed surprised I'd slipped back to the table without his noticing. "Is it your birthday? Have we missed the celebration of your birthday?"

"No, why?"

"We can hear you singing "Happy Birthday" to yourself in the bathroom!" He repeated this to Michel in French, and they laughed together. But I wondered, if they had heard me sing "Happy Birthday," had they not also heard Pierrette moan about her husband?

Pierrette bounded in with a smile and a great platter of greens, arugulas and radicchios and butter lettuces that adorned chunks of the most perfect tomatoes I had ever seen. Pierrette offered the plate to me first, with a look that, to her step-nephew and husband, might pass for friendship to a stranger, but appeared to me as desperate entreaty. And also: if I got the plate first, I would have to wait again as the others filled their plates, and then they would wait expectantly while I fumbled with my inelegant American hands (Jean-Marie had taught me just a week ago how to hold a knife and fork in proper European manner and I had felt like a child, *goo*) and I thought, all right, all right, don't rush me, and I spooned a half dozen chunks of lightly dressed tomatoes onto my plate.

Jean-Marie was swift and thoughtless. Michel stabbed one at a time, and I realized he too was a child in Pierrette's dining room, and was controlled like one. It came to me that she was torturing her new husband. "That's enough," she said in French. "You know what the doctor said about *moo*." Michel immediately obeyed, and put one slice of tomato back. I stabbed one of my own, not thinking about its taste but forced, suddenly, to do so once it entered my mouth. It reminded me that scientists call it a fruit, not a vegetable. It was also some kind of animal, the firm fleshy chambers held the guts and seed that burst in my mouth, and I had the feeling I was a caveman, one that had killed and sunk his teeth into a still-warm beast, and my hands clenched my knife and fork and my head pitched back and the flavor ran down my throat like blood. Jean-Marie's eyes widened; it was just a tomato, he said with his eyes, don't upset Michel.

To hide my pleasure, I put another tomato in my mouth. But I was eating too quickly. When playing the role of the lost penny, I'd learned to spread my meals out in artificial ways to avoid sitting listlessly, awkwardly at the end of a course. I'd take a bite, count to five, swallow, count to five, stab again, one-two-three-four-five, BITE, one-two-three-four-five, CHEW, one-two—but this only heightened the pleasure, here, of the perfect tomatoes. Nevertheless—onetwo-three-four-five, BITE, CHEW, one-two-three—

"Brian! I asked you if you wanted the last two tomatoes so that Pierrette can remove the plate." Swimming at the bottom of the bowl were two half-moon slices. I wanted them for their taste, for something to do while they talked of departures and deceptions.

But wait (one-two-three-four-five), why would Jean-Marie offer me the tomatoes? For my birthday? He knew they were delicious. And he was a businessman, never too timid to take what he wanted (one-two-three-four-five). Was this some sort of strategy? Was something even better coming to the table, some new magical course that would also have two bites left for somebody, two bites that would have to go to Jean-Marie, or I would seem rude? *Quelle déception!*

As if in answer, Pierrette slipped quietly into the dining room with perfectly dressed duck, obviously a duck that had been waddling around in the yard earlier that day, slow-cooked in a deep stone oven. The aroma was golden, too. I stabbed the last two tomatoes anyway. Michel watched my boarding house reach, appalled.

"Delicious," I said, and immediately regretted it.

Pierrette flashed me a version of my tight business smile. Jean-Marie did not.

The Duck

Pierrette gave Michel the duck to carve. He took his knife—was it the same knife he used for the bread? For killing ducks? For paring his horny nails? For scraping sheep shit off the soles of his shoes? Michel carved the bird as if it needed carving, but the meat simply fell off the bones. Pierrette had taken even that master-of-the-house task away from Michel, for it was sufficiently cut. Michel put some on his nephew's plate. Then Pierrette gave him some more broth, and took the platter of duck to the center of the table. There were potatoes in their skins, too, and warm white asparagus.

Jean-Marie looked up to his uncle just then with eyes narrowed by an indulgent smile, and once again I could see light coming from his nose, through it, from the eternally setting sun out the window. He was mostly in silhouette, and the pinpoint glint was striking. He was a man who'd had a nose ring, completely capable of rebellion, of acts cruel and anarchic—tattoo-getting, city-wall-tagging, middle-of-rural-France-ditching, and me left to be eaten by Coco the gorilla dog.

"Eat, eat," Michel suddenly shouted. It was supposed to be a fatherly hostly command, but it sounded resentful, and after I let it slip out that I'd been enjoying the tomato (that little easily trans-latable "delicious" had been like a floorboard's squeak during a nighttime jewel heist), Michel was watching me. The duck pieces were bite-sized. To cut it in two would be a fuss. I stabbed. I cut. I tasted. I forgot to hide my pleasure.

To replace any withering word he might have for me, Jean-Marie let his fork clatter to the plate.

"Moo moo moo moo seventy years *moo moo."*

Jean-Marie translated for the first time that evening, "My uncle says he has been eating ducks every day for his whole life, and he still enjoys them!" This seemed both possible and wistful, for Michel couldn't eat them any more, if Pierrette had anything to do with it. And I was having trouble enjoying the—yes—succulent quality of the duck because he had succumbed to flavor.

Pierrette caught Michel putting salt on his broth and she nearly screamed at him, "You know what the doctor told you!"

I looked over at Pierrette. She'd been seated for no more than two minutes, enough time to spoon a little of her own food onto a plate, when Michel *moo*'d another request, feeble retaliation. She fought for a moment, saying it was something he shouldn't have, but stopped in the middle of her protest, stood, and took the long way around the table, duck-duck-goose, tilting toward both Michel and me, for we shared the corner at the end.

When Pierrette leaned toward us, her eyes rolled on the incline like two marbles, aswim within with violet fins, though only I could see this, and I wondered, was she signaling me to follow her, or telling me to regard the slave driver that was her husband? Or was she simply rolling her eyes sarcastically at the ridiculous task/man/situation?

Jean-Marie and I had remembered, earlier that day, a night in Spain on our last pilgrimage, when we were having a laugh at our Iberian hosts. We'd looked for a vegetarian plate for Jean-Marie and flummoxed the locals—what was vegetarianism? they wanted to know—you eat a first course and then, what? a first course? We only found on the menu a thousand things that came out of the sea, octopus the most recognizable. Jean-Marie capitulated to the "vegetable salad," which was flaked with tuna.

And here in France, after he had expressed his dread of returning to the cuisine of Spain, I had reminded him of the vegetable salad. *"Éxito!"* I had said, to cheer him up.

He had asked me, as we walked along, whether *"éxito"* was the Spanish word for "Let's exit," because he was ready to make an *éxito* any time now.

"*Éxito* is Spanish for 'success.'" Spanish, I knew, and I looked forward to a time when Jean-Marie would depend upon me, for a change, and I would feel like, well, a man, not feckless, on the run.

But we'd been in Spain together before. Jean-Marie had found his own solution, back then, to the problem of sitting alone at a Spanish table while I and the others *habla*'d on and on. Jean-Marie told me after just such a dinner that sometimes he would listen to our conversations and take one or two of the words he knew or thought he knew and conjure the conversation: "My friend (my lover?) was an embarrassed bullfighter but he ended up in the pharmacy business until he broke his toe (finger?) and worked with prisoners (and himself?) for his goats in the trees." Jean-Marie said of this, "It can be surreal, but it can also be accurate."

"That's the silliest thing I've ever heard," I'd said, even though we had talked about goats getting into the trees. "'*Embarazada*' is a false friend, too, and doesn't mean embarrassed. It means pregnant."

But here at the dinner table in Chateau La Rigalle, I'd run out of opportunities for counting to five, wearied of the mooing, and the duck was gone, so I tried Jean-Marie's trick myself.

Jean-Marie was saying, perhaps, "Pierrette, if she were a man, would be a master of the ducks."

Michel perhaps said, "Only a man can be master of the ducks."

"You must be careful," it seemed Jean-Marie was saying, "or Pierrette will depart from you as well, what a deception!"

Michel laughed and reached for his nephew's glass of wine. He held it out to him, naughtily, and said before he drank deeply from it, "And where do you think she will go to make her omelettes?" Maybe that's what he said: omelettes.

Pierrette reentered and let clatter onto the table before Michel a platter of noodles smothered in a simple sauce—a béarnaise. Beside it, a bowl of wild rice, and smaller bowl with gray lentils. Food meant for the poor and desert fathers. The béarnaise looked great, though.

Michel looked pleased. He saw that I was eyeing the plate, too. He said, "Would you like some?"

Pierrette snapped, "No, I made *moo* for you." And then I thought she may have muttered, "I hope the béarnaise burns through your internal organs," in English. And that's when I began to wonder whether Pierrette might be poisoning her husband, weakening him and blaming it on his delicate condition. I watched the old man eat directly from the bowls, because they were his alone. It was as if he'd been starved. He inhaled the food, paying no attention to texture or taste; Pierrette may as well have set the bowls on the floor for Coco. Before long, the energy drained out of Michel, and he was as gray as his lentils. She must be killing him.

Michel began to talk with food in his mouth. Now it didn't even sound like mooing to me. I often elect not to rent the headphones for in-flight movies, but will sit and piece together the pantomime story, nonetheless. That was what it was like to watch Michel now. The way Michel contorted his lips and nose while he chewed made it impossible to know whether he was complaining or praising, and whether the dis/pleasure was for the food, Pierrette, his health, or the *Américain* Teep next to him.

Jean-Marie would not converse with me. He was too busy eating, and probably couldn't understand his uncle either. But Pierrette understood him, for he said something mid-bite, and I was able to hear, loud and clear,

"No dessert for you!" Pierrette said it in French, and got up to get the dessert.

Michel pulled his filthy handkerchief off his lap, wiped the corner of his mouth, rolled the handkerchief up again, and slid it into its silver ring with the nubbin pinky. He got up and said something about closing the barn, before the *moos* got out. Coco skittered out with him.

The Dessert

At last, it was only Jean-Marie and I together in the dining room. But Jean-Marie only half smiled. He stabbed the last two bits of duck on the platter, just as I suspected he'd do. If only I could drink a little more wine. Life always required just a little more fine tuning. To kill time, I looked at the bouquet of wildflowers Pierrette offered the dining-room table, common daisies, but of different colors, all messily stuffed into a tall vase. They wilted, leaned, hung. They were beautiful. What confection, I wondered, would Pierrette unveil for dessert?

I was about to say something to Jean-Marie, something conspiratorial, but outside, I could hear Coco barking like a maniac, with one single-syllable admonition from Michel to quiet her: *"Moo!"*

"I'm going to carry some of these empty plates in for Pierrette," I said.

"She can handle it," Jean-Marie warned, but I ignored him.

There were sauces all over the plates. In Spain, it would be impolite to lick plates or daub them with bread. Jean-Marie hated Spain soon after learning that, on our last pilgrimage. I put the plates down on an empty counter while Pierrette, absorbed in dessert preparation, kept her back to me, perhaps not sure who was with her in her kitchen. I ran a finger across the béarnaise bowl—a life-risking gesture. The flavors of pickled capers, sharp parsley, and tarragon and lemon, all separately discernable but also married, made me stick my finger in again.

Pierrette said, without turning from her work, "I want to go to Paris tonight. I have a sister there. But I have no money and I have no credit cards. I would be able to pay you back when I get to Paris."

I stepped into the hall separating dining room from kitchen. "I don't know," I said, "I'm not sure."

"I want you to take me to the train station, and drive the car back for Michel. Michel needs the car. Then hike back and travel with me to Paris." I wanted to go south, to leave France, to get into Spain. She was asking me to go in the opposite direction.

"Perhaps." One of my misgivings, one she could not know about, was my need for purity on this pilgrimage. I had not been in a car for over a month, and wanted to make sure that all the movement I ever made was on foot. I couldn't drive standard transmission, either. And still I said, "Perhaps."

"Go back to Jean-Marie. Michel is returning from the barn. I will bring something sweet to you very soon."

Dessert was, at first, a disappointment: ice cream. But then, it was not just ice cream, but homemade ice cream with nuts and a perfumed honey with orange blossom and rose and something else, what?—chestnuts, Jean-Marie explained in a quick aside when I nudged him, like a child interrupting the grown-ups, honey made from chestnuts.

We were silent after that, listening to Michel outside, yelling at the ducks. I kept thinking of Jean-Marie giving me the slip. He had the maps! He had the guidebooks! And they were all in French: the direction *"tout droit"* meant "all to the right," and I would have turned right at every intersection. But *"tout droit"* really meant "go straight." Lost, I thought, I'm lost.

"Will you help me with the coffee?" Pierrette asked in simple enough French. Now that I had carried in the plates, breaking the rules about men in the kitchen, I was being invited to smash away at etiquette. Jean-Marie smiled warmly, to encourage me to follow Pierrette, because he did not want to seem insensitive to my forlorn presence, counting to five and spreading out the potty breaks and bolting my food. I hate pity, almost as much as I hate being mis-understood. But I knew what Pierrette wanted. I followed her into the kitchen once more.

She began as if she had never asked me to take her to Paris, nor grabbed me by the button and made me tuck in my pants. "Where have you been walking from?" she wanted to know, as she tapped little spoons against this carafe and that.

"Vézelay," I said, and that had been nearly four weeks ago, ancient history.

And Pierrette, being French, replaced honesty with brutality, or mistook the two, when she patted my belly and said, "But you're still fat!" Perhaps it wasn't such a brutal thing to say in French. In any case, she had done the thing: I would now need to prove myself to her, would need to show her that I was more than met the eye. What did she want? She wanted me to help her get away.

"Are you poisoning your husband?" I asked, holding up the emptied plate with the drying béarnaise glaze. We could both be direct; time was short.

She laughed. "He is poisoning himself. I do not have to do anything."

"Didn't you know what you were getting yourself into before you married him?"

She pouted, let a tiny spoon patter out of her grip, as an example of powerlessness. "You are cruel," she said, "how can you know a person until you have been intimate with them? He was a prosperous farmer! His name is Daccord! I have always wanted to be the Madame of a *chambre d'hôte*! I wanted to make his life happier." I looked out the window and deciphered a sign while she sang her lamenting aria: "The picking of mushrooms is strictly forbidden here."

"Where would you go to make your omelettes if you left Michel?"

"My omelettes?"

I could hear Michel coming in through the side door; the ducks were in their place. So were the sheep. "Pierrette, I want you to help me, if I am going to help you," I said.

"But you will help me? Then good!"

"I think Jean-Marie wants to ditch me."

"Ditch? Throw you in a ditch? I have just washed all of your clothing."

"No, I think he's tired of me and wants to get away from me while I'm not watching."

"Oh," she said, picking up that little spoon again, then: "Oh! Yes, well. He has said something like this to us at the table, as well, I think." Then she picked up the coffee service and headed toward the dining room. I had nothing to carry, and I felt foolish following her, a servant to a servant.

Michel and Jean-Marie had been talking quietly when we came in. They stopped abruptly. Jean-Marie said to me, "Would you like more of the ice cream," as I sat down and began to fool around with my coffee, putting sugar and cream into it. I like my coffee black.

"No," I said, and thought I'd try a little French. When we'd gone to hotels that were full, They told us that they were *"complet."* I was full, too. I said, *"Je suis complet."* I smiled.

Pierrette began to giggle, then Jean-Marie looked down into his coffee and sputtered into it. Michel did not laugh but made a face at the *Américain* Teep that spoke volumes: What an Idiot.

"What's so funny?" I appealed not to Jean-Marie, but to Pierrette, under my breath, as if this were not a dinner for four but one for twenty, and only those closest might hear me ask.

Jean-Marie answered, "You just said that you were pregnant."

Pierrette got up again and left the room, laughing like some cruel girl in an opera, given an entire laughing song to show off her coloratura. She only laughed once she was out of the room, however, as if being polite.

The Cheeses

From far away, from a place perhaps beyond the kitchen—the barn, the forest itself, I heard a cart role ever closer to the dining room. It was a dreadful sound, one I'd learned about in the past few weeks. It was the cheese course coming, after all these rich foods, and I would be expected to select from among the mushroomy Camemberts and tangy Roqueforts and chalky Camemberts and nutty Cantals. There'd be grapes, too, and probably a sugary bottle of Sauterne, and then I would have to eat it all, even when I was paralyzed with so much food and isolation and drink and stimulation. I would moan and it would be mistaken for a sound of pleasure, and they'd serve me more, or, if Jean-Marie mistook me for making another yum-yum sound tonight, he would, indeed, depart from me, what a deception!

The cart trundled closer. I could hear its rickety wheels rumble along uneven slatted floors, drop silent as it passed over a hallway rug, clatter back to life on the floor, silently run again on another rug. It was like that little boy on his Big Wheel in *The Shining*.

"I must go to the bathroom," I said, interrupting whatever it was that Jean-Marie was saying to Michel, and I skittered off. I met Pierrette at the door of the dining room and was blocked, trapped, by the cheese cart. Everything I had imagined would be on the cart was indeed there, and more—an Armagnac and those melons I'd seen, sliced in quarter moons, baby-aspirin orange.

"Where are you going?" she hissed. Did Michel know she could speak English? Did Jean-Marie?

I didn't answer, but ran on, locking myself in the bathroom. I sat on the toilet, not taking down my pants. I felt breathless and dogged. In a basket at my side was a booklet of crossword puzzles, most half done and abandoned. I had such a basket in my bathroom. A familiar sight made strange—the worst thing that could happen. France would have been easier for me if there had been no samenesses, no cognates in the language, no comparable table manners—if their favorite food was a dog dish, their heads green, their feet blue, setting sail daily in a sieve. But no: *crossword puzzles*. And, if the answers were any indication, idiotically easy ones, with words like *"noir," "fidelité,"* and *"aussi."*

Oh the French, I thought; but what bothered me most was that if I had been French, I would have been the most insufferable Frenchman of them all. I would have ruined myself long before Michel on pleasure.

Pierrette knocked on the door. She said in a low voice, "Tonight, you will meet me? We will take the Renault to Périgueux and board the train to Paris. If you come with me, I will show you all the sights of Paris. I cannot go alone!"

Beyond the door, beyond Pierrette, beyond the cheese cart, I heard Michel and Jean-Marie burst into conspiratorial laughter. I was sure they were discussing my pregnancy again, or my birthday, or the developing plans to abandon me. I'd had enough of Jean-Marie! He drank beer at ten in the morning! He brushed his teeth the way I hated! How could he do this to me? I opened the door only a crack, even though there was nothing indecent about me. I spoke through the wedge. "I'll leave my backpack in the hall," which was supposed to be some sort of assent, only indirect, only, I hoped, misunderstandable: Not "yes," not at all.

"Three o'clock. In the morning."

I sighed. She blew me a kiss as I closed the door. Was that to be expected as well, the kissing?"

Digestif

After I washed my face in the old farm sink where the hot water boiled out of one spigot and the cold came out of the other, I found the dinner abruptly over; Jean-Marie already retreated to his own bed. There'd be walking to do tomorrow, as usual.

The big window was over Jean-Marie's bed. To look through it, I stood over him and crossed my arms. If I looked menacing there, to him, then so what. It would have been the first time this trip. Outside, I could see, in the perpetual gloaming that seemed to be the *lux aeterna* of southern France, Michel shooing two ponies. As purple shadows, they looked overfed, balloon animals. I said so to Jean-Marie. "It's as if he doesn't know that by feeding them too much, he's not caring for them, but harming them. They're not like his ducks, you know."

Jean-Marie was quiet for a moment, and I thought he had fallen asleep already. Then he said, "He knows." It was funny, how I could not see Jean-Marie in the dark of the room, but I could see Michel just fine, though he was grainy like a black-and-white photo made from blowing up a negative too much. He tapped his ponies with a stick. Jean-Marie said, "He's old, Brian. He wants to be a farmer and run his *chambre d'hôte* and live a life as he has always done, and he cannot do it, not without help. It's humiliating for him."

Just as Michel almost coaxed the horse in, Coco bounded out of the house, barking, spooking the beasts. Michel grabbed Coco roughly by the collar and dragged her into the house without saying anything, but knowing as anybody would know that Coco was a worse than useless animal. He had to go searching for the horses.

Jean-Marie made little mousy movements in the dark below me, trying to make a comfortable place in the cotton batting for himself. In the dark, I could almost forget about his nose-ring hole. I asked him, "Tonight, at dinner, you were talking about something with Michel, what was it?" Perhaps he would admit it. Perhaps I could get him to bring his disenchantment into the open, for once, and I could thwart his plans to bolt.

"About something?"

"About something that was *'quelle déception.'*"

Jean-Marie laughed with his mouth shut. "Oh yes. Last winter, when there seemed no hope that you and I might ever get together, I cheered myself up by going to Sri Lanka. On the first day there, somebody stole my camera. *Quelle déception!*"

I watched Michel plod back toward the house. I knew Michel could not see me, not in the dark, not with his bad eyesight. Nevertheless, I made a single sliding step away from the window. Michel suddenly stopped—aware of my movement? But no. He clutched his stomach, bent over for a minute, and coughed. It took Michel another minute before he could stand up. Tomorrow, I thought, he'd be doing all this completely without Pierrette's help.

Faux Amis

I took pleasure in feeling the little calluses at the base of each finger from the walking stick, from wringing out my own clothes when washing them—except for tonight, when, as a helpless child, I let Pierrette wash them in her machine. Wait! I couldn't go to Périgueux in the car—my clothes were still on the line.

I stubbed my toe trying to find my own bed: the furniture here was ponderous, yet fussy, like Michel. Sitting on the edge of my uncomfortable bed, I wished Pierrette had offered me a nightcap of some kind, after all that sugar and caffeine; it would be hours before I'd be able to fall asleep. And she would be coming into the hall at three in the morning, beckoning to me with her damn perfect English, impossible to misunderstand.

"Jean-Marie," I said in the dark, "we have to talk about something." He didn't answer right away, and I wondered if he'd fallen asleep.

 In Friesland

Raphael Kadushin

When they got to Amsterdam the light was as dense as Dutch syrup. In the morning it bounced off the Herengracht and swam around the walls of their apartment, in wavering ripples, so the tiny room seemed drugged, or submerged, like something about to float away.

"It's so tranquil," Jonah said to Matt. Matt stuck his head out of the window and Jonah took his picture. Later, when he studied the photo, he saw Matt's soft face, backed by a halo of April trees and bell gables, and he looked as guileless as a little boy in wooden shoes. But Jonah also saw the sadness, because Matt didn't really like to travel. He preferred to stay home and paint for the sweetest reasons; his portraits flattered people.

Jonah, though, couldn't sit still.

"You're just jumpy and you're the only one," Matt said. He was right. Everyone else in Amsterdam seemed sleepy and mournful.

"The girl is too sick to rise," their friend Nienke called, the day they arrived. She sent a fistful of tulips to their apartment but she couldn't bike the five blocks over, because her luck wasn't changing. "Some days," she told them, "I can't get out of the bed and open my curtains. I don't know if it's raining or if the sun comes out."

She had passed over four times already—once her car hit a tree, and once there was an angry boyfriend with a loaded pistol and bad aim, which had something to do with Nienke's missing poodle—and she got used to gamboling girlishly down the tunnel of light. "It's so peaceful when you die, like floating on your back," she told them, the first time they met her, years before. "You are at rest in space and you know the other tiny specks that swim past you, because you see that they're all your dead friends. They're just little dots but you know them."

Still, she kept turning toward the more transparent light, flying out the wrong end of the tunnel, booted back by the ether. Though it seemed to be Nienke's choice too. "Why do you keep returning then?" Jonah had asked, thinking of all those molecules trailing through space, time on their hands, doing their lazy cosmic laps. "Well," Nienke said, "once I came back for the crab dinner at Haeje Claes. I think I miss the excitement."

Jonah wondered if cracked crabs and a lobster bib were worth all that transmigration, and Nienke didn't seem too excited now. Now she was sick with something she picked up during years of traveling, when she danced in Africa and Asia, where every tick knew her name and pursued her, like incubi, until all her blood had turned to lyme. And they still found her, even when she was holed up incognito in her one-room flat off the slumped end of Harlermerstraat. "I came home the other day," Nienke said, on the phone, "and I have a pregnant tick on me. When I shook my coat the little ones flew off everywhere."

Most days now she sits in front of a black box that is supposed to goad her lazy immune system, but every time a little crackling whiff of energy returns there is another bite, the red puckered kiss, sitting on her skin like sabotage.

"The girl," Nienke said, "is so tired."

The girl, Jonah thought, might be crazy but he didn't know for sure. He had never seen the bites and he didn't want to. "She got them," a friend told Jonah, "after her boyfriend left. Though maybe that's just a coincidence." Jonah would scan his body whenever they were in town, and he'd scrub his face quickly, running to the bathroom, soaping the inside of his mouth, after he and Nienke did the Amsterdammer's three-cheek kiss that seemed like an in-joke, because everything else in Holland was sparing. Maybe the third kiss was meant as a wry critique, or maybe it was supposed to quietly erase the other two.

But Jonah and Matt didn't have to kiss too many people this time. Instead they spent the first few days back in Amsterdam cleaning their flat and walking up and down the canals, through the light that drowned the gables and the hunched bridges, until they looked spectral. The Dutch would bump by on their bikes, as graceful as ballet dancers. They cycled steadily, and thoughtfully, but their backs stayed still and straight, so that their elegant heads seemed indifferent to their lower halves—the spellbound legs, pumping slowly, forever, in circles. They always had scarves wrapped around their long necks, trailing behind in the wind. They came one after another, like the corps de ballet, a row of people who were self-contained, dreaming maybe of a Frisian cottage or the grandmother who wore the white winged bonnet, starched like a nun's hat, or maybe of a lover. Sometimes they had their whole family piled beside them: a dog in a basket, a baby up front, a boyfriend behind, all of them sailing along together, smoothly dipping and rising over the cobblestones they knew by heart.

Those were the real Dutch. The rest were just a lot of sloppy wrecks ("you can call me a metaphysical snob," Jonah's psychic told him, "but I can see right through them") who could have been wandering any strip-mall, half-cracked and full of platitudes. They peed in the canals and rode their rental bikes side-saddle, the way amateurs do, holding their big joints proudly, like fat men with stogies, weaving in and out of traffic, screaming "watch it" instead of using their musical bicycle bells. They didn't know tradition and they seemed bent on undoing the delicate, origami folds of Dutch etiquette until nothing was left but drag queens in wooden shoes and candy wrappers in the water. Jonah and Matt sided with the natives and when they'd see a man pull out his dick and spray the canals they would roll their eyes, like hausfraus who still scrubbed their front stoops clean, though sometimes they'd take a picture first.

But when they tried to get to know the Dutch they didn't have much luck. Aside from Nienke, most of the people they met on their past trips were the sort of Americans they had always known, only even more vague. The year before they had met Lou. Someone they knew, though they couldn't remember who, had given them his phone number and when Jonah called, Lou launched into his monologue because it didn't really matter who was listening.

"I'm a culture queen," he said. Jonah pictured a bunch of gays at some tearoom dance performing their own version of etiquette; the wife-beater tank comes attached to the trucker cap comes attached to the nipple ring and the mouth that calls itself a queen. But when they stopped by Lou's apartment it was filled with books and his Bar Mitzvah picture. He looked good in a *yamulka* though he hadn't aged well. "These are my boyfriends," he said eagerly, holding up photos of two handsome boys, his drum roll. "They both killed themselves." He looked sad in a proud kind of way.

"Oh no," Matt said.

"Yes. The last one committed suicide because his other lover—I suppose the real one—left him and he didn't know what to do." He fingered a photo of a dark-eyed boy with bangs that curled at the tips. "My current boyfriend I met on a chat-line. He had never slept with anyone, either a man or a woman, and he keeps hyperventilating until he passes out. I told him, the first time we talked, that he wasn't dying and he seemed relieved, so he came up from Utrecht and we met at the train station. I don't think he's all that attracted to me but we slept together and then he couldn't catch his breath and he cried through the night. His name is Thiebauld."

Jonah thought he'd cry too if Lou revealed what was under his T-shirt; he pictured a busy intersection of thickety hair, boils and flesh. "You shouldn't have done that," he wanted to say. "He thought you were his father and anyone can see that Thiebauld doesn't take things lightly." But Jonah didn't begrudge the man. At least he seemed honest.

"I hold thee as a thing enshrined," Lou said, holding up a new picture, of Thiebauld, whose face was braced under a blonde bowl cut. "It's a poem, by Keats I think, or Shelley. One or the other. 'I hold thee as a thing enshrined and sainted.'"

Jonah thought Matt might be sainted but he had another shrine too. At first it all seemed forgettable. "You're just his type. Tomasz is fun," his friend Evan had told Jonah, when they met for drinks in England. It was a month before Jonah and Matt's return to Holland, and Jonah was already restless. "Plus he likes to meet Americans. He's trying to improve his English." Jonah was airy about that sort of thing—all the fuss—so he called. But when Tomasz showed up he thought it was a mistake. The man didn't look like fun. He wore an orange vest and he trailed the whiff of a cologne that had turned so its original scent—florid or citric—was flattened out into something different. Now he just smelled like dope and sweat. But who cared? Jonah thought, until Tomasz stuck a fat finger in Jonah's mouth, and then two. He felt like he was being strangled, that all his words were being shoved back down his throat, where they belonged, and later, like his tongue was growing out of the other man's mouth. The man's eyes were very long and brown and watched everything, every moment. He never closed them but they never settled on one thing. "Living *la vida loca*," Jonah thought.

He told Nienke about it, because she lived so far away, and he sent her the man's photo. "Oh honey," she wrote, "you want vibes. Just remember you ask a housewife's vibes, not an expert. I can see what is attractive. He is sparkling and there is a strong sunlight coming out of him. Nothing wrong with that. But he is running two ways all the time. He should go into the jungle and cry like a little kid. Or up to the North Pole."

Jonah didn't know what this meant but he saw the jungle thick with all of Nienke's ticks, flying in formation, waiting their turn. He pictured Nienke and Matt and Lou and his dead boyfriends, and himself too, all bawling like babies, in a big wet huddle, under a canopy of umbrellas splattered by jungle rain. But he couldn't imagine the man crying. He'd kill the ticks before they got him, or he'd pass them onto Nienke, who would give them one last pint of blood despite herself.

After their second day back in Amsterdam, when the apartment had been aired, Jonah and Matt decided on a loose kind of schedule. They planned to stay longer this time. Matt would paint in the mornings. That's when his face settled into itself. His hair would dry in curls, and his cheeks would fill out, like a Renaissance putti with a head full of wind. "Mr. Cheeky," Jonah would say, watching Matt mix his colors, "where did you get those pillow cheeks?" Jonah thought Matt looked like a boy who knew the dam was bound to break but kept on painting anyways: windmills, and canal houses, and women sprouting snakey tendrils of hair. "You gotta bang something," Jonah would tell him, because they were too tender with each other, but Matt would get embarrassed; he was still the way he had been, when they met.

After Matt got cranky Jonah would go sit on their front steps, like a voyeur, and take blurry photos of the Dutch passing by on their bikes. Then he'd shop for souvenirs. Anything Dutch. He bought a farmer's daughter doll, dressed in a blue apron, balancing milk pails on her manly shoulders. He bought a plaster miniature of Rembrandt's house with a hinged door that swung open to reveal the painter himself, looking sheepish and stunned, because he seemed to be holding a big internal organ in one stubby hand. ("I think he ripped out his liver," Jonah said. "No," Matt laughed, "that's supposed to be his palette.") He bought a Hans Brinker oven mitt, and a wooden-shoe corkscrew, and an old green chest painted with a village scene so faded the cottages seemed buried in some freakish sandstorm. Then he bought a postcard of a fat, crumpled Dutch woman sitting on a stool milking a Frisian cow, her skirt hiked up around her blubbery thighs. "Me working off our rent," Jonah wrote on the back, and then he sent it to Tomasz. After he mailed it he knew it wasn't a good idea. He bought a dreamier one of Chatterton, lying on his bed after his suicide, because Matt thought the poet looked like Jonah, but that was the one that probably got lost in the post. Think breezy, Jonah told himself when he scrawled on the second card, because he didn't want the man to picture him wringing out tissues, or watching himself tear up in the mirror. "The bellboys at the hotel kept asking for you after you left," he wrote, "especially the old grizzled one who chews on his bow tie." But it didn't matter. Jonah knew he'd slowly become, in the man's memory, a loutish farmer's wife milking away at a teat, dreaming of a big pancake dinner. Or maybe he'd become the grizzled bellboy himself.

Weekends, they decided, would be for side trips. "I want to go to Friesland," Jonah told Matt, thinking of the year he had lived in Groningen, when he was a little boy and his father took a sabbatical. His parents rented a white cottage with a red tiled roof and there were dwarves in the meadow Jonah had to cross when he walked to school. "Some will eat you alive," his friend Elsie told him, "starting with your feet, and some are good elves though you can't tell the difference." They called her Elsie the Clothesline, but Jonah didn't remember why. He would run home from school every day, as soon as they closed the front door, and the women along his route would take turns calling his mother. "He's rounding the corner of Bluemenstraat now," one or the other would tell her. "The Dutch were so nice to us," Jonah's mother would say, for years after, though it was clear what she thought at the time. They were wondering about all those missing neighbors and Jonah's family was concrete enough, and reassuringly aquiline. What Jonah remembered was the smell of the candy stores and the low rise of the land to the dikes and the feeling of being gently cradled, safe, between all that water. They were like an Eskimo family in an igloo. The children next door were named Hansel and Gretel and Jonah's mother and father would dance around the living room. When Jonah and his sister took them back, years later, they held each other, in front of the cottage, and cried.

"Let's go to Friesland," Jonah kept telling Matt, but they couldn't find the time. During the first few weeks back in Amsterdam Matt mostly worried about their house in the midwestern college town where they lived, between trips. They had rented it to the contessa, though that wasn't his name. He was a visiting medievalist from Venice who was giving some lectures and they had never met him, because he sublet the house after Jonah and Matt left. But they pictured him, clearly, as one of those bloated, big-hipped contessa-like queens wearing pastel cashmeres and elaborate rings, a cheap means of distraction, and who sang along to Mozart arias and knew the lost language of graying poufs. Hilda Handcuffs, Jonah read in a book of old gay slang, used to mean the police; eek was a face and omee-palone was a homosexual.

Matt started calling the contessa. Every time he called there were sounds of a party and Jonah and Matt would picture the Meissen shattering against their bleached wood floors. They would see crack pipes smoking on the front porch and farm boys dancing in a tipsy conga line around the house and big circle jerks gumming up their industrial living-room carpet.

The contessa, though, didn't sound so happy on the phone. "Is everyone in this place blonde, blue-eyed, and twenty-one?" he asked.

"No," Matt told him. "Only if we're out of town." Then the contessa started to complain when Matt would call. "You don't have any pots and pans," he said, in an accent Matt couldn't define. "Where are all the pots and pans?"

"That's odd," Jonah said. They started to picture spaghetti blowing across the kitchen and exploding microwaves and naked orgy boys in chef's hats stepping over the legal line with whisks and lumberjacks going slaphappy with the spatulas, the way any spirited omee-palone would.

But Matt, who liked to keep things friendly, kept calling and finally the contessa said they could take his house in Venice for a week. "Just let my maid know. He lives in. His name is Marco."

Matt worried that this was some sort of pay-off, for the smoking hole they once called home, and Jonah's friend Billy, sending updates, didn't try to calm him. "Went to the contessa's dinner party," he e-mailed. "He's not Italian though it's hard to say what he is. But after dinner he opens your closet doors for all the guests and says, 'look, it's the same black coat. Ten versions of the same black coat.'"

To get Matt's mind off the imploding house Jonah started booking the weekend trips. First they went to Yorkshire, where a woman named Megan took them on a tour. The blue eye shadow caking her left lid sat in a perfect arc but on the right one it shot up like the Dow indicator. She walked stiffly and lurched slightly so from a distance she resembled Bigfoot in a dress and crocheted vest. "I had a stroke last month," she told them. "I was in a restaurant with friends and suddenly the left side of my mouth went numb, like when you're at the dentist, and the water I was drinking dribbled out onto the table." She had a sheep farm in the Dales that she ran alone, with a sheepdog she mistook for her husband, and she seemed upbeat as she showed them the sights, though she believed in tours with an edge. In York they skipped the cathedral ("too showy," Megan said) for a drive around a very tall, green hill that looked like a burial mound. It was.

"This," Megan told them, wistfully, as if she were remembering her campfire days, "is where they herded all the Jews of York and burned them, every last one."

Then she drove them to Haworth, where the Brontë parsonage was dwarfed by a cemetery so big it looked like a Mexican village of the dead.

"They think," Megan announced, "that the dad had dormant TB and infected all the girls. Or maybe that the rotting corpses in the cemetery poisoned their water supply."

"It's amazing any of them survived into their twenties," Jonah said. He saw the four sisters wandering the moors, calling for Heathcliffe but only bumping into each other—damn, you again—stumbling past flocks of sheep and one-eyed farmers, leaving a delicate trail of blood behind them. "Heathcliffe" they would try to shout, practicing hopefully, but every time they opened their mouths funnels of blood would pour out over the heather.

The air still smelled fetid and rotten in the parsonage. Jonah coughed into a handkerchief and looked for his own ripe spot of red.

"They were really just crazy girls," Megan suggested, before she took them to the moor-top village where the townsfolk once killed witches who were as far-gone as the Brontës, pulling the spinsters' parts off limb by limb, like sloppy butchers, and yanking their tongues out with pincers.

Matt seemed alarmed by this, and dreamt of their house finally crumbling in on itself, so when they flew back from England to a rainy Dutch afternoon and checked the apartment Jonah said let's just keep going. Then they went to Italy for the sun. The contessa had sent directions to what he called his palazzo and they thought it was a joke until they found the quiet canal, and saw the big old villa. Above the front door there was a stone panel of a medieval man sitting on the edge of his bed. Was he going to sleep or waking up? "Let's pretend he's getting up," Jonah said.

Inside the floors were marble and everything smelled of garlic and bad fish. "We could hide all his pots and pans, except for the ones we pee in," Jonah suggested but Matt, never prone to whimsy, was still trying to make amends. When they crawled into the frozen bed at night the palazzo was as cold as an ice palace. "Where is Marco the maid?" Jonah suddenly remembered, sitting up in the dark, but Matt was already asleep, his legs cycling restlessly, rehearsing something. Jonah looked at Matt's face and thought of the stone man getting out of bed and then he thought about the other man. Tomasz was half Italian and half Polish. "People don't think I'm Italian," he told Jonah, the second time they met, in the hotel in London. "They think there isn't enough hair, and I don't have a mustache."

"What are they picturing," Jonah asked, "an organ grinder?"

Tomasz didn't understand. "It's a puzzler," he admitted. "I got that from TV, from *Frasier*. It's a puzzler." He was still learning English and it wasn't until later that Jonah realized why the man's e-mails were so coded. "Looking 4-ward to c-ing u," the man would write, working on his alphabet. At first Jonah thought this was sheer laziness, as if entering whole words was too much work, something he saved for his real lovers, but then he realized it might be the lack of words themselves. Though he was never really sure. "Looking 4-word" was as urgent as things got.

But when they did meet, the man's tongue was fluent and Jonah would think you can't fake that as he watched Tomasz's eyes looking all around the room, restless as Matt's legs, the pupils always dilated.

"What," the man asked, "is humane?"

"It's like very human," Jonah told him. "It's like human only more so."

The man raised his eyebrows and his smile was long and curved up. That's what he did when he didn't know what to say. But otherwise he seemed so generous and deft, like someone who got at least one thing right.

"I meet all kinds of persons," he told Jonah. "Writers, businessmen, counts."

That, Jonah thought, seemed like a big leap, writers to counts, and he wondered if Tomasz had gotten it wrong. Were there any counts left?

"Now I'm happy," the man told him. "I have an apartment and a car and everything is in front of me." The writers, the counts. His biceps were as hard as a coconut. Jonah took a picture of him spreading his arms wide like someone about to take off.

"You can put that on your Web site," Jonah told the man, hoping he would replace the oddities that popped up on the screen now, like a cultural misunderstanding. There was one shot of Tomasz in a Santa's cap—Jonah wondered if he mistook it for some jaunty S&M headgear—and one in which the man's face rotated slowly like a lazy susan, as if he were illustrating a racial type in a Nazi training film.

"You have such a big cage of ribs," Tomasz said one time, when his English got better. "What's behind it?"

"It's a puzzler," Jonah said.

In the morning, after Jonah slept a few hours, they woke up to the Venetian sun, which seemed bleached out, as if it were tired of all that busy rising and setting, the whole unyielding cycle. The streets were filled with Italians grinding up against each other, tweeking the cheeks of babies, talking at once so loudly it sounded like a din after the quiet Dutch. Hands went flying and everyone was kissing and after awhile all the touching began to look like a mauling. On San Marco Square they passed a man charging money for photos; he stood next to a pyramid of trained animals, a mouse sitting on a cat sitting on a dog, like a carnivorous totem pole. "There's an accident waiting to happen," Jonah said, but Matt, who missed things, was studying a shop window filled with marbleized papers. The back of his head looked as soft as an eggshell.

When they returned home in the evening the palazzo's marble floors were glacial. They got into bed again and Jonah fell asleep quickly this time, without the Ambien. But then he woke up to a sound, something like a long moan. "I'll be right back," he whispered to Matt's curled body, heading for the staircase. At the bottom of the steps he stopped. There was a thin bald man on top of a dark-haired boy, who was sprawled face-up on the wobbly love seat in the hall. The bald man was pumping away too fast, so his bony ass looked graceless. The boy was groaning and his head was flopping over the side of the couch and banging against its wooden frame. His eyes were closed. Then the bald man let out a weedy shriek and the boy raised his head, suddenly alert, to see if he was done. When they heard Jonah's stage cough they both seemed nonchalant, though the boy let out a half-hearted *mama mia*.

"Sorry," Jonah said.

"Oh for the days of keyholes," the bald man said, in a vaguely British accent, pulling up his shorts, smiling. "I wondered if you'd get here. I finally ended up buying some pans but I left the receipt on your dining room table."

The next day the contessa gave them a tour of the town. Matt lagged behind because he didn't want to hear the contessa but Jonah didn't care; he'd already given up on the man. The contessa talked as fast as the Italians, though he had, it turned out, been born in Manchester.

"I love Marco and he's going to move in with me for good once he finishes school."

"Uh-huh," Jonah said.

"Yeah. I'm tired of all the melo-theatrics and I'm ready to settle really. The last boyfriend I had locked me out on his balcony hand-cuffed to the rail and didn't come back for eight hours. I was naked and freezing out there. When he got back he acted like he'd just for-gotten. 'You still there?' he asked me. Talk about condescending. But he was a man of substance."

"Sounds," Jonah said, "like substance abuse." They leaned over the side of the Rialto Bridge—an old thing that still felt fake—and watched the gondoliers row by in the straw boaters and striped shirts that looked loud to a Dutch eye; they were, you could easily see, just a siren call, as tacky as fishnets and stilettos.

"You know," the contessa said, "it's true they're all promiscuous but they mean it at the moment and when they fall in love it's pure for that moment and it gushes, nothing closed off, like they're de-vouring each other, like the walls of the house blowing down. It's like the way they eat with so much greed, the spaghetti swirling out of their mouths and the wine soaking through the tablecloth and the lamb chop over the shoulder and all the bravado. They don't hold back. My last boyfriend said to me 'I will cut your cheek with a knife so you'll have a big red scar, because that's the way Latins mark their lovers.'"

"And I was just going to settle for a tattoo," Jonah said. They sat down for coffee and the contessa kept talking but Jonah stopped lis-tening. The last time Jonah saw Tomasz was his final day in London and they were in a car. A friend of Tomasz's—a big henna-haired cockney—picked them up at the hotel and when they got into the back seat of the car Jonah could see the driver watching them, in his rear-view mirror. He looked angry and Jonah was nervous, and kept his distance in the back, scrunched against the door. But then To-masz brushed a hand against Jonah's cheek, while Jonah watched the eyes in the mirror, and then the car stopped and Tomasz stepped out onto a curb near Piccadilly. It was one of those London days when the sun is muted and almost Dutch and there was a little triangle of gold that fell on Tomasz and Jonah could feel the same light glazing his face too, so when the car drove away it seemed like his eyes, and Tomasz's, were both lit a cat's eye amber and that they had finally settled on the same sight, for one split second, at the same time. "I see you," Jonah thought.

"You know, he treats everyone like that, every toff," the driver said, speeding up fast. "It's like a bad tic."

"I c u," Jonah thought, turning to watch the receding view.

Back in Amsterdam, after the Italian week, Jonah and Matt opened the windows of their apartment, so the breeze from the Herengracht blew in and some green buds floated onto their bare wood floors. "It's like living in a tree house," Jonah said, feeling hopeful, but the next day he was mugged on the tram.

"What's in your pocket?" the foreign man said to him and suddenly Jonah saw he was sandwiched tightly between two of them. They were standing so close and straight on either side of him that he thought the three of them must look like some bad Riverdance road show, the kind that would play Head Start classes and public transportation hubs. Or maybe they looked like a triple date. Finally, he thought, men fighting over me, as one of the thieves held Jonah's hands behind his back, in an almost comforting clamp, and the other ripped his chain wallet off its belt loop.

The day after that Jonah slipped in their undersized bathtub and broke three ribs. They snapped clean and easy, like three wispy wishbones from a defeated chicken, or a humming bird, and as he crawled to the bathroom door, trying to breathe, he felt a rush of relief. Matt had to start pulling him out of chairs and every time he drew a breath or laughed he felt the reassuring pain, like another rib was giving way; he knew what that was. The Xanax helped, and other drugs, though he'd get woozy sometimes. "It's not the quantity of the blackouts," he told people. "It's the quality." But he couldn't move fast and he could feel Matt always watching him, closely.

"Now," Jonah said, "is the time to go to Friesland." They got as far as the central station, where they had to squat inside a photo booth to take their train-pass snapshots. Jonah thought they both looked good under the booth's bare bulb—us two toffs—but when the strip of pictures curled out the side of the machine their faces stared back at them, pale and drawn. "Look," Jonah said, "it's

Mr. and Mrs. Uriah Heep. At least they won't need dental charts if we ever commit to that murder–suicide scheme."

Matt didn't laugh. He studied the pictures and then he looked up. "It's too long a trip to Friesland with your ribs, Ebenezeer."

Instead they stayed that last week in Amsterdam. At night they rented videos—*Sunday Bloody Sunday, Mrs. Miniver,* and *Darling,* and then *Camp Poka-hiney, Forest Rump,* and *Boneanza.* The sky had turned gray and it drizzled all the time. Finally the drizzle turned to rain and the old stones of the city looked happy, soaked clean the way they liked it.

"I want to go home," Matt said, thinking of their salt-box house with its blue shutters. He pictured their pine sleigh bed and his little studio, and he knew they were almost out of time. "There's no money left," he told Jonah.

"Well when they serve dessert," Jonah coached, before they left for one of their restaurants, "just tip the table and run."

But by their last weekend they were reduced to cafés, and Matt was already packing. On their final Friday they got two letters in the mail. The first was from Megan, who seemed to be researching her next tour. She had enclosed a photo of a ruined abbey and on the back she wrote, "this is where they found Braveheart's actual heart buried in the dungeon. Some people say it was squeezed right out of his chest, while he watched."

The note wasn't signed, which lent it the breezy air of a death threat. The second letter was more surprising. It came from an old friend in San Francisco and it was addressed to both of them, so they didn't open it until they sat at a canal-side café table under a momentary sun. "I found this when I was moving," the friend wrote, on a Post-it attached to an old photo of Jonah and Matt hugging. Jonah had turned, so only the back of his head was facing the camera, and Matt's face was resting on his friend's neck, looking straight out at the lens. Matt's lips were slightly parted and his eyes looked as if they were seeing something for the first time, maybe Icarus falling from the sky or some kind of annunciation or the view from the top of the Westerkirk. He resembled a Sicilian boy, in a photo they had seen in a book, with tangled black hair, holding a hand to his bare chest and staring out so intently, stricken or elated, that he seemed stuck, forever, in the only moment that mattered. Very brave, Jonah thought, and he ran a finger down Matt's cheek. "Mr. Lashes," he said.

Matt pulled on his nose, the way he did when he was embarrassed, because the Dutch watch so closely, even when they pretend not to. When Nienke got to the table her face looked pale. "My big day out but I should have stayed in bed. The girl," she said, holding out her arm, "is bit again, four times." Here was evidence, two puckered bulls-eyes dimpling her skin, though Jonah thought they could have been track marks or hickies. But they looked real and he knew that they'd never stop now, they'd just keep biting, and Nienke knew it too.

"I thought I saw my old boyfriend on the street yesterday," she said. It was the only time she had ever mentioned him. "He wasn't good for me."

Jonah shrugged. "Not like he killed anyone," he offered, doubtfully. They all stared at the canal, below their legs, and waited for the sun to go back where it belonged, behind a cloud, as a long boat slid past, filled with three girls drinking wine, their hair curling out behind them.

The next day the drizzle turned to rain again and then it didn't stop at all. "We're not going to Friesland are we?" Jonah said. He sat by the apartment window watching the rain and he thought of the north, where the lowlands are so low they sink altogether and the meadows turn into seaweed. Those, he thought, are the real netherlands, something so ethereal they could disappear in a second, sliding under the surface of a wave or just evaporating in a little liquid cloud, like the bubbly sighs babies sometimes blow. The netherlands as ether, a mix of the soft and the hard. When he was young his parents would drive out through the Frisian country. A farmer once opened his armoire to them, to show off the Dutch linens folded into tightly wrapped shapes—hearts and ribbons. In his cottage there was a painting of a grandmother or a great-aunt. It looked like the Golden Age portraits of burgher's wives who knew how to hold steady gazes, the straight-faced answer to all those coy French countesses dressed up like Dianas, and those pompous English ladies sniffing roses but smelling nothing. The Dutch sitters had settled into their lives; they had claimed their triangles of light, their letters by the open windows and their clean front stoops. They didn't need to put on shows. The farmer had some old hats too and he told them that the side-pins on the headdresses signified social status. Jonah, though, couldn't remember the code now. It was something like round pins meant you were Protestant and straight pins meant you were married. Bent pins meant you would bust up some marriages, burn the pea soup, show up in church with a sawed-off pistol, and, in a sudden moment of regret, slip out of town. I'd be the one who sat on her pins or lost them, Jonah thought, staring out the window. I'd be the hatless village idiot.

"We're not going to go there, are we?" he asked Matt again, while the rain kept coming, and Matt said no, it seemed unlikely. Jonah thought about renting a car but he couldn't see himself driving all that way, his ribs sticking up against his skin. Instead he stayed by the window and he tried to imagine it. He would get in the car and drive along the Amsterdam canals, in Celtic spirals, because the grachts all wound in on themselves, and he would finally find the one straight road that ran out of town. He'd turn onto the highway and he'd drive until he passed Edam and Enkhuizen. The rain would splash against the window but he'd keep driving. He would drive from Broekoord to Medemblik. He'd drive through puddles as big as ponds, past wooden shoes so waterlogged they were turning to mulch. The women's winged bonnets would flatten down into dripping earflaps, so the Dutch widows would look like old salty dogs, calling out "thar she blows." He would drive straight across the enclosing dike, a thin strip of concrete running through the North Sea. He'd keep driving until he got to the top of Friesland, past Harlingen, and then he'd crawl up onto the tallest embankment just as the dikes cracked so the water would sweep over everything, the way everyone knew it would. And then he'd see what he wanted to. Beside the uprooted trees and drowning cows, the man would be swirling by on a cresting wave, not kicking but resigned, while the water filled his mute, stupid mouth, and his tongue curled back down his throat, and his eyes finally shut for good.

My Father-in-Law Has Two Names

David Masello

Sometimes when I travel to cities like Nashville, arriving late at night when the downtown streets are empty, I want to leave in the morning without exploring because I feel there is nothing left to see. That is my inclination when I hear long, low train whistles my first night in a Nashville hotel-room bed and remember there is no depot in town for the trains to pull into. But I will stay for a few days because I have come with my partner, Mac, to visit his father, Neil.

After we land, Neil leads us from the airport to his house. We had met once before, but as I drive behind him, I see the way the back of his head—how the ears stick out at slight angles—resembles Mac's. But I can't imagine Mac's neck fossilizing with the same deep creases. Beside Neil sits Michael, a man younger than Mac. And while Michael is not the man Neil had left Mac's mother for, he is indistinguishable from those who preceded him: as young as a son, minimally educated, dependant and undependable, and with an insatiable desire to distance himself from his past and background— "To live a life he'd had no sense of before," Mac's father has said before about Michael.

Soon, we are in a working-class Nashville neighborhood, the streets lined with postwar ranch houses, each tagged with a TV satellite dish. Rusty cars and pumped-up trucks with blackened windows fill the driveways, though some vehicles are parked on lawns near the front doors. Mac has been to this neighborhood before but still finds it depressing.

"We always lived in college towns, sometimes in student ghettoes, but I just can't believe my father lives in a place like this now," Mac says. "These aren't people who could be his friends. My father, university dean, professor, has always sought out the neediest men he can find to be his boyfriends."

Blocks before we reach the house, Neil puts on his signal and slows almost to idling. In the rearview mirror, his eyes, wincing from cigarette smoke that curls from his mouth, catch mine. We pull into the driveway, at the end of which is a car without tires, hubs sunken into the ground.

"That must be the latest car Michael wrecked," Mac says. "My father told me some story about Michael having a blowout on the highway. Tell me the last time you heard of someone having a blowout. Cars don't have those anymore. I think that's the fourth car so far. What do I think happened? Michael was drunk and speeding and hit the curb so hard it bent the axle."

Even though it is mid-November, grinning, flickering jack-o'-lanterns, their orifices curling inward, stare from the windows and concrete steps of the house across the street. A scarecrow, dressed in a black pointed hat and cape that the wind has twisted about the body, stands slumped on the lawn. Dried-out onion eyes, knotty garlic nose, and scallion-stuffed mouth are fashioned so realistically the figure is like an effigy ready for sacrifice. Explosions of blue TV light flash behind the house curtains.

"They're our resident Satan worshipers," Neil says when he sees me looking at the house after we get out of our cars. "I understand they hold black-Sabbath meetings. They put all those props out in September and they remain there until winter. She's Asian and he's Caucasian and so they don't seem to care about Michael and me being, you know, a mixed couple."

From our room in the Hermitage Hotel the next morning, I see the main elevation of the pre–Civil War Tennessee capitol and I know then that some integrity remains on Nashville's downtown streets, a fact I wouldn't have believed the night before. While Mac and I are later exploring government buildings that occupy capitol hill, we come to a series of bronze plaques affixed to an outside wall of the War Memorial listing the World War I Tennessee dead (2,965). The engraved names, illuminated by the morning sun, fill a façade.

Scanning the plaque containing the R's, Mac says, "Look, the same spelling—that's really rare." He points to his family name, just one, on the brass roster. He then begins calculating who the fallen soldier might have been, a cousin? from which branch of the family? which part of the state or country would have come? had he been a city boy? The name and all it conjures up is the kind of information found in a city's downtown.

Most of the remaining old buildings in downtown Nashville have embossed at their tops their dates of completion, most in the early 1900s. All of those World War I dead, it seems, would have come through the state's most important city on their way to the war. They had seen these buildings. For them, the small, dark-redbrick structures that filled the dense cluster of downtown streets were Nashville. That was how the big city, the state capital, appeared to them. And certainly they had wandered through the Nashville Arcade (1903) that runs from Fourth to Fifth Avenues between Church and Union Streets. The two-story, skylit arcade has more life now than any other downtown street. The three-starred state flag blazes at one end of the expanse, the U.S. flag at the other, and those of other states in between. The arcade, with its first floor of little stores and an upstairs of offices and workshops, is an ideal urban space: a place both of the outside and indoors, melding with the street fabric to draw people in and bisected by an alleyway, down which beeps the occasional delivery truck.

Passenger trains no longer stop in Nashville. The station has become a hotel and the vaulted shed where the trains had arrived is a dusty open site running with earth movers, plows, and cranes that reach to the iron spokes of the building's framework. Elaborate wrought-iron staircases leading down from the main waiting room, the steps of which once banged with suitcases and steamer trunks, are stranded in this featureless urban field. Their landings are look-out points from which we can see, as if through the rib cage of a giant carcass, the baggage building, its façade marked by rusticated stone arches that repeat rhythmically above windows. The tracks have been dug up. Little mounds of earth, like not-yet-settled burial plots, mark their former course.

Mac's father, a Nashville native who lived for many years in Alabama, Pennsylvania, and Indiana following a line of academic jobs before coming out, divorcing, and returning home, tells us as we walk from the Hermitage to Church Street that the last department store downtown has just closed. "There used to be four," he recalls. Arriving at Church he says, "This used to be the main shopping street and they just tore it all down. Nothing's left. It was always so busy."

When we reach the intersection of Church and Capitol Boulevard, Neil says, "I'd always heard as a boy that the sides of this church were marked by Civil War bullet holes." We scan one of the walls, which becomes larger as it follows the downhill site, and finger round holes in the stones. But no literature inside the church or on the plaque outside mentions them, only that the building had been converted into a Federal hospital.

Inside, the church has a flat, coffered ceiling and in the balcony are raked rows of iron seats upholstered in maroon velvet. There is a meeting in progress of Historic Nashville, Inc. About forty people have gathered early on a Saturday morning to discuss ways to halt demolition of what remains on Church Street. There is talk of how the street has already gone through many incarnations in its long development. Now, Church is a mere lane narrowed by a widened brick sidewalk meant to encourage pedestrian traffic, its north side mostly parking lots—except for a Presbyterian church, a Greek Revival Catholic church, the portico of which is closed off by a fence ("the homeless were coming inside and urinating in the pews," someone tells me later), and a pit as deep as a quarry, soon to be the site of a twenty-eight-story apartment tower. The latter is a sign of the hoped for revival of the street, but the artist's rendering on a billboard depicts a building shaped like an Aztec pyramid, more appropriate to the Vegas strip than a mid-sized southern city.

From our balcony perch, the people in the church appear like huddled survivors of a bombing campaign. I am reminded of the movie *The War of the Worlds* I had seen as a kid in which fleets of attacking spacecraft land in the world's great cities. By the time the aliens succumb to earthly viruses, they had left behind a twisted, smoking Eiffel Tower, a toppled Big Ben, the domes of the Taj Mahal broken through like egg shells, and I couldn't imagine how the world could be interesting again with all of those landmarks gone.

"We have the right to proclaim Church Street as one of our pivotal downtown streets," says one speaker grandly. Others invoke the names of stores and destinations that had been on the fourteen-block-long street—Candyland, the Castor Knott department store, the Watkins Institute—as if they were fallen leaders.

"They're forgetting the mother of all: Woolworth's," Neil

whispers. "My reward as a boy for sitting with my mother while she tried on hats in Castor Knott was a milkshake at the Woolworth counter."

On the short walk back from the church to the hotel, construction workers march, like occupying troops, in and out of empty buildings. I ask one of the men standing in the center of the trafficless street and looking up at a white office building from the 1920s, its façade covered with friezes and gargoyles, what is happening to the building. I expect him to say it is a gut renovation or restoration. "It's being demolished," he says.

"Why?"

"Why? It's being torn down for a parking lot."

"As if the city needs another," I say.

"Hey, you try to find a parking space around here."

"It looks like a great old building," I say. "What a waste to tear it down."

He steps further into the street, white dust puffing from his boots, puts his hand atop his hat, looks up, and says, "Yeah, I guess it's real old."

A co-worker joins him, an older man with steel-gray hair shooting from the sides of his orange hard hat. He stares at me with the blunt resolve of a union man challenged, his eyes narrowing. "What's it to you?" he says to me. "You some funny decorator type or something?"

From where we are, the Ryman Auditorium, a.k.a. the Grand Ole Opry, stands amid blocks of yellow parking-zipper tracks; it, too was once presented to developers as a potential garage site. The weapon-sharp Gothic windows of the former tabernacle are divided into three stacked panes of solid opaque colors. Later, we discover in a back stairwell of the auditorium a single clear pane in one of those windows that rises above a stamped-steel landing. Through the point of that window, the frame of which casts a prayerful shadow on the landing, we see a fanciful molded streetlight, an alleyway, and the back of a bar: elements of real Nashville. And I have to believe that Patsy Cline's high heels reverberated in this space.

Because I am interested in cities and their demographics, I ask Neil if Nashville has a black mayor.

"Why would you ask something like that? What difference would it make?" he says with an edge.

"I'm just curious. If you tell me the city has a black mayor it tells me a lot about the state of the city—whether it's got a black majority or not, usually."

"Well, it doesn't."

"Doesn't what?"

"Have an African American mayor or majority. We do have a lot of people of color, though—lots of Mexicans and Vietnamese. I guess there's something a little uncomfortable for me about that question you're asking. Do I detect a judgment being made—that people of color aren't good for a city to have?"

I don't pursue the issue. Though Neil is a model of political correctness, he is full of contradictions about social and sexual matters. When Mac had told him that the daughter of an old family friend lives with her boyfriend in New York, Neil said, "I don't approve of that, at all—a couple living together, not married." And when describing the efforts of college administrators to recruit inner-city youth, he derided them as "classic university liberals without a thought about how a bunch of ill-prepared youth impacts the rest of the college."

That Neil only chooses uneducated, underachieving black men as mates is another form of racism because it excludes the possibility of others—that is, educated, responsible black men of his caliber, not to mention white or Asian or Hispanic professionals. It seems Neil's repeated decision to partner with the men he chooses indicates a desire for boundaries—of race, class, and education. The limitations of his mates imbue him with substance. His role as mentor is confirmed.

Sometimes, during the visit, when I catch Neil looking at Mac and me, witnessing our easy banter, I feel a sadness for him. His life with Mac's mother was a good one, filled with prestige, professional advancement, and academic socializing; she was his intellectual and social equal—he has never replicated that with a man, perhaps deliberately. Just as I feel slightly guilty around Mac's mother who has had to witness the "coming out" of her husband and only son and, thus, reckon with the familial limitations imposed by those facts, so

I feel uncomfortable around Neil. Mac and I are well teamed, with common interests and an ability to converse that defines a truly happy couple, gay or straight. How could Neil not envy us?

Everywhere we drive with Neil, he has a story and a recollection. On the steep road to the Nashville Reservoir, he tells us of his grandmother who remembered when a section of its great stone wall gave way one midnight in 1906. A torrent of water—an inland tidal wave—washed away blocks of frame houses. The rebuilt circular wall before us is of dark rusticated stone and topped by a section of brick into which are interspersed a steady rhythm of narrow, Gothicized slits.

We drive the circumference of the reservoir. Its solidity betrays no sense of the watery tonnage within, the cold turbulence of it all—though ominous tricklings of moisture bleed across the stones. The reservoir stands like a fort above Nashville. I think, if I lived in Nashville, this quiet hill with its hypnotically wrapping stone presence is where I would come often. But as I consider this, I look through an edging of trees and see battered, plywood-windowed units of a housing project just below, young men "hanging," dressed in urban hides of thick, segmented down coats, voluminous pants bunched like accordions at their ankles.

"It's five-thirty, time for my 'garden club' meeting," Neil says as we get into his car. "'The garden club,' that's what I call the piano bar I go to certain nights of the week."

"You mean a gay bar?" Mac asks.

"You could call it that."

In the parking lot, on the way into the bar, Neil stops us and says, "By the way, they know me as Jim in here, so don't be surprised when you hear me called that. You should call me Jim. Just try to remember that," he says, looking at both of us.

"Why Jim?" Mac asks with irritation, registering another unsettling change in his father. "Why not your real name?"

"It's just how the fellow members of 'the club' have gotten to know me, that's all."

The piano bar is an annex off a bigger bar–disco–game-room complex, with a separate glass-door entrance. The deep bass of disco mingles with Andrew Lloyd Weber tunes on the piano.

We take our places on stools at the bar.

"Jim, let me get the first round," I announce as a way to make Neil feel at ease and to remind myself to use the new name.

After we order, the bartender sets before us six glasses, two each.

"It's happy hour," Neil says, noticing my bewilderment. "Two for the price of one."

"But at the same time?" I say.

"The trick is to sip from one glass, then the other," a man next to me says. "That way neither one of the drinks gets too watery from melting ice." I consider the logic of that strategy.

After Neil finishes one of his drinks, he introduces us to his friends. "This here is my son, Mac," he says. "And this is his friend — of several years," the last fact said with special emphasis.

From the way his friends suddenly unbend from the bar, rise like animals detecting a predator, it's obvious that Neil has never mentioned a son before. Two of his friends stand from their stools to shake our hands, as if we're celebrities.

"Does that mean you're a father-in-law, Jim?" one of the men says.

"I guess you could call me that," Neil responds. "But you won't be calling me a granddad some day."

All his married life, Neil was used to having two identities: a married man and a gay man. Now, his dual identities are as an attached gay man and a single gay man, *or,* more precisely, an attached gay man with a companion not reliable enough to present in public as his mate and a gay man with a past and present no one need know. How could someone using a changed name ever become an intimate friend of someone? Surely, Neil's interaction with his happy-hour buddies cannot carry beyond the confines of the bar. To invite them to his house for socializing risks discovery of his real name and real identity as a man with a companion who is much younger and of a different race — the latter, possibly a troubling issue for some of the men.

Through the glass door facing the disco, I see young, attractive guys entering the main bar, some hand in hand. Many of them peek through the glass, cupping their hands to deflect glare. The moment they see our crowd, though, mostly older men in unstylish shirts and off-brand sneakers, some clustered around the piano singing, they turn away and vanish into the thumping, flashing darkness of the disco.

When asked by my friends about my trip to Nashville, I say it is where my partner's father lives. At the bottom of Neil's backyard, freight trains pass regularly; his is the first house I've ever visited where that happens. Near the tracks are Osage orange trees that litter the oily ground with their mottled, brainy green growths.

Mac was so taken with the appearance of the inedible fruit that he suggests we gather several and put them in glass bowls for dining-room centerpieces.

"I've never thought about doing *that* before," Michael says, one of the few times he has been with us during the visit. Michael stacks them in his arms, carefully examining the surfaces for worms. Those that are infested are cast aside and where they roll they become perfect Shakespearean death props.

Before dinner, our last in town, much fuss is made by Neil about the automatic bread maker, a gift from Michael one Christmas.

"All of the ingredients are simply thrown inside the machine," Neil explains. "The mixing, kneading, rising, and baking are all done automatically. Every stage of the bread's shaping can be viewed through this tiny window. Michael is fascinated by this. I predict the smell of the bread baking will bring him right out here," he says, nodding toward the locked door of Michael's room, where he has gone, presumably to drink.

I've eaten bread from these machines and never find it satisfying. Each loaf comes out a perfect square and the crusts are thin and brittle. When the timer sounds three hours later, Mac's father is less enthusiastic about the finished product than he was during its preparation. He drops the loaf on the kitchen counter, immediately wraps it in foil, then into a plastic bag and, as it is still spinning from the twist-tie, hands it to us.

Later, Neil lays out on the dining table an assortment of family heirlooms brought down from a closet shelf. He wants Mac to have them. He pleads the need for more room in the house, but Mac thinks it's because there are so many break-ins in the neighborhood. The goods include Neil's mother's wooden musical bread bowl, a chest of silverware, a skeleton pocket watch minus its gold fob, and a set of department-store tea cups so thin they are nearly transparent.

Mac is grateful to receive the items but sad for his father who has no choice but to relinquish them to save them. Before we say good-bye, Neil walks to the end of the hallway and knocks on Michael's door. "Michael, you awake? Mac and David are taking off." There is no answer.

"He falls asleep early," Neil says when he comes back to the kitchen. "That's his habit."

So, after the final night's visit, our new items in hand, Mac and I return downtown along the Pike, past the flag-rippling car dealer-ships and the spotlight-washed brick housing projects of "an eco-nomically disadvantaged community," as Neil had said earlier. Later, we sit with a drink in the Hermitage's mirrored lobby to discuss the day and the others before. The room's programmed player piano eventually stops its tunes, the invisible player toying with musical phrases and then, finally, single notes—as if he is getting tired and a bit melancholy.

Goodbye Vienna

Wayne Koestenbaum

In January, for one cold week, I sojourned in Vienna with my boyfriend. We traveled there for opera and concerts but also stole time for useless pleasures, like buying a deodorant stick at Knize. Knize is an elegant clothing emporium, its interior and exterior designed by architect Adolf Loos; that means it looks like the inside of an ocean liner in a 1930s M-G-M film, and that Adolphe Menjou once shopped there. I suppose that the woman selling shirts, behind the Knize counter, considered me a cheapskate when I said, "A stick of Knize Ten roll-on deodorant, please. No shirts, thank you. Just deodorant." Knize Ten smells of hay, an elevating odor, sharp as a violin tuned for maximum penetration. Ever since Vienna I have been applying Knize Ten under my arms, as if Franz Schubert had been the "nose" in charge of inventing it.

I went to Vienna because Schubert—the divine, the borderline, the unclassifiable (is he romantic or classical?)—lived and died there, and because of other great Viennese composers, too, whose legends are part of the town's trade: seraphic Mozart, titanic Beethoven, happy Haydn, schmaltzy Strauss, aphoristic Webern, serious Schoenberg. (Schoenberg died in Los Angeles. That is another story.) It may seem preposterous to travel thousands of miles to hear dead composers, but tone-pilgrims like to see the rooms in which the requiems were written.

Until my trip to Vienna, I had never visited a German-speaking country. My father is a refugee from Hitler's Germany. That hasn't stopped him from revisiting Berlin, his birthplace. But any sane person would agree that a stellar performance of Richard Strauss's *Der Rosenkavilier,* with its nostalgic waltzes, can't erase history.

Morbid, sentimental, I ended my first day in Vienna with a trip to the cemetery. Right before sunset we went, my boyfriend Steve and I, and our guide, a voluble woman named Irene, whose late husband had played in the Vienna Philharmonic. We'd never before hired a *Cicerone,* but someone else was paying, and Irene knew the facts and had the power to take us, in her car, to inconvenient and esoteric places. That afternoon, she'd driven us to the house Beethoven lived in when he realized he was going deaf, when he looked out the window and saw the church bell oscillating but couldn't hear it ringing. We, too, stared out Beethoven's window at the silent steeple;

in our thick winter coats we had the bourgeois massiveness of sport utility vehicles, and I longed at that moment for a glass of young Viennese white wine, Grüner Veltliner, a desire I did not immediately satisfy. Did you know that Vienna is surrounded by vineyards?

We had Central Cemetery to ourselves. The sky's violet light was punishingly beautiful, like the conclusion of a beach day. I let Irene and Steve mosey along and I went alone to Mozart's grave, though Irene told me that the composer's actual remains were probably elsewhere. Frozen, I waited desperately for emotion to shake me, and yet I could summon no transport; Mozart was a speck of nearly nothing, far away. I remembered the last scene in *Don Giovanni,* when the stone statue comes to life and drags the profligate lover down to hell. Mindful of my potential damnation, I went to Schubert's grave, heavy with bouquets the winter air had kept vivid. The sky darkened, and there was barely time to find the grave of a soprano whose voice had the force of a Concorde jet taking off, and whom I'd heard, live, in San Francisco and in New York, singing Wagner: Leonie Rysanek, Vienna-born. I'll never forget her Elisabeth in *Tannhäuser* at the Met in 1987, the way she rushed onstage for her opening aria, her arms pell-mell, her chest thrust valiantly forward. When I reached Rysanek's grave, I was disappointed to see that it was modern and austere, like a tire-track sculpture by Robert Rauschenberg.

Vienna's main opera house, where Rysanek often sang, is called the Staatsoper, my pilgrimage's epicenter. From the outside, the Staatsoper is filthy. (Vienna, unlike Florence, is not soot-marred; overall, Vienna's stone monuments remain an unpolluted gray-white.) My boyfriend and I showed up at the unclean Staatsoper a half-hour before the evening performance, and the plaza was deserted, as if a curfew had been announced. Once we penetrated the unfriendly exterior, however, inside was all plush invitation, and we felt at the dubious center of European operatic aristocracy.

In the Staatsoper lobby a boy's choir was singing "We Three Kings." The three little boy kings were wearing blackface, and no one surrounding us seemed to find it odd.

Walking into the theater itself, I understood what architect Adolf Loos meant when he said, "Ornament is crime." Loos was reacting against the Viennese tendency to gussy up facades, to underscore the imperial, to make buildings aspire to the condition of noodle pudding. Loos cleaned the Augean stables with the broom of the so-called Jugendstil, Austria's version of France's Arte Nouveau or Spain's Modernismo. Jugendstil practitioners aimed to unite every aspect of visual culture (furniture, tableware, interiors) into a *Gesamtkunstwerk;* in their hands, organic forms like leaves and garlands became abstract, geometric fantasias, in thrall to modernist dogma.

There was no trace of Jugendstil inside the opera house, for it was the usual gold-laced whipped cream with burgundy velvet trim, the ceiling a flat elliptical dome with a crystal doughnut chandelier. Even during the performance itself, the house was not entirely dark, so I could admire the boxes, which looked like a sugary creation from Demel's, Vienna's fanciest pastry shop. Every inch of the Staatsoper's interior had been meticulously decorated, as if the architect had doodled with gold leaf on its surface. In the regal vernacular of a European opera house, good taste and bad taste are indistinguishable.

Tonight's opera was Verdi's *Nabucco;* the next night we saw Gounod's *Roméo et Juliette.* The imaginative productions surprised me; I'd forgotten that European opera houses were more intellectually intrepid than North America's. For *Nabucco,* Hebrew letters were projected on the scrim, and half the cast wore orthodox Jewish garb. In the first act of *Roméo et Juliette,* the heroine, played by the skinny Stefania Bondinelli, shimmied and gyrated and wore a dress apt for Björk. The audience liked Bondinelli but preferred Angelika Kirschschlager, the attractive mezzo who played the pants-role of Stéphano. I wondered why everyone was so excited about Kirschschlager, and then I remembered that she was a native Viennese. Both nights, however, the applause was moderate, not hysterical. I did my part, in the *Nabucco* curtain call, by letting rip a loud American "brava" in honor of gutsy Eliane Coelho, who'd sung Abigaille, a role whose stratospheric intervalic leaps seem a musical equivalent to jumping off the Empire State Building.

I found the Staatsoper's acoustic dry: not the hot-tub immersion that live operagoing can be. The voices didn't invade my body, as they do at La Scala, where the listener is *force fed* the arias, like a hunger striker with mouth jammed open by the police. Someone unofficial told me that the Staatsoper uses a secret amplification device: unverifiable rumor.

During intermission, I promenaded through large Versailles-like rooms and ogled the women I still consider, in my childish nomenclature, "fancy dames"—international ladies with ski tans and expensive hairdos, women whose glamour is tactful as first snowfall. I like to circulate incognito among them, to observe their ostrich formality, their shellac, their calm.

Another night, we paid a visit to the city's second opera house, the Volksoper, or the People's Opera. My fondness for Viennese operetta, a sentimental anachronism, embarrasses me: don't ruin—by interrogating—my love for the Elisabeth Schwarzkopf recording of arias by Lehár and Millöcker and Zeller. The Volksoper is the logical place to see this gorgeous schlock performed idiomatically, with the requisite uncloying lilt; we had missed Carl Zeller's *Der Vogelhändler (The Bird Seller)* and Emmerich Kálmán's *Die Scárdásfürtin (The Gipsy Princess)* this season, so instead we attended a commedia del'arte production of Rossini's *La Cenerentola,* the production barebones, the acting slapstick, the Italian impure, the singing imperfect but charming, and the orchestral-playing impeccable. The Volksoper's interior, intimate as Broadway, looked like the dream-theater in *Mulholland Drive* where a singer performs a Latin number. A family atmosphere prevails, the dress code lax; I felt like I was at a picnic or a circus. In a parterre box sat a girl with pink hair.

More acoustically responsive and more architecturally exquisite than the Staatsoper or Volksoper is the Musikverein, one of the world's perfect concert venues, constructed in 1870 by architect Theophil Hansen, of whom I had never heard. The building contains two halls, one large (Grosser Musikvereinssaal) and one small (Brahms-Saal). The majestic Grosser Musikvereinsaal is unmitigated gold, a vast, decadent Baroque shoebox with crystal chandeliers, the ceilings decorated with the obscure August Eisenmenger's gaudy paintings of Apollo and the nine Muses. At the theater's opening a tetchy critic wondered whether it "was not too sparkling and magnificent for a concert hall." Perhaps it is, but I subscribe to excess. Acoustically, the hall behaves like a seashell: at a performance of the

Wiener Symphoniker (Vienna's second orchestra, after the Vienna Philharmonic) conducted by music director Vladimir Fedosejev, I could hear, as if microphoned, the piano soloist (Oleg Maisenberg) groan while he played. My boyfriend was appalled by the noise—it sounded like the pianist was having a nervous breakdown—but I enjoyed its late-romantic extremity, appropriate for the Rachmaninoff he was performing; Maisenberg's platform manner recalled the hero-lunatic's conniptions in *Shine*.

Pianos in Vienna do not sound like pianos in New York. In New York, most pianists play Steinways. Maisenberg, at the Musikverein, played a Bösendorfer. If you are not a pianist or do not care about piano music then you will not appreciate the esoteric differences between the American Steinway and the Viennese Bösendorfer, but I am an amateur pianist, and I have dreamt my entire life about the sound of a Bösendorfer, which I have never had the privilege of playing. A Bösendorfer embodies the studious lyricism of Vienna, that city where music is not *plein air* celebration but a matter of interior rigor, introspection, refuge from the quotidian. A Steinway is brash like Manhattan, bright and virile and confident and meaty and also, when it wants, sweet, while a Bösendorfer, which you will never hear in America, is muted and easy and evasive and subtle and accommodating and does not ever sound like a cannonball, a hammer, or Niagara Falls. A New York Steinway sounds like a piano built for a robber baron. A Vienna Bösendorfer sounds like a piano built for a psychoanalyst.

The names of the Wiener Symphoniker members were not listed in the program. While it's customary in the United States to credit each ensemble member, in Vienna a group ethic obtains: individuals, serving the gods of music, are erased, like the workers in Fritz Lang's *Metropolis*. The mood at a Vienna concert is sacred, a cross between the quiet tension of a rare book room, where you must wear gloves before you touch the manuscripts, and the public-spiritedness of a natural history museum, where you gamely go to admire the dinosaurs. Once the house lights were dimmed, the players filed onstage in a formal row and shook hands with their stand-partners. I was grateful for the politeness of the Viennese audiences, respectful and silent, never wiggling, whispering, snoring, or rustling candy wrappers. At a concert or opera, I am usually the disciplinarian who turns around and tells my chatting neighbors to shut up. No need for vigilante justice in Vienna.

Another night, we attended a chamber music concert by the Altenberg Trio, a piano, cello, and violin ensemble based in Vienna. They performed in the Musikverein's second hall, the intimate Brahms-Saal, which seats only six hundred. The hall itself, the most beautiful I have ever seen, is exquisite as an Esterházytorte or an enameled snuff box, and sitting inside it, you feel cosseted and enclosed and as if nothing in the outside world could ever disturb you.

I'd noticed, on the staircase landing outside the Brahms-Saal, a marble bust of Clara Schumann. Her husband, the composer Robert Schumann, has always been one of my favorite romantics: exactly twenty years ago I wrote a doomed short story called "I Want to Be Robert Schumann's Daughter," and my title was in earnest: I longed to be the loyal child who might save the insane composer, prince of the fragmentary and the carnivalesque, from jumping into the Rhine. His wife Clara Schumann, née Wieck, was also a great pianist, and a composer who never got her due. I feel at home near busts honoring overlooked women.

Have you ever seen a loden-coat? In Vienna, a loden-coat is considered classy. But the loden-coat cannot escape its nature, which is never to be an object of beauty. The loden-coat implies good circulation and hydrotherapy and suppers of wild boar stew. In the Brahms-Saal, the loden-coats were out in force, incongruous among the caryatids and Ionic columns. The women in loden-coats were practical, however. During intermission, they combed their hair and refreshed their makeup not in the private retreat of the lavatory, but right out in the open, facing the lobby mirrors, as if an invisible rest room had been constructed, like the Emperor's New Clothes, its walls a convention respected by all.

Seated to my right at the Brahms-Saal was an elderly Viennese woman who looked like novelist Jean Rhys, author of *Wide Sargasso Sea,* in the last years of her life, with a wrinkled, beautiful face, and an expression of spirited, ruthless concentration. The Viennese woman wore a blue pleated skirt and during the concert kept her cane positioned between her knees. I decided that she was an emissary. I cast her in the part of *messenger from the dead*. I am not certain what message she was entrusted to give, but she seemed sufficiently spooky and memorable for me to believe that destiny—or synchronicity—had placed her next to me. She didn't know that she was symbolic. She didn't know that she was embodying, for me, the paradoxes of old Vienna.

Before the concert began, she asked, in English, to see my program. (They were for sale in the lobby.) She held my program close to her eyes but couldn't decipher one of the composer's names. "Friedrich Gernsheim," I told her. (An obscure composer, nearly forgotten, he was a German Jew who lived from 1839 to 1916; the Third Reich had banned his music.) I repeated the name, but she still didn't understand, so I wrote "Gernsheim" in large block letters in my notebook and passed it to her. She shrugged: "I've never heard of him." After Gernsheim's trio was over, she leaned over and confided, "It was not exciting, but it was *correct*." Without knowing a thing about my neighbor, I found myself taking umbrage, as if I were Gernsheim's descendant, and it were my duty to defend his music as more than correct, and to teach this woman that correctness was not life's purpose and would never, by itself, bring pleasure.

The program continued, wave after wave of controlled expressivity, the kind that erases invidious distinctions at the same time as it fosters them. She nodded to the music. She seemed to be closely judging it, and I imagined she had heard a multitude of concerts, some of them great, in her long life. Before a Brahms trio began, she turned to me and said, curling her fingers archly to her lips, as if she were assessing a piece of coffee cake, *"Aimez-vous Brahms?"*

I responded, *"Oui, je l'aime."*

She smiled, and after a long pause, corrected my error: "You are the young generation and can't remember Françoise Sagan's novel, *Aimez-vous Brahms*. I don't know if she is still read."

"Bonjour Tristesse has its fans."

She dismissed *Bonjour Tristesse*. She mentioned other titles, other Sagan feats. She said, conspiratorially, "Sagan was one of the starters of the *woman-power* movement." She hastened to add: "But not the political aspect."

Goodbye, I thought. Goodbye, sad, beautiful, compromised Vienna. Goodbye, city of Brahms and Clara Schumann and their unacknowledgeable love. Goodbye, city of Beethoven's deafness and the psychopathology of everyday life. Goodbye, woman-power movement. Goodbye, long afternoons waiting for the barbarians to arrive. Goodbye, Friedrich Gernsheim, and your banned, forgotten, correct music.

Sigmund Freud, like many Viennese Jews of his time, was intensely devoted to Germanic high culture (Goethe's *Faust*), but, unlike many Viennese Jews, he was not especially musical. I have never undergone a proper psychoanalysis, but I can't extricate my world view from Freud's controversial formulations, and so, while in Vienna, I paid my respects to his apartment and office at Berggasse 19, now a museum.

As I walked up the stairs from the street to the second floor, where Freud lived and worked, I noticed the way the light entered and did not enter the dark stairwell, and, by only half entering, gave the walls the friendly, dingy look of a nightmare put into perspective by reasonable explanation. Here, I thought, were the stairs that Dora, the Wolf-Man, and Little Hans, Freud's famous patients, once climbed, filled with an expectancy and love and dread that the doctor called "transference." What does one ever feel, visiting a city for the first time, but transference? Am I seeing Vienna, or my own phantoms? The light in the stairwell seemed *uncanny,* one of Freud's crucial concepts: the unhomelike. Light adequately infiltrated the not-total darkness; and this barely there illumination gave me a haunted sense of climbing stairs *always already* climbed.

Upstairs, in the museum, I saw important as well as unimportant things. I saw the furniture in the waiting room, the very chairs his patients had sat in. I saw home movies of Freud, in London, where he lived after escaping Vienna. In these silent films, Freud leaned on pillows and kibitzed with his sister Mitzi, who was later killed in a concentration camp. I saw Freud's cigar cutters, his family Bible (in German and Hebrew), and the manicure case he used when traveling. The apartment's modesty and ordinariness overwhelmed me, and I thought of Vienna's Prater, a Ferris wheel, which we'd passed on the drive back from the cemetery. (The Prater appears in the Orson Welles film *The Third Man*.) The wheel, when we saw it, was not spinning, and its paralysis seemed a token of all that ghostly baggage that will never budge.

Freud understood the power of relics and fetishes, and he certainly would have understood my compulsion to visit the house in which Franz Schubert was born. It is difficult to explain the musicological importance of Schubert, but I can suggest it by saying that his melodies are both longwinded and succinct. Seemingly endless, they finally stop, exactly at the point when you realize that you will never be able to conceive of a future without them. Schubert was born at Nussdorferstrasse 54, on 31 January 1797; he never grew to be very tall, and he died of venereal disease at the age of twenty-eight. In his house museum, I saw his school report card, his guitar, and his eyeglasses—tiny spectacles that little Franz actually peered through. The house is not special. It is just a house. It sheds no light on the composer of "Erlkönig," one of his greatest songs, set to the Goethe poem about an abducted child. If you don't care about Schubert, his birthplace is not a wonder of the world. The glasses are just someone's glasses, and they might not even be Schubert's, though the guidebook promises they are. The eyeglasses, trustworthy and enigmatic as a photograph, tell us that there was once a person named Franz Schubert who gave us melodies that infect us with a sadness and a precision that nothing in the visible world can approximate.

This train of thought is melancholy, like Vienna in January, the buildings white and gray—sometimes more white, sometimes more gray, sometimes resembling a hatbox from a Paris shop in the 1930s, when women still wore hats, and sometimes resembling a Roman sarcophagus. A disquiet surrounds the buildings, an aura that makes one wish to inquire *what happened here?* but also makes one hesitate, because there is no one to ask, and how, in the first place, would we phrase the question?

Memorials suffer from abstraction: if you want to animate a fossil, to imbue it with life, you need to be willing to hallucinate. An ordinary plaque is enough for me, if it is the right plaque. Two plaques in Vienna arrested me. On the front of a house, Kohlmarkt

9, which happens to be a stone's throw away from the best pastry shop in Vienna, a plaque explains that Chopin once resided here, the Chopin who wrote, in a letter from Vienna on 12 August 1829, "it is being said everywhere that I played too softly, or rather, too delicately for people used to the piano-pounding of the artists here." Delicate Chopin, the epitome of the neurasthenic and sexually ambiguous artist, did not like to accommodate himself to the loudness of the diurnal world. And on a house, Schönlaferngasse 7A, now painted a color between ochre and coral, a plaque indicates that the composer Robert Schumann lived here for nearly a year, 1838–39. Robert Schumann died from syphilis after a long spell of madness, but that is not what the plaque reports. The plaque is correct. Ornament is crime.

On our last night in Vienna, my boyfriend and I ate at Pfudl (Bäckerstrasse 22), a traditional *Beisl*: the word *Beisl,* from the Yiddish word for "little house," refers to old-fashioned home-style Viennese food, including *Tafelspitz* (boiled beef rump with fried potatoes and apple and horseradish sauce). I ordered a light, large Wiener Schnitzel—not unlike a veal version of tempura, containing hills and dales, fried undulations.

We returned to the hotel, and in bed, we split a room-service slice of Sacher torte, served with a huge cloud of unsweetened whipped cream: the moist soft chocolate cake almost but not entirely capitulates to the harder chocolate exterior, though by the end of the bite, the layer of jam, with its mysterious orange-liqueur flavor, rules, and leaves the last trace.

Postscript: Over a year has passed since I wrote this essay. Now my new favorite writer is Thomas Bernhard, Austrian, who hated Austria, and who is teaching me to respect minimalism, rancor, monomania, and the art of remaining exactly where you already are.

 No Man's Land

Matthew Link

In the days after my return from Antarctica, I was cross, confused, dazed. I was discontented. I lay in my room, unable to simulate animation. Vague images of lonely icebergs and unnamed bays floated around the room. It wasn't like me to be comatose, and I hadn't expected to feel this way at all. I had heard that astronauts fall into this state after a trip on which they leave the earth and see the whole thing for what it is.

It was one of my boyhood dreams, traveling to Antarctica. When I was sixteen and living in New Zealand, I called the country's Antarctic government division and bluntly asked what paperwork I needed to fill out to join a science base at the South Pole. Ever since that rebuff, I've been determined to visit my beloved, mystical continent. But the depression upon returning was more than just a post-trip malaise, or the vague hollowness felt after achieving a long, drawn-out goal. It was a creeping sense that somehow nothing would be the same again. I wanted my life to come rushing back in its familiar colors, but this it refused to do.

I spoke with Jerri Nielsen, the doctor who had been airlifted from the Amundsen-Scott South Pole research station after a self-administered biopsy revealed she had a vicious form of breast cancer. A television movie about her ordeal starring Susan Sarandon was soon to broadcast. Jerri was a vivacious, vital woman, who seemed to rip off life in big chunks. I liked her.

"Life is easier there, you know," she told me. "You either do or die. There are no choices. It's just you and the land. You truly know people there—the shedding of all the pretenses frees up energy to be who you really are. You know, it takes up a lot of energy being who you aren't."

Maybe that was what I was feeling. The ice of Antarctica had scrapped a layer of false skin off me without my knowing.

When I originally told Arthur Frommer, my boss at the magazine I worked for, where I was going on my vacation, he shot me a quizzical sidelong glance.

"Antarctica?" In his mind I was undoubtedly violating one of his precious tenets of the type of democratic, budget-focused travel he had pioneered for so many years.

"Uh, yeah. Antarctica."

He sort of rolled his eyes and shuffled out the door and said, "Okay."

I mumbled something to his back about the fact that over fifteen thousand tourists a year now go to Antarctica, and that tour prices have come down considerably. He responded, but kept walking. Who could blame him? I might as well have told him I was going to Jupiter.

Most of my friends were equally flabbergasted. But a photographer friend, Len Prince, told me flat out, "I'm going with you."

"I don't know, I'll have to see," I backpedaled.

"Find out if they need pictures. I'm sure the company who is arranging the trip would want some."

"Okay." I wasn't sure if I wanted to share this intimate experience with anyone. I'm closer to the world when traveling without another buffer-person. But I pictured myself having dinner alone every night on the ship with a hundred other strangers, and bringing Len along suddenly made sense. The only time I ever feel alone is in a group of people anyway.

On our long vertical sojourn south, Len and I spent a couple of sparkling late summer days in Buenos Aires, giddily enjoying the sights like soldiers on leave before assignment to the bitter front. Then we bundled our snow gear and flew to the town of Ushuaia, at the tip of Tierra del Fuego. It was a little village sandwiched between snow-studded peaks and deep channels, with one busy main street filled with shuffling tourists wrapped up in bright parkas and scarves, embarking on or disembarking from their Antarctic cruises. Over 90 percent of all Antarctic tourists left from here, and nearly all of them visited the northwestern arm and dots of islands of the Antarctic Peninsula. Rare was the tourist who spent the tens of thousands to fly to the innermost South Pole itself.

Ushuaia could have easily been a small Alaskan port. Except for the proud signs everywhere proclaiming *El Fin del Mundo.* I looked down the Beagle Channel, squinting past rocky islands off in the distance, trying to glimpse past the unknown sea where the great southern continent lay—the fabled land that everyone from the Greeks onward sensed was there and placed on maps for centuries despite lack of any proof. I had read everything I could get my hands on about Antarctica's enigmatic role in human exploration. Captain Cook circumnavigated the entire continent in the 1770s in vain, never setting eyes on it. He wrote in his logbook that Antarctica must be " . . . a Country doomed by Nature never once to feel the warmth of the Sun's rays, but to lie for ever buried under everlasting snow and ice." No human even set foot on the ice continent until 1821, the year Napoleon died. No one owns Antarctica to this day. It never had indigenous people. It's a perfect vacuum, a no-man's-zone. I loved the purity of that.

Antarctica was the place that white men felt they had to conquer, in order to find their souls. But the place only belonged to itself. And they risked their very lives flinging themselves against its closed door.

A behemoth Norwegian Cruise Line ship called *Norwegian Dream* was docked at Ushuaia's dinky dock. Its shiny hull glinted in the sunlight, its layered height seemed twice as tall as the highest building in Ushuaia. "It's more like *Norwegian Nightmare,*" I overheard a passenger remark as we boarded our more authentic, smaller Russian ice vessel. The *Akademik Ioffe* was almost four hundred feet long, came with Cyrillic signs everywhere, and had the requisite stern but handsome Russian crew who seemed even icier than the waters they sailed upon. It had been built as a serious science vessel, not for tourists, and the crew's frosty expressions hammered home that point.

Cheerful Australian, Canadian, and British travelers filled the boat, and I kept repeating "I'm Matt, this is Len." Did we stand out as a couple of gay guys? It was my problem—no one really cared. Everyone was espresso-level hyper, fueled with anticipation for meeting the Great White South.

Our first day out at sea was on what the voice over the loudspeaker in our room described as "the Drake Lake." The swells were gently rolling, and the *Akademik Ioffe* took them in stride, like a young actress naively confident at a life-and-death audition. Len and I climbed up the narrow rocking stairways to the top deck. We stood and gazed into the enormity of the watery expanse, clutching the slimy, salty railing.

"My God, the earth is huge," Len finally stated.

The horizon slowly slanted this way and that. "I don't trust the ocean."

"But you grew up on it."

"I know. All those years as a kid on my dad's boat didn't make me love it more. The sea is a bitch. She can turn on you at any moment. Especially here."

Len shot me a worried glance. We had already had our lifeboat drill, at which we filed like ducks to stare down into the dark covered boats that looked too much like caskets. I was glad how easily he had kept his calm. I remembered September 11 in New York and how Len and I had raced down to Ground Zero and had taken photos, watching buildings burn in front of us. His anxiety was often thankfully delayed. I patted his back, "Don't worry, these Russian ships are built for Arctic weather."

"Oh, I know. I'm not worried," he lied.

Out of the corner of my eye a wandering albatross glided through the gray seascape, dipping and reappearing behind waves. Its four-meter wingspan was like a small glider plane's. The voice on the loudspeaker in the room had told us the birds live for years out in the ocean without touching ground. It was the creature of good luck that the narrator of the "The Rime of the Ancient Mariner" shot down with his crossbow, bringing destruction upon his ship and crew. I always thought the poem's mystery was why he shot the bird down; that was never made clear.

"I'm glad you brought me here," Len said. He leaned against me and gave me a hug. His body was warm. I hugged back, but not too hard.

The Drake Lake didn't last for long. The seas rose as I had anticipated and began to reveal their true nature. We were entering into no-man's-land, and the earth was trying to tell us to turn back. Meals, safety seminars, and wildlife lectures were all served in the rolling dining room, which Len dubbed "the seasick dungeon." During one mandatory safety briefing on a rough day, a wave hit the boat and sent a girl flying clear across the room; I caught her with my arm and barely kept her from smashing into the wall. In her lunge, she had knocked over another older woman who loudly explained in her Australian accent as she clawed her way up from the corner "I'm right! I'm right!" Antarctica was no place for the casual tourist.

I lay queasy in my cabin unable to sleep and thought about all the weeks spent on my father's boat when we never saw land. I told Len stories about having dry heaves while on watch, being yelled at for forgetting to move a line, and having to steer the boat through dangerous shipping channels at night. I always just wanted the thing to end, as I did now.

Len snuggled in the narrow bed next to me, gently purring on my neck as the icy waves hit the porthole and the drapes slid back and forth on their tracks, making a soft hissing sound. I could feel his erection pressing on my leg, keeping me company. I felt safe and secure from the elements raging outside.

The first sight of the seventh continent was just around the long, languid Antarctic dusk. Fairytale mountains and bays, completely covered in thick ice, began to shift from peach to pink to purple. It was richer, more tangibly remote than I had pictured. Why hadn't anyone told me about how the icebergs looked like floating sculptures, with curves and differing hues of white, blue, and green? The bay was a heaven of ice, as if Maxfield Parrish had brushed it himself.

I heard there was a daily kayaking option. Having run my own kayak tours in Hawaii, I signed up. We were to don waterproof dry suits for paddling around towering icebergs and fifteen-story ice flows that regularly shed apartment-building–sized chunks into the ocean like bombs. "If you see a shelf drop, point the nose of your kayak into the oncoming wave," explained our soft-spoken Canadian leader, Kathy.

I gingerly asked how long one would last in the near frozen water if one were to flip over the kayak? "I'd say about twenty-eight minutes," she answered flatly. And without the dry suit? She thought for a second. "Oh, about six minutes or so." It didn't seem to phase her, this being her umpteenth trip to The Ice.

When Len found out I was going kayaking, he said, "I thought you were going to help me take pictures?" He had brought along his signature old-fashioned, large-format camera with a curtain drape. The negatives were huge, the pictures extraordinary, and the equipment heavy and awkward.

"I'm sorry. I signed up for it." I wasn't going to miss the chance to kayak in Antarctica.

"Okay," he said. I felt selfish.

As I kayaked around the bay encircled by white mountains, I spotted Len setting up his camera on the dark rocks next to a penguin rookery. I waved. He barely waved back. It was a bright and clear day, and the ice took on a new depth through my orange goggles. The chocolate-fudge peaks drowning in powdered sugar rose before me, and I tried to focus on how mind-boggling it was that I was actually here, and not on Len and me. I slowly kayaked past small icebergs, paddled up to stoic penguins, touched the floating ice chunks with my paddle, and fished out some clear squid egg sacks with my numb hand. I sighed and thought about how my grandmother had told me many friendships end during shared holidays. Alone in our cozy cabin, I saw how well Len and I had been getting along on this trip, unpacking our bags together, following each other to meals, looking out for each other. We were automatically closer out here. I was hoping my grandmother's words weren't true.

I asked Kathy a question about the kayaks, and behind her head, as if in slow motion, a huge chunk of ice slipped down the shelf toward the still water. I pointed. "Look!"

Another kayaker was just in front of it, his back turned. "Paddle!" Kathy screamed. He looked and started to move, but the chunk slid into the water and made only a minor wave. We laughed, our voices slightly shaken. Kathy afterwards gave us a mini-lecture about always having to stay "frosty" and alert when in the water. We listened.

The days quickly folded into a militaristic routine. The constant voice over the speaker told us when to eat, when to get dressed for the Zodiac boat trips, when whales were visible and on which side of the ship, and when happy hour at the bar started. I futilely looked for a knob to turn the volume down, finally resorting simply to pointing my middle finger at it whenever it came on. I was grumpy in the mornings, shoving back against Len's pokes to wake me up with annoyed grunts. In the afternoons Len would refer to how he couldn't get any shots because he couldn't transport all the equipment by himself.

We had dinner with the other perfectly pleasant people, and I couldn't stand talking to any of them. Why did I loathe making chatter, think I was wasting my time finding out information about them since I would never see them again? Len was happy showing people his large glamour book, filled with famous Hollywood stars he had photographed. Everyone was duly impressed. Why was it that I was always more content being alone, not the center of attention? I could have mentioned to people that I was writing about this trip for *Time* magazine, but I kept quiet. My whole life, I had been the perpetual orphan, the outsider, the loner. Len knew this. And I couldn't seem to stop from hurting him by being who I was. The camera, the big bulky thing that couldn't be moved by just one person, was the whole relationship between us. I was the one who wouldn't help move it.

"How long have you two been together?" Anne, the nice Australian lady who had fallen down in the dining room after leaving the Drake Lake, asked me at the lunch table when Len left to get something.

"We aren't boyfriends," I answered, a little embarrassed.

"Really? You seem so close together." She wasn't prying, just factual. Her ruddy face grinned good-naturedly.

"I think Len would like us to be. But I'm not really interested in that. I was with a guy for ten years before. I don't really want a boyfriend right now."

"You just seem like boyfriends to me. I thought you were."

I wish it were as easy as she made it sound. I wish Len and I could have loved each other without any expectations. What I needed was the great world, the continents, the unknown lands. And I needed it alone. In some egotistical way, I wanted to be Antarctica itself. I wanted to be the land no one owns, the pure island, the one in a vacuum. And I was prepared to pay the price.

That night seventy of us camped out on the ice. The odor of penguin feces hung over us, and the termperature was below freezing. I tried to get comfortable in my sleeping bag with all my ski gear on, but finally gave up on sleeping. Instead, I watched the overcast sky pressing upon me for hours as the cold night dragged on. Antarctica was so giant. And I was so tiny, lying in my cocoon.

I thought about what Jerri Nielsen had told me, "In Antarctica, there is no real future or past. You just can't imagine the end of it." As the clouds cleared and I stared up into space, I realized that we were dangling on the edge of the globe, the bottom of it, ready to fall off. This was the last step before the cosmos. And out there, the endless space was even colder than Antarctica, colder than humans could comprehend. Astronomers say the universe will expand and ultimately die a "cold death." That night, I could feel it. I could sense how delicate the little earth we inhabited was, so exact in its temperature range, keeping us little creatures alive on this speck in space. And yet we—I—took it all for granted. If the people around me, the ship, the sleeping bag, the leaders, the clothes weren't here, I would be dead. It was as simple as that. I saw the real world, the real universe, as a freezing and fatal place.

Len told me with wide eyes the next morning how one of the leaders had left him on a small rock island to take pictures. But he hadn't been alone. At his feet had been a penguin carcass and two huge skua birds (huge, vicious creatures that attack anything). He had taken his photos, then had used his tripod to fend of the birds' swoops to his bald head. The skuas had finally calmed down, and then he had spent an hour standing and seeing nothing except himself and Antarctica.

"Matt, it was like I was seeing something no one else could ever see. There was no boat, no wires, no roads, nothing but glaciers and mountains and sea. It was amazing, awesome."

I agreed, with equally wide eyes. I told him about camping on the ice. "This place is like the land before humans, like looking back into deep history. It's like we're not even here." We smiled at each other. Humans became bigger in Antarctica, too, like under a great magnifying glass.

I began to help Len take pictures from the top deck, pointing out what I thought was a great peak, ice shelf, or iceberg. We took photos of each other with the pure landscapes behind us. We both looked through his huge viewfinder, which seemed to heighten the detail and crystallize everything. It was like we were seeing the same exact thing. A land where all we had was each other.

I could feel something happening to me. On one kayak trip, I almost burst into tears. I was afraid I would never experience such clean beauty again. I don't think we were supposed to have seen it. It was too raw, too real. Yes, nuclear fallout from bombs had been found in Antarctica's ice, as well as Northern Hemisphere pollution. Ice shelves the size of Liechtenstein had broken off its body. Its temperature was rising. It was ever so slowly dying, melting. Humans were bound and determined to destroy this last vestige of purity on the earth. And they eventually could. But looking up at her unending grandeur from my kayak, I had an inkling it would put up a good fight.

Our last days on Antarctica were spent visiting an abandoned whaling station and a Ukrainian science station, watching leopard seals bloodily devour penguins, and witnessing ice caves six stories high collapse before our eyes. The wind was so bitter on one boat trip that I couldn't feel my feet for forty-five minutes, even after a hot shower. Antarctica didn't care about us. We weren't supposed to be here anyway. We had sneaked into the back door of a palace. And we wouldn't be staying long. Winter warned us it was approaching with every icy gust.

When we left the last anchorage, Deception Island, Len and I quietly watched a dark green iceberg float by the porthole. He embraced me from the back, and I rested my head on his shoulder, and we stood like that for some time in silence. It was the last we would probably ever see of the great southern land.

We made it back to Ushuaia after another strenuous journey, passing back through the zone of no return and its malicious sixty-foot waves. We heard that a sixty-two-year-old man had been swept over the side of another passenger vessel. No one was sure whether the guy had committed suicide, but he hadn't been the first tourist to end up overboard, we were told.

On the way back from Buenos Aires to New York, war was declared on Iraq while we were in the air over South America. We had hoped it would have happened while we were in Antarctica and stranded us there, safe from the world. I thought about Frank Hurley, the photographer on Shackleton's *Endurance* expedition whom Len admired so much. He had returned from Antarctica to bombs dropping on London, and had written, "Emerged from a war with nature, we were destined to take our places in a war of nations. Life is one long call to conflict, anyway."

Len and I hurled forward through the air, back to our predictable worlds and our imminent post-trip depressions. Life would look so different now that we had seen the other side of the true earth. I wondered if now we could become who we really were? I squeezed his arm, and thought about holding his hand between our seats, clutching it all the way home as our craft careened softly through the night. But I didn't.

Perhaps love is one long call to conflict as well.

Death in
the Desert

Edmund White

They rented a car and headed south through the mountains. The highway was just two lanes. What appeared
on the map to be a straight line turned out to be hundreds of hairpin curves. At first the landscape was innocent enough—the melting snow in the mountains was flowing into
the irrigation ditch beside the road and making it into a clear, clean
stream, leaping and cascading from step to step down the slope, the
flow was thick as a cable. At some points the falling water was so
capacious its splashing was audible through the closed windows.
The fields were just beginning to take on a bit of spring color. The
two men drove through a village of charming old wood houses,
neatly painted.

And then they began to climb, up and up. At a scenic spot high
in the mountains they stopped for gas; they could see their breath.
A little girl came toward them with something for sale, a small,
stoppered vial of attar of roses. Along the roadside three men were
crouching beside sections of quartz geodes. The amethyst-colored
points made Austin think of sharks' teeth.

With his peripheral vision Austin was constantly monitoring
Julien. He was aware of how Julien was sitting up or slouched down
in the car, whether his mouth sounded dry when he spoke, whether
he was in pain or developing a cramp.

Their car climbed higher and higher. They drove through clouds,
which they could see from below as they approached them. No one
was living up here, not even shepherds, and they encountered only
one vehicle, a bus barreling down from a higher peak and pushing
them perilously closer to the edge of a ravine. When they got above
the clouds they saw an eagle wheeling past, its wings spread, looping
in slow, majestic circles.

At last they descended onto the plain beyond and by dark they
were at their hotel in Taroudant, a small city east of Agadir.

Julien loved the hotel and they spent four days there. He was
worried when he saw the room with its bed on a mezzanine, fifteen
stairs to go up, but in fact he managed them well, if sometimes with
a little push from Austin. The hotel, which occupied the former palace of a local ruler, was built against the old mud city walls. In the

evening, sitting out by the modern pool in deck chairs, they watched the starlings swooping into and out of the square niches set into the thick terra-cotta walls. The pasha's massive wood gates were thrown open and the noisy, chaotic road was dimly visible behind an intricate metal grill. The blue pool was lit from within. Four tall, skinny palm trees in a row soared up above the walls and their parapets. Outside the walls they could hear the clip-clop of horses and the gruff voices of a driver, and even see a cart moving, dusty, behind the grill. A muezzin, his voice tinny and amplified, called the faithful to prayer, while by the pool the bartender tuned in a little radio to dance music. The bartender was wearing black knee breeches with a tiny waist, the *sarwel*.

Every meal was torture. There was a European dining room and a Moroccan. Nine times out of ten they chose a table far from the other French tourists in the formal European dining room. There they'd sit in nearly total silence. Julien would take a long, long time to eat. Usually the other guests had left and their dishes had been cleared while Julien still faced a full plate. Julien would try to eat a few things, just several sips of clear broth, or a bit of dry toast, but within a few minutes his diaphragm would start to heave, his face would lengthen and he would grab one of the sacks from the plane and throw up in it. Austin would fill the silence and try to lessen the feeling of defeat by saying something absurdly general and pleasantly genteel, what he thought of as "dowager chat," but in the midst of his babbling Julien would suddenly stand and totter out, walking with his slow, dragging tread. Often Austin was impatient with Julien for walking so slowly but revealed nothing. He remembered hearing that "toward the end" even if some nourishment got down nothing was absorbed, the digestive system could no longer extract any benefit from food—but could this be the end?

Some evenings they stood by a pond and looked down at big wet boulders that would suddenly crack apart and slide: turtles. One of the turtles was so lazy, almost inert, that they nicknamed it "Lucy." As the evening came in, the cold arrived with it. Julien was cold all the time and he bundled up in several layers of clothes; when Austin touched his hand it was always icy. Julien wore pale tan jeans that rode very low in the back; Austin turned quickly once and saw two Arab bellboys laughing and looking at Julien's skinny ass, nudging each other in the ribs.

In one of the big sitting rooms some of the local notables sat around the fireplace with their beads, eating from big plates with their right hands and watching television. On the screen, the king was participating in a religious ceremony in Rabat, in a building that was projected to be the world's largest mosque, but was only partially finished. The king wore a white silk cloak and hood. So did the *imam,* whose big black glasses looked disconcertingly modern under his hood. Austin asked the clerk behind the desk what the holiday was. "We're toward the end of Ramadan," he said.

Ah, Austin thought, that's why the notables are eating so late and the hotel staff looks so pale by day. No food until sundown, not even any water, and of course no cigarettes. It was hardest on the smokers, people said. Usually Muslims slept as much as they could by day and then feasted till midnight. Then they set their alarms for four in the morning so they could eat breakfast before dawn and a new bout of fasting. The thought flickered through Austin's mind that the whole population must be partying now, eating and making music and talking and laughing. He could imagine slipping out of the hotel once Julien fell asleep and trailing through smoky streets past open doorways giving onto rooms lit by kerosene lamps and crowded with robed figures. . . .

The next morning a guide, who spoke fluent French, attached himself to them as soon as they came out of the hotel. He lined up a carriage (undoubtedly the driver would slip him a commission later). The carriage was painted green and was bedizened with dangling hands of Fatima cut out of black plastic and spotted with red and yellow stars. They asked to be shown the outside of the walls. The carriage rolled past low olive trees with small gray-green leaves. Children were playing with a rubber tire. In some places the walls, which were medieval, had started to crumble. The carriage lurched when it went across a deep rut and almost turned over. Austin let out a little cry ("It's going to turn over!"), and Julien laughed at him with his deep but no longer resonant laugh. The driver called out something like "Geesh" to the horses in a reproachful tone, as one might say, "Giddyap." They went past some crudely fashioned cages in which rabbits were being raised. Then they passed a tanner. An old man was washing skins in a well of foul-smelling green liquid in which he was standing waist-high in rubber hip boots. When their carriage turned in through the gate, into the winding narrow streets, few people were out; the demands of Ramadan had driven the lethargic but uncomplaining population indoors.

One day they rode out to a chic hotel compound where millionaires vacationed and played golf. The hotel itself was empty. At the end of a long walkway beside a stream was a swimming pool, surrounded by English people, bright red and fat, slathering in suntan lotion. They were eating hamburgers; the smell of the cooking meat on the grill was heavy and wintry, nauseating. Five or six of the English had been talking all at once, fluty and merry, until they caught sight of Julien and Austin. The bathers were wearing swimsuits, but Julien and Austin, intimidated by the reputation of the place, had put on coats and ties. The English guests just stared at Julien with hostility. Austin became very nervous and said he wanted to go back to the main hotel dining room, which was deserted. But first Julien had to make the grand tour of the grounds—fields planted with vegetables, rose gardens, tennis courts, individual bungalows. He had the strength for all that. In the distance they saw the greens under the wide-cast arc of sprinklers. Julien hadn't noticed how his presence had reduced those English men and women to appalled silence.

At lunch they were waited on by an old, dignified Moroccan who treated them with a deference that concealed a certain tenderness. They were self-quarantined in the formal dining room, which was painted pistachio green and hung with chandeliers the shape of grape clusters. Julien started with a melon and went on to broiled fish and steamed potatoes. It turned slightly cold and they took their coffee (mint tea for Julien) in the dark, empty *salon,* looking at a television program from France.

On the drive back to town they were hailed by the guide from the day before, a skinny man in his early thirties who smelled of old tobacco. He'd overheard them saying during their tour of the city walls that they were interested in buying an old Koran. Now he showed them a well-preserved hand-written Koran with glossy illuminated letters at the beginning of each *sura*. He said a friend of his needed to sell it in order to have enough money to pass his driver's test (the *baksheesh* apparently ran very high), but Julien said to Austin, "We can't take on the world's problems," and added to the guide, "I don't like this copy, I don't think it's beautiful."

Back at the hotel they sat beside the pool and looked at the starlings rushing out of the old wall like sparks up a chimney. Thinking of their life back in Paris, Julien began to criticize Austin's friend Rod, whom he had never even met. "You like him just because you two can gossip all night long like housewives. But he sounds to me like a ne'er-do-well and a drug addict."

Indignant, Austin said, "At least his conversation is lively and interesting."

Julien was quiet so long that Austin, against his will, looked over to verify his expression, which was stony. But when at last he spoke, his voice sounded deeper and more vulnerable; "It's too bad I didn't die six months ago when I was still interesting. Now you'll remember me only as I was at the end—boring and drugged on morphine."

Austin said, "You mean too much to me to judge you as either dull or interesting." And it was true, true that Austin was so *enthralled* by Julien's health and survival that he never thought he was dull, even though sometimes he became irritated when Julien started nodding off. Apparently he needed the morphine to mask the pain in his back and to calm the impulse to vomit, but the drug meant that he was alert now only for a few hours each day.

On the way back to their room, Austin said, "I think you're a bit better."

"Well, I didn't vomit my meals today. It's not exactly miraculous but I can't complain."

A furniture dealer in Paris had told Austin to be sure to see the Berber Palace that was just off the road between Taroudant and Ouazarzate, before the turn-off up through the mountains back to Marrakesh. "It's completely out-of-the-way," the dealer had said, "and very beautiful. We ate lunch there."

Julien and Austin drove there with the guide. He had another Koran to show them, badly battered, perfectly square, slipped inside a leather satchel that folded shut like an envelope and could be worn on a chain around the neck. "You put a chain through this hoop," the guide said. Then he laughed, showing his stained teeth. "Not *you,* of course, but *one.*" His laugh turned into a cough. Julien shifted away from him, afraid of being exposed to tuberculosis. Austin was *certain* that that fear was going through Julien's mind.

Despite his fears, Julien bought the Koran and was never seen without it afterwards. He fell asleep with it on his lap, usually still in its scuffed and water-stained leather case with the coarse stitching. Sometimes, when he was drowsy from morphine, he'd thumb through the pages with their long, cursive comet-tails and their bug-track vowel signs which looked like those radiating dots in comic strips that indicate delighted surprise or sudden enlightenment. It was the perfect book for a weary, dying man—pious, incomprehensible pages to strum, an ink cloud of unknowing.

Julien was wearing a cotton caftan with tan and white vertical stripes over a T-shirt, under a gauzy white caftan and a white wool sweater he'd draped over his shoulders. He kept the sweater close by in case he began to shiver. He'd abandoned his jeans since the seams cut into his fleshless hips and legs. Only in these robes did he feel comfortable. His black hair was thin and oily, pressed into a cap on his head; many white hairs were scattered through the black. Seen from behind his ears looked immense, especially if the sunlight was shining through them, perhaps because his neck had become so scrawny. His eyebrows had grown shaggy and his nose looked much bigger, as if old age, frustrated by his quick decline, had decided to rush ahead and hit him now.

Although he walked very slowly, he was still game. He wanted to go places and see things. If he sat tranquilly in one place the morphine would make him fall asleep. He smiled sweetly wherever he went, though he spoke so softly people couldn't hear him and Austin would have to repeat what he'd said. When he smiled his face broke into hundreds of lines that hadn't been there six months earlier.

The guide, who knew not to wear them out with his talk, kept silent in the back seat and spoke only to indicate the way to the Berber Palace. Austin appreciated his discretion; he obviously sensed that they were living through a difficult moment, but he didn't ask questions or let his curiosity show through. The day was hot except when a breeze blew; then they were reminded that winter had just ended and that the mountain peaks on the horizon were still deep in snow. They slowed down as they rolled into a village of low houses and teeming streets. The pedestrians' dull-witted stares were the look of grouchy nicotine withdrawal.

They took the road to the right. A little farther on, the macadam gave out to be replaced by gravel. Soon they came to the massive structure of the Berber Palace with its alternating square and rounded arches, its tile roofs, and its pale blank walls. Sometimes a small window, barred, was pierced into a wall, always at an improbable place, as if the rooms inside were of madly varying heights. As soon as they'd gone down two steps and along a walkway redolent of thyme, they were in an immense garden planted with palms crowding up from geometric plots of clipped bushes. The walkways were lined with white and faded blue tiles. A few tiles were missing. The inner courtyard was still large enough to seat a symphony orchestra.

No one was around. Caged birds hanging in doorways were singing and flickering in the shadows, twitching shuttles of gold through the gloom. A small fountain drooled into a clear basin. Through the water green moss could be seen, waving from black boulders like hair on drowned heads. The thrown-open doors here and there were carved and painted wood decorated with abstract sunbursts. Like a bored shopper at the bazaar, the sun itself was feebly fingering the dusty lusters of a chandelier far inside a room, with no intent to buy. They went in one door and could smell stale smoke from last night's banquet. An empty plastic water bottle had been thrown on the carpet. A tile dado lined the walls all the way round at shoulder height.

Their guide, Ahmed, clapped loudly and called out something in Arabic. At last a white man in his fifties could be seen crossing the courtyard. He was wearing sunglasses and had a full head of graying hair cut short and spiky that grew low on his forehead. He had a goatee that emphasized the squareness of his jaw. His loose orange sweater was decorated with wide black bands on the sleeves, like an exaggerated sign of mourning. He seemed self-conscious walking toward them in sunlight as they watched from the shadows. At least his stride looked unnatural and he hung his head until he'd come within calling distance. He tried to speak French but with a German accent. Within a moment they'd all found their way into English.

He explained that he was German and a friend of the owner, who was Muslim and sleeping through the difficult Ramadan day.

"Do you think we can eat something?" Austin asked.

"An omelette. I'm sure they could make you a cheese omelette and a green salad. Would you like to eat outside? In the sun?"

Austin turned to Julien; would he be too cold? The German suddenly shrugged and said, "I don't work here. I'm a guest." He smiled. "I don't know why I'm interfering." He looked at Julien. "You won't be cold. It's protected from the wind." Julien asked where the toilet was and shuffled off toward it with Ahmed. The German said in a low voice, "I can see how ill your friend is—is he your son?"

"Friend."

The German, who said he was called Hermann, touched Austin's arm. They were seated at a rusting white metal table on the pale blue and white tile floor. Unseen birds were chirping from within the stand of trees toward the entrance to the grounds.

"What's that delicious smell?"

"Orange blossom," the German said, then added, confidingly, "I know what he has. My friend just died of it. Your friend is not long for this world."

"Oh?" Austin asked nervously. He felt a flutter of panic play like fire over his solar plexus. The early spring was so calm with all the daytime torpor of a small Moroccan village, and even though it was noon the sun seemed veiled and remote. Was Julien about to die? "He's come so close to dying before, but he always survives. He has miraculous powers of recuperation."

"No," the man said, shaking his head, "he's dying."

This is "German coarseness," Austin said to himself, quick to label the offending stubbornness, although he knew few Germans and usually detested the almost inevitable generalizations everyone made about national character.

Hermann added, "I'm a doctor. I watched my friend—" He interrupted himself and touched Austin's sleeve again, "It's all right, we needn't say the name of the disease, but I know what he—do you say, what he suffers *of*?"

"*From.* You say *from.*" Austin put on a bright social smile. "And what brings you to Morocco?"

"I will tell you all," the man said solemnly. "I am bisexual. I have a good wife I live with since thirty years. But my real love was my friend. I am a doctor, a *Narkosearzt.*"

"Anesthesiologist?"

"Yes, but a doctor of that. But my friend was a famous surgeon. You see?" He pointed to a neat scar fifteen centimeters long buried in his clipped hair. "I had a brain tumor, most unusual. That's why I have trouble speaking. I know English very good before, but now I forget and only slowly, slowly the words come."

For a moment Austin was confused. He thought the "friend," the surgeon, had been a brain surgeon and had removed the tumor, but a moment later Austin had reshuffled the kaleidoscope and saw the same elements in a new configuration. He smiled and said, "Your English is perfect. Don't worry. Did you know your friend for many years?"

"Yes, yes, all my life. He was twenty years older than me, but age means nothing to the souls—"

"Kindred spirits."

"Yes. That."

"And did your wife know him?"

"Oh, yes, we were all very close. You know, in Europe we do not go into details, no, but she knew. Ah! Here comes your friend."

Julien was slowly coming down the long *allée* of trees and box-wood hedges. He stopped to gather a mass of orange blossom in his arms and to breathe in the fragrance. He was smiling as he walked with tiny, stiff steps toward them, accompanied by the deferential guide, who was frowning. Julien's outer robe was faintly dama-scened, which made it shine when it caught the light.

Over lunch Hermann talked on and on. It seemed that his older lover, the "friend," had fallen for a Berber from this very village. "My friend bought this palace and installed Ali in it. His plan was to turn it into a hotel that Ali could run. But Ali, who is thirty now—ah! How time, like a bird . . ." He mimed flapping wings.

"Flies?"

"Yes, how time flies." He said that Ali had never learned how to run a hotel. He'd become obsessed with sports-car racing and had never concentrated on ordering food, supervising the staff, holding down expenses.

"When my friend was dying he asked me to look after Ali. Now I'm here, although I have had much mental loss with the tumor. Ali's family is challenging his inheritance of this palace, as is the commune, as are the pasha's original descendants."

This man with the unsmiling mouth, the big, unironic eyes and the look of confusion traceable to his scarred skull, seemed disturbingly intimate and real. For so long now Austin and Julien had been rocked in the comforting arms of French gaiety and discretion, the illusions made possible by silence or elision. Now here was a flat-footed (if unsteady) German with a metal plate in his head and a verbal problem in several languages who was, with all the misguided kindliness in the world, making them look at the inevitable, from which they'd so long averted their eyes.

"It's strange for me," Hermann said. "I'm here to recuperate but all I can do is worry and worry about Ali." With a familiar Teutonic gesture, he performed an immense shrug of his shoulders and let his lifted hands collapse rhetorically onto the slats of the chair he was sitting on. With the same gesture he propelled himself into a standing position and said, much more loudly, "*Gut!* We go?"

"Go?" Julien asked, blinking. He'd been smiling into the garden and looking at his uneaten omelette as though he were a mild-mannered child to whom the gruff natives had offered an inscrutable toy. "Where are we going?"

The German said, "I don't have a car but you do. I thought we could all take the dirt road up into the mountains to Ali's village. They'll make us mint tea, which for them is a great luxury, and you can meet Ali who you'll see has lost his looks and become fat as a *you-nook*."

Oh, Austin thought. As a eunuch. What a drool-making temptation. . . .

They drove a few miles out of town into the foothills where the gravel road gave out and there were just two continuing ruts in the mud. After another mile Austin decided they couldn't continue because the bottom of the car was scraping against the turf.

Julien said, "Go on! Go on! I want to see the village."

"No, we can't," Austin said. "We're scraping the bottom of the car. We'll destroy the motor. We'll be stuck here. Our insurance won't cover the repairs—it will so clearly have been our fault."

Julien, who was sitting beside him, said, "Oh, I'm so disappointed, you have no sense of adventure. I wanted to go there."

Something about the way he said it made Austin think he was referring to the foothills of death. No, that was a fancy way of putting a simpler intuition, that Julien was expecting something to happen to him up there that now would never happen.

Julien left them and went walking across the valley. Somewhere, out of sight, over the next hill possibly, several men were hammering something and all talking at once. "What are they doing?" Austin asked.

"Building a house," the guide said, though how he knew exactly Austin wondered.

The sound was peculiarly close and present, irregular but frequent blows of hammers on something hollow-sounding, perhaps stakes being driven into the earth after all.

A soft breeze was blowing and tossing and gathering the folds of Julien's white robes as he walked. The ground up here was stony and barren, the color of sand though the pebbles and rocks would need another ten thousand years to be ground down to grains that fine. Green trees, wind-trained and full as giant bushes, were dotting the tan hills all the way down to the distant, verdant valley. There were no clouds in the sky except along the horizon; at first Austin wondered if they might be snow-covered mountains, but then they drifted slightly.

The guide stood apart, as if afraid of disturbing them with proximity. He suddenly hunkered down in a crouch, with his back to them, and looked off to the valley. Hermann stood near Austin, kicking a pebble with his right foot. Austin looked at Julien, whose white caftan was glowing with the suffused daylight and was floating in the shifting but constantly flowing breeze. Austin took three pictures as Julien walked back toward them. Austin thought, Julien's such a romantic boy, he's probably communing with nature in preparation for his death.

And then he thought: That's exactly what he's doing, it's not a pose, it's a reality. He's communing with nature in preparation for his death.

Do You Join in Singing the Same Bigness?

Philip Gambone

For several years after my lover Bill died, I wandered the world—or at least a small, gay part of it—looking for something. I traveled to New York; I traveled to Provincetown and San Francisco. Two months after we buried him, I went to Italy, where I rented a car and drove through Tuscany and Umbria, visiting museums, cathedral towns, Etruscan ruins. At night, after delicious but solitary dinners, I visited gay bathhouses. I cruised parks and shadowy fields under the walls of Renaissance cities. Sometimes I took guys back to my hotel. One guy in particular left me totally smitten. We spent the night together in Siena. He had a body like Donatello's David—lithe, smooth, boyish. A lot like Bill's before he got so sick. We made plans to see each other again the next night, but he never showed up.

"This trip has been a kind of practice run for my life as an older gay man," I wrote in my journal just before I flew home that summer. "A practice run for how to be middle-aged with dignity, for how to live with diminished prospects for romance, sex, beauty. I've become aware of how the Italians accept the fleetingness of youth. Once it's over, *giovinezza,* once the body begins to deteriorate, once the good looks go . . . well, *finito!* Italians don't seem to dwell on this fact with much sadness; they've accommodated themselves very sanely to the irreversible reality of lost youth. They see old age not so much as a horrible thing but rather as merely another stage along the way with its own patterns and perquisites. I find this extraordinary."

But then, not quite ready to resign myself to those diminished prospects, I added, "And yet, I still expect some big romantic thing to happen to me. Yes, I'm still on the prowl for it—*that big romantic thing.*"

The following spring, I went back to Europe, this time to southern France. In Nice, a guy I met at the baths took me back to his apartment, fed me dinner on his balcony overlooking the city, shared his bed with me. The next day, he drove me to the station, where I had a train to catch for Barcelona. He kissed me goodbye. A few months later, he showed up on my doorstep in Boston, wanting to be boyfriends. I wasn't ready. Politely, I suggested he check in at the gay hotel on the other side of my neighborhood.

The next summer, I took off for another stay in Provincetown, sharing a house with several friends. The morning after I brought someone home—a kid whose swarthy Brazilian complexion and curly black hair made him look like one of those angelic rough-trade types in a painting by Caravaggio—one of my housemates told me I had a sex problem. "Your coming to Provincetown is like an alcoholic moving next door to a brewery!" he told me. At the end of our vacation, he broke off our friendship forever.

One more spring—it was now 1996—and another trip, again to Italy. In Florence one night, I came back from the baths only to find that I was locked out of my hotel. I took myself to a bar, intent on picking someone up who would take me home for the night. Within half an hour, I had met Stefano. Distantly related to the exiled Italian royal family, he lived in an elegant apartment overlooking the Duomo. Stefano spoke impeccable English and had impeccable, princely tastes. I thought I could fall in love with him. But a few minutes after we had adjourned to his bedroom, Stefano asked me if we could move back into the living room, because, he explained, this was the bed he shared with his lover, and it made him uncomfortable to be having sex with me there.

That summer, I drove across the country to Taos, New Mexico, the capital of New Age America, where I spent six weeks at an artists' colony working on a book of interviews with gay writers. A cross between a desert outpost and a latter-day hippie haven, Taos disappointed me. It was small, quiet, and closed up by ten. "Where, where, *where* is the gay life here?" I wrote in my journal a few days after I arrived. Already Taos felt more foreign than any foreign country I had ever visited.

I spent a lot of time in coffeehouses, keeping my antennae out. In one, I found a copy of New Mexico's only gay newspaper, the *Rainbow.* I called a couple of the personals. The guys I spoke to—one in Santa Fe, another in Albuquerque—told me there was no gay life in Taos. At an alfresco restaurant, a waiter I mooned over a bit too obviously yelled at me to get lost. Another man, the owner of a small art gallery, shamelessly flirted with me, then called the next day to say he really needed to make a sale and wouldn't I buy something and put it on a credit card? I placed an ad in the *Rainbow*. A few men called me. I met them for coffee or sex or both. On the weekends, I would drive to Santa Fe for the opera and chamber-music festivals. All the gay men I saw there seemed to be paired up.

When I wasn't obsessing about men, I wrote, or read, or just tried giving myself over to the Zen-like quality of the desert solitude I was immersed in. At one of the bookstores in town, I picked up a copy of Mabel Dodge Luhan's memoir *Edge of Taos Desert*. A salon hostess of the New York avant-garde, who had moved to New Mexico in 1917, Luhan fell in love with the Southwest, especially the deeply spiritual culture of the Pueblo Indians. "In New York," she wrote, "I had learned to use the name of sex for that strong autonomous serpent in the blood that once unleashed took full possession of all my other activities, and rode me unmercifully." Once she moved to Taos, where she lived the rest of her life, Luhan experienced what she called a "spiritual therapy," the result, in part, of her falling in love with Tony Luhan, a Pueblo Indian. "What a miracle," she wrote, "and how little we understand it that a human being will be brought across the continent to the right one, that she may be changed truly almost in the twinkling of an eye by being with him."

I copied those words into my journal. They described so perfectly the longing I felt, the *something* I was after. But it was not the crossing of a continent that would end up changing me. It was an ocean.

A week after I returned home from Taos, in late August 1996, I took off again, this time for a semester in Beijing, where I had accepted a teaching position in a program for American high-school students. I went to China fully expecting to lead a celibate life, if not by choice, then certainly by circumstance. For if the "strong autonomous serpent" of sex was in my blood, then the harsh realities of the gay scene in Beijing—"it does not exist," one informant told me—would surely send that reptile into deep hibernation for a few months.

My job afforded me plenty of time to explore the city. In 1996, Beijing had not yet been named an Olympic venue. And though its transformation into a glitzy, high-rise international city, where Deng Xiaoping's injunction, "To get rich is glorious," was fast becoming the new mantra, there were still plenty of vestiges of a slower, more amiable culture to be found. Every morning, dumpling vendors set up their steaming woks outside the gates to the university where I lived; women in long indigo smocks swept the curbs with brooms made of rush; pairs of off-duty soldiers, looking as young as boy scouts, wandered the crowded outdoor markets, strolling hand in hand. ATM machines were virtually nonexistent.

On my bicycle, I learned to negotiate the rush-hour avenues so dense with cyclists that we moved as one, a steady-flowing river of rickety "Flying Pigeons." Afternoons and weekends I would visit temples and palaces, pagodas and mosques, ancient observatories, sleepy parks, crumbling old neighborhoods of gray-brick courtyard homes—the surviving remnants of what, less than a hundred years before, the French writer Victor Segalen had called "the superb production . . . of the capital of the greatest empire under the sun." Westerners were still a curiosity in 1996, which meant I was stared at all the time, gawked at, smiled at, laughed at. More often than not, these reactions, rude by Western standards, were well-meaning and friendly and often led to awkward, but delightful, attempts at communication.

"It's a gray, foggy, dusky November afternoon," I wrote in my journal one Sunday, "and I've stopped at my favorite café on Sanli-tun Road for coffee. The waiter I like here greeted me with his usual warm, shy smile, and we tried having a conversation—once again, a frustrating effort. He wrote a question in my book, and I asked him to transliterate it into pinyin, but even that didn't help much. All I could make of it was something like: 'Do you join in singing the same bigness?' Huh?"

Beijing was full of such sweet young men—waiters, clerks, delivery boys, the guards at the university. "They charm me with their gentle smiles, their courtesy, their sweet shyness," I continued in my journal that day. "Right now, I'm watching one of the three boys behind the counter peeling a potato and it nearly breaks my heart. His delicate fingers, the way he so gracefully, so patiently goes about his domestic work. Yes, these boys are breaking my heart."

In large measure, my affection for Beijing increased in direct proportion to the number of gay men I met there. As the weeks went by and my courage increased, I began to find them through the city's rudimentary gay infrastructure—a cruisy park near the Drum Tower off the Second Ring Road; a neighborhood bathhouse with a reputation that proved to be accurate; and a tucked-away pub, the only exclusively gay bar in the entire city of twelve million. The bar—its English name was the Half and Half—is where I met most of my gay Chinese friends. They were doctors and accountants, waiters and government workers, a dancer, a cosmetologist, an AIDS worker, a publisher, a graduate student, and a few from the nascent entrepreneurial class. Some told me stories that were full of sadness and pain and resignation; others spoke more optimistically, with a modest hope for their personal future as gay men and for the collective future of China's quietly emerging gay subculture. Everyone I encountered seemed to be "trying my best," a phrase I heard repeatedly and one that for me came to stand for the courage, dignity, and fortitude of the Chinese people in general and gay Chinese in particular. It was that beautiful and enticing combination of modest dignity and erotic appeal that totally won me over. There was something about these guys—both the ones I only talked to and the ones I slept with—that attracted me in ways that most of the guys I had met since Bill's death did not. They had something I wanted to tap into.

"You're turning into a rice queen," one American friend told me. But there were connotations to that phrase that I didn't like. "I want to travel a road that's harder than fantasy, than erotic play," I wrote toward the end of my semester in Beijing. "I want to be more than someone who passes through the world skimming the surface, merely seeking enchantment, the picturesque, the pleasantly titillating. These boys are people, not Kewpie dolls."

On my last Saturday in Beijing, I stopped in at the Half and Half to say my goodbyes to friends. It was a bittersweet evening, full of reminiscing and embraces, posing for snapshots, and promises to keep in touch. Around eleven, I decided to call it a night. On my way out, I passed a striking mustachioed guy, a Chinese man in his early thirties, whom I'd seen at the bar on a few other occasions. We began to talk, and soon I was inviting him back to my place.

In the cab, we held hands. He began to tell me his story: he was a doctor from another province, on a research grant in Beijing,

married, and miserable. He had tried to tell his wife, who still lived
back in their home province, a thousand miles away, that he was gay,
but she had only laughed and refused to believe him. They had a
daughter. Back in my dorm room, we made love. As with so many of
the Chinese men I slept with that fall, bringing each other to orgasm
seemed incidental to the tender hours of caressing, kissing, and
cuddling that we enjoyed. Eventually, he fell asleep, softly weeping
in my arms.

In his provocative and quirky book, *Great Mirrors Shattered,* John
Whittier Treat suggests that homosexuals have often chosen Asia—
"its antiques, or its boys, or its very far distance"—as a place in
which they could "refashion themselves." While it had not occurred
to me that I was aiming to "refashion" myself when I went to China,
in many ways that is exactly what I was doing. Just how refashioned
I had become, I was still to learn.

On a blustery day in early December, my students and I boarded a
train at the Beijing station for a two-week, end-of-the-term field trip
to Vietnam. The fifty-five-hour journey, which took us across the
Yangzi River, through southern China and, with a layover at the
border to change engine and crew, into Hanoi, was one of the high-
lights of my semester.

From the moment we disembarked at Ga (from the French *gare*)
Hanoi, I was utterly captivated. We were immediately set upon by
dozens of women in conical hats who sold us loaves of hot French
bread, the first good bread I'd tasted since I'd left Boston. The tour
guides call Hanoi the Paris of Southeast Asia, but in its vibrant color
and chaotic bustle, in the wild motor-scooter traffic that plied the avenues, in its unregimented street life so oriented toward food and a
relaxed mixture of generations, the city struck me as a second Naples.

We settled into a little hotel in the old quarter. In the morning,
the other faculty and I would hold classes in Vietnamese history
and culture. As their English teacher, I had the kids read Graham
Greene's *The Quiet American* and Tim O'Brien's collection of stories *The Things They Carried.* In the afternoons, we explored the city,
visiting its museums and historical sites, including the Ho Chi Minh

mausoleum and the enchanting Hoan Kiem Lake, from the depths of which, legend has it, a golden turtle arose and presented a Vietnamese patriot with a sword by which he defeated the invading Chinese.

Everything I saw delighted me—the plethora of flower shops and art galleries, the crumbling French colonial architecture, the lush green foliage on the trees, a welcome respite from the frigid climate of the North China Plain. Some days, we gave the students the after-noon to explore on their own, and I'd sit in the open-air hotel lobby, watching the life on the street outside: children gleefully playing together; men lounging over a cup of *caphe sua*, Vietnamese coffee sweetened with condensed milk; women in silky, pajama-like clothing trotting along, steadying the poles on their shoulders from which were suspended pails of food; other women squatting before charcoal grills, fanning the coals with banana leaves.

Our first Saturday in Hanoi, after dinner with my colleagues, I made my excuses and went in search of a gay bar, the Golden Cock, which was listed in a gay guidebook I had brought along. The spring-like weather, the romantic appeal of the city, and the fact that Vietnamese men seemed even more attractive than their Chinese counterparts had once again stirred that serpent in my blood.

Having no luck finding the bar, I headed off to an area on Hoan Kiem Lake that the guidebook promised was a cruisy place. Sure enough, within minutes I was being chatted up by two young men, who whisked me off to what they claimed was a gay bar. Small, cozy, and nicely appointed, it was a karaoke club with a clientele that looked pretty straight to me. As soon as we sat down, the guys ordered up a round of expensive beers. Soon snacks came to the table, too. In no time, they had racked up a bill for two hundred thousand *dong*—about twenty dollars—which even I knew was a small fortune in Hanoi. An argument ensued. I insisted I wouldn't pay for things I hadn't ordered. The cashier and I finally settled on thirteen dollars. Furious, I left. Was this what gay life in Hanoi was all about—money boys, con artists, hustlers? I was seeing the other side of gay Asia, a side I had, for the most part, not encountered in Beijing, whether out of luck or because I was more savvy to the scene or for some other reason, I wasn't sure. All I knew was that I was already missing my sweet boys at the Half and Half. Gloomily, I headed back to the hotel. In ten days I'd be home. It was all I could think about.

My route took me by the lake again. And it was there that I met Minh. He followed me into the public toilet where I had gone to take a leak (yes, I'd drunk a couple of those expensive beers). The way he cruised me was heartbreakingly timid, almost frightened, totally unlike the unctuous, self-assured manner of the duplicitous duo who had led me to the karaoke club. In the dark recesses of the public toilet, Minh and I started to kiss and embrace, until we were interrupted by someone else coming in. I motioned to him that we should leave. Outside, we introduced ourselves, and I invited him to take a walk with me.

We strolled around Hoan Kiem, surreptitiously holding hands. The low-intensity street lighting—as much a factor of economy, as of intentional design—allowed us to get away with it. It was easy to convince myself that this was the most romantic situation I had ever been in. There was a hushed mildness about everything: the evening air, the dim lights shimmering on the water, the leisurely pace and conversations of the people passing by. In the center of the lake there was an island connected to the shore by a delicately arching wooden bridge. And on the island, a Buddhist temple. Clouds of incense—or was it the evening mist?—rose up from the temple grounds. I was feeling blessed, smiled on by whatever gods inhabited these precincts.

Minh's English was limited, but the gentle smile on his face and the demure ardor in his eyes communicated all I needed to know. No boy in China—indeed, I wasn't sure any boy in America—had ever looked at me that way. He seemed ready to hand over his life to me. For the most part, we were silent. I was reminded of holy silences I had known: church, yoga classes, visiting certain hushed rooms in museums I loved back home. Occasionally I would ask Minh a question, not so much because I was curious for information but just to break the silence, which felt overwhelmingly vast. What was his job? A computer programmer for a bureau of the government. How old was he? Twenty-six. When he asked me my age, I knocked off two years. Even so, a twenty-year gap seemed to make no difference to him. If anything, he seemed amused that I should care. "I think you are very beautiful," I told him. He reacted with bashful pleasure. Eventually, achingly, we said good night, with plans to meet the next day for dinner. It was all I could do to hold myself back from telling him, "I love you."

He showed up! Those were the first words that came to my head when, the next evening at the appointed hour, I saw Minh patiently waiting for me at the street corner where we had agreed to meet. When he recognized me, his face lit up with that sweet, shy, trusting smile that over the years would never fail to do something magical to me. From then on, I began to think of that look as his Buddha face. We went out to dinner, stumbling and laughing through another rudimentary conversation. He drank Coca Cola; I drank Vietnamese beer.

For the next week, Minh and I spent almost every evening together. We would meet for dinner, then stroll around the lake or sit at a bistro and eat *kem phap,* delicious French ice cream, the many exotic flavors of which—mango, durian, carambola—we would sample night after night. Minh took me to his house to meet his parents, who served us tea and were as gracious and kind as their son. I was introduced as his "new American friend." With the blessings of my faculty colleagues, I moved out of the hotel and into another hotel where Minh registered us as American businessman and his translator.

"I want to marry you," I told him on our final night together. Like the doctor in Beijing, he wept in my arms.

"My head raises a thousand objections," I wrote in my journal a few days after I returned to Boston. "You were just needy, *he* was just needy; he's twenty-two years younger than you are. He'll grow out of this, he'll find someone younger, sexier, more virile. He's twelve thousand miles away; you're just feeling guilty (the guilt of the Western exploiter) and that's why you need to prolong this affair, to prove it wasn't just an affair."

It was a reasonable litany of objections. I knew my friends would raise similar ones. "But I'm sick of reasonableness!" I continued. "It's bankrupt as far as I'm concerned. I've done the reasonable thing for years now: dated men, tried to understand when they didn't want a relationship, told myself that in the meantime it was okay to settle for sex. I've observed the reasonableness of South End gay dating, gay courting, gay relationships—men who measure out their emotions in coffee spoons, who have trained themselves to take it slowly. All that is fine. Yes, I approve. I've done it, too, known its wisdom, cautioned myself about how prone I can be to flights of fancy. And yet . . . why do I trust that what I feel about Minh is not infatuation? The truth is, I have the power within me to let this not be an infatuation."

I sought out the advice of an acquaintance of mine, Pratap, a man from India who had a much older American lover. They had traveled this road. What could he tell me? To my surprise, Pratap grilled me—gently, but firmly—about Minh. Did he speak much English? What was the level of our communication? How cosmopolitan was he? Did he know who I was? It was a good dose of reality testing, but when you are feeling as alive, as whole, as deeply imbued with blessedness as I was, Pratap's words seemed to miss the point.

Over the course of the winter, Minh and I wrote to each other, first via letters, which sometimes took over two weeks to be delivered, and eventually through his company's e-mail account. Minh didn't have his own screen name, so he had to use a colleague's, explaining to his friend that the person sending him these electronic love letters was an American girl he knew.

Then, in late March, I returned to Vietnam to see him. We traveled together, visiting Hue, the ancient imperial capital. We went via a tourist mini-bus. Our traveling companions were all Westerners—Americans, French, Australians, Germans. Early on, I sensed that a few of them were giving us the cold shoulder. I assumed they thought I was a sex tourist and Minh my rent boy. I didn't care. Let them think what they wanted. They had no idea how deep our love was for each other.

"Eros is everywhere here," I wrote from Hue in my journal, "—in the extraordinarily beautiful, *heartbreakingly* beautiful bodies and faces of the young men; in the cool, loose clothing everyone wears; in the food, the cleanliness, the colors; in the way these people are so comfortable and unselfconscious in their bodies. The idea of 'personal space' doesn't seem to exist here—like the *xichlo* drivers who practically make love to you with their eyes and voices, the way they get so close." In their raptures for the South Seas, could Melville or Gauguin have felt any more deeply the holy intoxication I was feeling?

While I was in Vietnam that second time, I interviewed for a summer teaching job. Everyone wanted native speakers of English. The job, at one of the foreign-language universities in Hanoi, wouldn't pay much, though enough that I could afford to rent a little apartment outside the quaint old part of town. In the end, I decided not to take it. I catalogued my objections in my journal: there wouldn't be enough to do or see in Hanoi all summer; the heat and humidity; the lack of privacy; the meager salary. Instead, I would come for another visit. Minh and I would go touring again.

Before I went back to Vietnam that summer, my mother told me a story: "During the War," she said, "there was an Italian detention camp in Taunton. Did you know that? Down toward Cape Cod. Your grandmother and I would drive there to visit the prisoners of war, bring them cigarettes or candies, speak to them in Italian. One of the prisoners—he was a lieutenant, very well educated, spoke beautiful English—well, we fell in love. No hanky panky!" Mom laughed here, the idea was so absurd. "This was 1944," she added. "When the War was finally over, all the detainees were shipped back to Italy. I never heard from him again."

I listened politely, but a "mother's perspective" on my international romance was not what I was looking for.

In July, Minh and I traveled to Ho Chi Minh City. When I got sick and had to be hospitalized, Minh stayed up all night by my bedside, quietly keeping vigil. *This is the man I want holding my hand when I die,* I thought to myself.

The following March, I went back again, my fourth trip to Vietnam in fifteen months. This time, Minh and I stayed in Hanoi. During the day, while Minh was at work, I would roam the city, revisiting favorite places—the Temple of Literature, the art museum, the lake. My guidebook talked about the "childlike serenity and sweetness" of Buddhist sculpture. It struck me that these were exactly the qualities that enchanted me about Minh. I visited the old Roman Catholic cathedral, too, a building I'd avoided my three previous times in the city. The interior was, for lack of a better term,

Gothic Vietnamese—a mixture of red and gold lacquer and stained glass. For the first time in years, I prayed, on my knees. The only other people present were a couple of old Vietnamese women silently fingering their rosaries. *Please let him come to America,* I whispered. *Please.*

By a miracle—there seemed to be no other way to understand it, especially after my lawyer had given him a one-in-ten chance— Minh was granted a student visa to study English in Boston for the summer. The night I met him at the airport, still not certain whether he had passed immigration in Los Angeles, was one of the happiest moments of my life. He arrived with a single suitcase. Around his neck, he wore a small pouch that contained his passport and other documents. He looked like a kid whose parents had sent him off alone to summer camp.

For the next four years, we kept extending Minh's visa—more ESL lessons, then graduate-school preparation classes, and finally acceptance into a state university for a master's program in computer science. Life became about keeping Minh enrolled in an accredited, full-time program so that we could stay together. When he'd get discouraged with the classes or—I had to read his silences here— embarrassed that I was shelling out so much money to pay for his tuition, I would remind him that I didn't like the arrangement any better than he did, but that it was only temporary. If he could just hold out until he finished the master's, everything would be fine. I encouraged him with the hope that once he got his degree, he would have a chance to work legally for a company that was willing to sponsor him for the Green Card. A real life for us, I kept reminding him, was just around the corner.

During the four years we were together, my globetrotting came to a halt. Minh seemed skittish about traveling very far. (Maybe it was the money thing again.) A fall trip to pick apples in central Massachusetts, a day's outing to the beach at Cape Cod—such was the extent of our trekking about. I contented myself with domestic pleasures—cooking meals, watching television together, helping him with his English lessons. None of this felt like a compromise. Indeed, there was a lot that I loved about the quiet, "married" life we were sharing. I loved watching Minh as he would carefully examine fruit at the grocery store, frequently putting selections that I had made back in the bin because they were slightly blemished or not ripe enough. I loved the way he ate rice out of his bowl, cleaning the sides of every grain as he fastidiously made his way toward the bottom. I loved the way he would giggle at American sit coms or exclaim, "Oh, my God!" at a great soccer play on TV. Once, while we were in the car, he scolded me for tooting the horn at the driver ahead of me who was taking too long to make a left-hand turn. "Why do you do that?" he chided. "It doesn't make him go any faster." *You can learn a lot from this man,* I told myself.

Because Minh was not one for long conversations, I frequently resorted to my journal to "talk" about our relationship. "I want to travel farther with him than I ever did with any of my other lovers," I wrote. I meant a journey into deep intimacy. It would happen, I persuaded myself . . . as soon as Minh got his degree.

Occasionally I would worry that sex was the only thing keeping us together. But then I'd tell myself that Minh and I were on an incredible journey together, one that we were making up as we went along. If sex was what we had now, so be it. Eventually, we would develop a deeper connection. I copied down another quotation into my journal, this one from Octavio Paz: "Love must violate the rules of our world." That idea seemed to capture the project we were engaged in. I had lived so long not knowing whether we could ever be together that a little more uncertainty hardly seemed like something to fret over.

When on the street together, I kept my eyes out for other interracial gay couples, hoping to make a connection that might help Minh meet more friends, develop a business contact, or just see how normal what we were trying to do was in America. I brought him to a meeting of the Long Yang Club, a worldwide social organization for gay Asians and their Western friends, but his shyness got the better of him, and he refused ever to attend another meeting. I introduced him to gay-friendly straight Vietnamese acquaintances, but here, too, Minh never followed up.

As the months wore on, his withdrawal became more and more acute. "What's wrong?" I'd ask him, interrupting our nightly silent meals. "If you don't tell me what's wrong, I can't help."

"Don't worry about me," he'd reply.

I took these retreats into silence to be anything but what they really were. I told myself that he liked being quiet, that it was part of his "Buddha nature." I told myself that he was a mathematician, naturally laconic. I told myself that, just as it had been for us back in Hanoi, we didn't need to talk so much. I told myself it was "very Asian" to be so sparing of words. *What's important is that you love him; the rest is details,* I told myself.

In the end, the details overwhelmed us both. A little over four years after he arrived, Minh dropped out of school, quietly, without telling me. It was only after a refund check arrived from the university that I found out. By then, I knew not to ask him why. I knew he would just go silent on me again. Besides, it was clear not only that he did not want to be in school anymore but also that he did not want to be with me. He moved out, as unobtrusively as he had moved in, carrying his stuff in that single, small suitcase he had arrived with.

I returned to China in the summer of 2002, my first trip back since 1996. In the six years that I had been away, I had turned myself into something of an amateur Asia scholar. I had amassed a collection of over three hundred books on Chinese, Japanese, and Vietnamese history and culture. I'd visited and photographed most of the important collections of Asian art in the United States. I'd studied Mandarin and Vietnamese and had published several articles and book reviews on Asian life and literature. At my school, I teach a yearlong course on China. My return visit was a time to reflect on why I had developed such a case of "Asia fever."

It was a month-long tour, made in the company of twenty-five other American teachers. We traveled a good portion of the country, from east to west, north to south. Of all the sites I visited, no place caught my wonder more than Dunhuang. Located in barren Gansu province, at the westernmost end of the Great Wall, ancient Dunhuang was a supply outpost for the trade caravans that crossed the scorching desert during the era of the Silk Route. And it was here, in the thousand years between the fourth and fourteenth centuries, that Buddhist monks carved out and decorated hundreds of cave shrines in the limestone cliffs south of town. Even today, the Mogao Caves are one of the most spectacular assemblages of Buddhist art in the world. Within the five hundred surviving caves and niches (at one time, there were close to a thousand), some forty-five thousand square meters of wall paintings and two thousand polychromed statues dazzle the eyes.

Scenes of Buddhist tales and legends predominate, but there are also many murals that vibrantly depict everyday life during the Chinese Middle Ages. You can see musicians, farmers, acrobats, soldiers, prisoners of war, people going about their daily work, hunting, fishing, wood cutting, pottery and wine making. Cave after cave presents a wonderful imbroglio of color and action, almost baroque in exuberance and detail. Even under the dim, eerily flickering illumination of our flashlights, the effect was astounding.

But of all the glories I saw, nothing peaked my imagination more than the statues of Buddha attended by his two disciples, Kasyapa and Ananda, that adorned many of the small altars and shrines within the caves. Kasyapa, the Buddha's oldest follower, was a devout ascetic. He is usually depicted with a kind of fierce, emaciated, but blessed, expression on his face. In contrast, Ananda, the Buddha's cousin and youngest disciple, is young, beautiful, and sweet. Quiet, unassuming, selfless, he was the Buddha's favorite. For me, the two disciples—old, crazed Kasyapa and young, pretty-faced Ananda—came to represent the two faces of monasticism, indeed the two faces of holiness.

In one of the caves, I noticed something rather curious: the statue of Ananda was missing. What had happened, I wondered. Had it crumbled with time? Been destroyed by vandals? Looted? I kept going back to this last possibility: that the Ananda figure—so charming, so . . . well, *fetching*—had been stolen. It felt reckless, letting this notion come into my head, the kind of interpretation only a gay man (one so enchanted by the winsome charms of young Asian guys) could possibly dream up. But I kept turning it over, this thought that once, long ago, someone had been so transported by Ananda's beauty that he had desecrated a holy site just to possess the beloved image. How curious, I thought, that desire, the emotion Buddhists see as at the core of all human suffering, should have played itself out so ignominiously right here. I thought, too, about my own desire for Minh, and the mental contortions I had indulged in trying to convince myself that our relationship was good, and still alive, long after it had expired.

Now as I write this, it is winter, the winter of 2002-2003—a hard one weather-wise, a hard one for the world. At night, I bundle up in a bed made lonely by the absence of my beloved and read books on Buddhism. "Interrupting our destructive habits and awakening our heart is the work of a lifetime," I read. I think about that. I think about a trip I will take to Japan in the spring. I think about all of the traveling I have done and all of the traveling I still want to do. I think about how, in spite of all the silly, pitiable, unhappy steps I have taken, I still love to roam the world. And when I ask myself why, what I come up with is this: traveling seems to put me in touch with a bigness at the center of my being—call it love, or joy, or wonder, or Buddha nature—a bigness that feels so much bigger than all the flashy, seductive, heartrending sights I keep settling for. That's where I want to travel now, deeper and deeper into that mysterious, ineffable bigness.

1001 Beds

Tim Miller

Travel is work. I mean that statement literally because I am one of those beleaguered grunts who makes his living out on the road performing. My life as an artist and activist is built around travel, twenty-five to thirty weeks a year doing gigs all over the world. Tokyo one week. Cincinnati the next. Glasgow right after. My life is that of the wandering queer performance artist minstrel, the Johnny "FAG" Appleseed! Believe me, this endless schlepping takes its toll: the constant time-zone confusion, the sleeping on the floor at O'Hare International during snowstorms, the permanent sinus condition I share with all flight attendants, and the "if it's Tuesday it must be Tennessee?" confusion. On the plus side, I can also see myself as a fierce culture worker out there nurturing those ever-crucial Whitmanic leaves-of-grassroots. But on the downside I can sometimes feel exactly as one "friend" once referred to me—I thought, insultingly—as "Tim Miller, the Willy Loman of performance art." As the son of a traveling salesman dad and a mom who worked for years behind the wristwatch counter at May Company department store, I took slight at that!

I did the math recently and figured that I sleep in a minimum of twenty-five different beds each year as I travel and perform. If I continue to tour as I have done for the last twenty-one years for another twenty or so, I will easily end up sleeping in at least a thousand hotel beds in my life. For maximum poetic oomph, let's say 1001 beds. This scary sum seems important, but we "do the math" on our lives at our own peril. What seems pleasurable in week-by-week doses can add up over a lifetime to an exponential horror show, an endless phalanx of beds extending as far as the eye can see. Yikes! It is this dangerous love of statistics that made me calculate when I was seventeen how much semen I was likely to ejaculate over the course of a lifetime. I figured the total amount, based on a reasonable per orgasm average of one and a half tablespoons, would fill two large Hefty garbage bags. This was *not* a sexy thought.

I was thinking about these metaphorical "1001 beds" as I checked into the Vernon Manor Hotel in Cincinnati for a gig I was doing at the Cincinnati Playhouse. The Vernon Manor is a huge old sprawl of a hotel. Designed with a Gothic cum Tudor confidence, the Vernon Manor is like the set for a well-funded touring production of *Camelot*. The hotel was built in 1924, as an escape and retreat for the then wealthy Cincinnati residents living in the busy downtown riverfront district. That part of Cincinnati was referred to as "Porkopolis" in acknowledgment of the squeals of protest from the pigs that were becoming hot dogs at the many pork processing plants of sharp-knifed Cincy. Over the years the Vernon Manor Hotel has hosted everyone from President Kennedy to Judy Garland, from the Beatles to "Barney," from Bob Dylan to Kevin Bacon, thus proving that "six degrees" theory and returning us to the pork-theme of Cincinnati. There are no coincidences!

As much as I would love to run into Barney in the Vernon Manor, hotels are not mostly about celebrities. As I walk down the long hallways of the Vernon Manor, I can't help but think of the hundreds of thousands of regular people who have laid their heads down in this hotel over eighty years. The people who have fucked here at lunchtime affairs, had dark nights of the soul here, celebrated their honeymoons here, had their final sucking down of booze or the barrel of a gun here. All of these scenarios are on the menu at the Vernon Manor, as indeed they are at every old war-weary hotel in the world. Every hotel is haunted. On some level, anytime we check in at the front desk, we are checking in to that hotel in *The Shining*. We may not witness Jack Nicholson's carpet-chewing performance of a psychopath, but the ghosts are everywhere nonetheless.

I checked into Room 626. Right next to 624—the Beatles Suite. There is a huge sparkly star on the door of 624 in honor of the two times the Beatles stayed there in the sixties. The Vernon Manor is a very popular hotel for performing artists who tour to Cincinnati, our Guild Hall Tavern in a way. It's used by many road shows and by all the Cincinnati Playhouse actors, directors, and designers. I sometimes think that there is no real difference between some actors' bar in Piraeus during the fourth century B.C. and the late night bar at the Vernon Manor where we can order our third Jack Daniels & Coke and the Beggars Purse appetizer plate! Those ancient Greek actors getting ready to head out to Samos for some Euripides premiere are in a direct genealogical line to me gearing up for my show the next night at Cincinnati Playhouse. I like feeling that deep historical link as much as I do the more recent histories of the Vernon Manor. Certainly the Beatles-who-are-lost-to-us haunt this hotel. John Lennon at the ice machine. The young George Harrison in 1966—a real look alike for my partner Alistair—running from the screaming teens outside the hotel.

But enough about the Beatles, back to me! How many stories the 500 or so beds of the 1001 that I have already encountered could tell if they hadn't agreed to the confidentiality clause! Just as every hotel is a haunted hotel, every hotel is also a sex hotel. Certainly a good percentage of my already-slept-in hotel beds have been sex beds. There was a time in my life when the main perk of the road was savoring the local brew of the boys of Edinburgh or San Antonio or Palermo. Finally in 1994 in a hotel bed in South Kensington, London, I met my partner Alistair and that put a stop to those sexy shenanigans with the boys o' the world!

But it's not just the hotel as erotic vortex that I'm interested in here. These 1001 beds today have become the symbol for the burden of these endless journeys. Each one of those hundreds of beds means I have to face the unbearable ordeal of prying myself out of the bed I have shared for many years with Alistair in our home in Venice Beach. Peeling my limbs out of the sheets and bedclothes, I then fling myself somewhere in the world far from my man. I am doing this partly because, on the practical level, I need to make a living but mostly because I have a deeper calling to run around the world and create queer space in small southern colleges or fading industrial cities in the Midwest of America or the Midlands of England. I believe that real, face-to-face culture is retail not wholesale. (Back to my traveling salesman motif.) It relies on us being near each other, in the same room.

My mission—and I have decided to accept it—is to be always ready to run around and perform my lean-'n-mean homo-drenched performances, cultural agitating, teaching, and generally being a way-out gay role model and/or target. Whenever I need to hop on a tiny plane for Des Moines or Chattanooga and show the rainbow flag, I am ready to do this. Sure, I usually feel blue on a Sunday night nested with Alistair knowing that the next morning I need to hit the highway. As I face my dread at getting up at 5 A.M. to make the journey to teach a workshop in Winston-Salem or to speak at a queer studies conference in Asheville (the next gigs as of this writing), my touchstone to shove through that resistance to leaving our comfy home and bed together is my artistic and political mission. I know that whatever cultural agency and visibility I have accrued over twenty years as a performer and sparring partner duking it out with American homophobia make me a useful cultural provocateur. This doesn't make me dread the actual nuts and bolts of travel any less though. In the two days before a trip I begin to feel depressed and anxious. The tribal anxiety-attack drums start to gear up as the stress and challenge of my travel schedule begins to impose and undermine any sense of a "normal" life Alistair and I try to have together. I stop being able to sleep, have limitless reservoirs of panic about what I will forget or which airport I will be forced to sleep in when snow cancels my connection.

I make a very unlikely traveler. I love my domestic patterns and I am incredibly disorganized in my travel preparations. I have never had that glacial travel cool that Joan Didion—my personal über diva of California first-person narrative—describes in *The White Album*. La Didion tells us of her precise checklists for travel and how she always has a bag packed ready to go to Viet Nam or Cannes. Not me. I am always scrambling at the last minute through the dryer for my costume, or wondering where I put my passport, or have you seen my mini-disc with the show's sound cues?

The comfort I can find in that scary statistic of those 1001 beds lives strongest in the knowledge that those beds have meant something, they symbolize a life and art that has been dedicated to reaching out toward folks from Bozeman, Montana, to Tampa, Florida. A life and art that has traveled widely and I believe reached a fair few couple of hundred thousand or so people with my stories of queer life and love. This legacy of connecting to other lives and communities is the only way I can stop seeing those 1001 beds as an almost Dantean third ring of hell, horrifying in their Sisypehan multitude. Is that really me carrying the plush Simmons double-king Postur-pedic on my back up a steep hill only to have it roll back down again and again? That endless parade of beds that mark the journeys of my life becomes my own personal Boy Scout merit badge for a life that has a strong sense of service and mission, especially when I consider how difficult it is for this homebody to fling himself about far from home and love and Alistair.

Aerogrammes

Alistair McCartney

I was born in Perth, Western Australia, in 1971. From an early age I dreamt of leaving my birthplace, known to be the most isolated industrialized city in the world. Twenty-two years later I finally realized this dream, arriving at London's Heathrow Airport on 4 July 1994.

Just two weeks after my arrival, I met the Los Angeles performance artist Tim Miller at the Institute of Contemporary Art (ICA) in the West End. I fell instantly and deeply in love. For the next year, we romanced one another in different cities. Some of these cities were interesting, exciting—Glasgow, San Francisco, New York—others less so—Hartford, Davis, Pittsburgh. But the locations of our meetings were of secondary importance. Both of us were more concerned with exploring that interior, placeless geography that exists between lovers.

In between these rendezvous, Tim and I talked on the phone and wrote aerogrammes, wooing one another, attempting to work out the exact nature and precise shape of the love that was growing between us. Apart from the obvious difficulty of distance, there were other complex factors to deal with—especially the fact that when we met we were both already in relationships.

My introduction to Tim bore an uncanny resemblance to the way my mother and father met. In the mid-1950s my mother went on a pleasure cruise through the South Pacific. My father was in the merchant navy and worked on the liner. Soon Beth Wildy from Adelaide, Australia, and James McCartney from Glasgow, Scotland, embarked on a shipboard romance. After the cruise ended, they wrote aerogrammes to one another and met up in different places, eventually marrying in Scotland in the spring of 1958. The love letters they wrote to one another were scattered in different books around our house. As a child they fascinated me, the spidery declarations of love concealed inside these pale blue documents.

The following love letters that I wrote to Tim Miller, from the time we met until right before I moved to Los Angeles, have been heavily condensed and extensively revised, so you are not reading exact transcriptions of what I wrote to Tim; I wouldn't wish the un-revised ramblings of my twenty-two-year-old self on anyone. Rather, I've used the original letters as raw material to create a new set of love letters addressed to my sweetheart. I have, however, kept the order and dates the same and have limited myself to "true" events. Most important, I've made every effort to stay true to the grain of the longing embedded in those pale blue paper rectangles, measuring eight inches by four inches.

27 July 1994

Just got back from swimming at the men's bathing pond at Hampstead Heath. The men there are either queers or orthodox Jewish fathers with their sons. Being in water reminded me of you, so I thought I'd write. I have to admit that I wrestled with the notion that I am writing too "soon," but the desire to write (my desire?) finally won out. I hope you had a good journey back to L.A. Did you jump in the ocean? Though the men's ponds are great, I would trade some of their duck shit and slime for your Pacific sea-salt any day. I have to confess I was really upset over your leaving. I felt a powerful connection between us, and then all of a sudden our time with each other was over. I hope we'll have more chances to be together. Things between Philip and I blew up as soon as you left. He was very angry with me for going off with you. What began as a day of sightseeing turned into a day of huge fights in popular tourist spots. The first one took place in Trafalgar Square while we were sitting on the edge of the fountains, right beneath Nelson. As we yelled at one another, a tourist tried to take a picture of us! We calmed down and sat there for an hour, watching this little boy blow up a huge inflatable globe of the world. Then we wandered off to St. James Park, where the next fight began, on the striped lawn chairs near the bandstand. We cursed each other as the brass band played old favorites like "God Save the Queen" and "On a Clear Day." We had planned on going to the Tower of London, but thought better of it. Anyway, the outcome is that we're going to see what it feels like not to be boyfriends. I hope I'm not spilling too much of my insides onto the page. Write me soon, soon, soon. Dip your tongue in saltwater before you seal your letter.

3 August 1994

I did some more sightseeing today, but of an unofficial kind. I retraced some of the steps we took together here less than a couple of weeks ago. Walked past the Jewish embassy in South Kensington, where the bomb exploded that first morning we woke up together in a hotel just a couple of blocks away. Watched some sexy dark builders repairing the structure slowly. Then I went to the ICA and looked at the memorial to that colonial general who massacred hundreds of Indians during the Sepoy Rebellion; stood in the same space where we made out after your workshop. There was a wreath of plastic poppies lying at the foot of the memorial. I imagined putting the wreath around your neck. I saved the best until last. I went back to Picadilly Circus and walked around the statue of Eros, counter-clockwise, just as we did that night when we had nowhere to go.

15 August 1994

I've moved from Kentish Town to West Hampstead. The mail has been redirected, but I don't seem to be receiving anything from anyone. Here's something strange: I just got a job at the Drill Hall, where we had our first date. Philip and I have decided to break up officially, and we seem to be getting on much better. We just looked after his gay (sadomasochistic/accountant) uncle's flat in Harrow for a couple of days. Went down to the famous boys' school; imagined sexy nineteenth-century boys being roasted over open fires by their brutish boyfriends. Everywhere you look in London there's a monument to war. I prefer the temporary monuments, the kind built out of plastic flowers, like the one in King's Cross memorializing the black boy beaten to death. Had a dream last night that Princess Diana called me up, to talk about the media trials. Maybe we should talk on the phone? I want to hear your sweet accent. Do you still want to meet in sunny Glasgow?

25 October 1994

I had been thinking about you so much today, so it was sweet to creep downstairs and find a blue aerogramme from you, with my name written on it in BIG red letters. I wish I could have sex with your handwriting. I've been thinking constantly about our time in Glasgow. It was something, wasn't it? Strange to think of my father as a young man, walking the same streets we did. The air smelled like him, of tobacco and whisky. I didn't tell you at the time, but that day we walked by the river Kelvin, past the spot where the gay man was murdered while he was cruising, I could have sworn I saw the ghost of my Uncle Frank, the soft shadow of his pork-pie hat. I thought the city was surprisingly beautiful, all that dark heavy stone. Though in effect we could have been anywhere—our sightseeing was pretty much limited to each other's bodies, the gray sex couch, the red-carpeted bedroom. I don't even remember the name of the street we stayed on. If I wanted to, I could calculate fairly accurately the number of hours we've spent together. But I don't want to. I'm more interested in the things between us that can't be measured: the amount of saliva we've exchanged, the number of kisses, the feelings spinning between us. While we were in Glasgow, if someone tried to find us on a map, I don't think we could have been found. This evades geography.

1 November 1994

I dreamt last night that we were back in Glasgow, in the little flat, making out on the couch. There was a bird hovering outside the window, but not your everyday bird, some kind of prehistoric bird. A pterodactyl? Anyway, it was floating outside the window, up and down—it would come into view and then it would disappear, and then it would come back into view, only to disappear again. And it was laughing at us, giggling. Then we were in the bedroom, getting ready to go to sleep. Instead of the blue bedspread we slept beneath, there was a huge map that we spread out over our bodies. Actually, it wasn't just one map, but all these little maps stitched together. I can still see the seams. It's hard to think I'm not going to see you again until spring, and maybe not even then.

14 November 1994

I have to confess I've been feeling a bit gloomy the last week or so. I think it comes down to two things: it's only now beginning to hit me that I've left Australia for good and I'm living here in London. I don't feel homesick exactly—I wish I did, but I don't miss Perth and I have no desire to go home. I am not Dorothy. If anything, I'm closer to the Wicked Witch of the West, who wants the bright object that will take her anywhere, who just wants to go and go and go. All

I feel is a kind of numb dislocation. I don't know whether I'll ever get used to this city with its endless rows of identical two-story red-brick houses and lines of identical queer boys, with their shaved heads, dressed in bomber jackets, boots, and combat pants. If I feel homesick for anything, it's for you. I feel homesick for the little house we shared together for those two weeks in Glasgow. The lease for the flat here runs out in February, and I've pretty much decided to look for another place to live, or maybe do a little traveling. All I need is those red shoes.

27 November 1994

I'm so excited that the prospect of traveling together for a couple of months in the States is beginning to feel more concrete, more real. It makes London and the winter seem more bearable. Someone told me today that London is still a medieval city-state. It isn't separated from the rest of England by a moat, but by a complex system of motorways. This morning to clear my head I went for a walk through Westmere Copse. I leaned up against a tree, only to notice that someone had carved the letters B.N.P. — British National Party, England's version of the Ku Klux Klan — into the tree's trunk. As I made my way back home down Kilburn High Street, a Caribbean woman with red lipstick smeared all over her face yelled at me: why don't you have five children like me and let the city eat them? As I go about my day I think of you enveloped in your day. That long bicycle ride you described sounded so nice. Maybe we can do that when I see you next? What color is your bicycle?

6 January 1995

Your letter arrived today, so it didn't get lost in the Christmas flood. Your time in New York sounded intense, so many memories and ghosts for you there. It would be good if we could erect our own public monuments to people and events we think deserve to be re-membered. I can't wait for you to show me around New York. I'm looking forward to moving out of the flat in West Hampstead and being rootless again, at least for a while. I found myself missing you intensely over the holiday season. I could feel something gnawing away at me. Had a lot of strange off-kilter sex to compensate: a man from Germany, Mikal, passing through town on his way to Cuba to look for his boyfriend who has mysteriously "disappeared"; a boy from Hawaii on his way to Nepal; and then this guy I met at Heaven, who lives in a house in Hampstead where this Jewish Marxist historian (an old lover of Susan Sontag's) used to live. But get this—apparently this historian guy hung himself from the rafters of the very bedroom I found myself in! Soon, though, I will see you and won't have to compensate. I am saving like crazy. It's like I've turned into Ebenezer Scrooge. I am even stopping myself from putting money in the coin-operated heater. It's freezing, but all this feeling I have for you keeps me warm.

11 January 1995

I'm so glad everything is coming together for our February trip. I loved getting your midnight call. I went straight to bed and jerked off, imagining us back in Glasgow, you fucking me on the carpet in the kitchen. Cum, carpet-burn. Yum! Then I fell asleep and dreamt about us meeting up again. We weren't meeting in any particular "place." There was this weird little boy hanging around us. He grabbed my finger and stuck it in what I at first thought was his mouth. Then I looked down and saw that it wasn't his mouth, but a neat little slit just above his eyebrow. An asshole? A mailbox slit? I withdrew my finger, and it made a sucking noise. Then the persistent little boy grabbed my finger and stuck it back in again. I would have preferred if this dream had involved a little less displacement, but I guess until I see you again (soon! soon! soon!) displacement will have to do. Send me your analysis.

31 January 1995

Thank god my letters arrived *finally*. I was beginning to think that the Royal Mail and the U.S. Postal Service were involved in a sinister conspiracy, actively trying to stop us from corresponding. Letters ARE really important, especially these. And one misplaced letter is more than enough. I wonder whatever happened to the first letter you sent me? I wonder who received it? Perhaps my last landlord has it; perhaps he reads it over and over again, swooning, imagining your sweet words are directed to him; perhaps he keeps it hidden from his wife, beneath a loose floorboard. I wonder what you said in that letter? I'm not doing much at the moment except working, working, working, saving up as much money as I can for our U.S. trip. It's hard to concentrate on anything at the moment—I'm so excited about seeing you. I'm trying to be patient, though. I'll be moving out of here on 11 February, and staying at my friend Mickey's house in Streatham. I'm not sure when the phone is going to be cut off, so I'll call you and give you my new number. At the risk of repetition: I can't wait to see you. This is so much nicer than "I miss you." Though of course I still feel that, too. I can't believe we'll be together again. And in America! It will have been almost five months.

4 February 1995

Stop the press! My friend Mickey has decided this is not a good time for him, so now I will be staying with my friend Nick in Bethnal Green. I'll call you as soon as I'm there to finalize where exactly to meet you in San Francisco. I can hardly wait to get out of this bitter city. I can't wait to see you, touch you, taste you again. When I open your aerogrammes I find myself wondering if your tongue licked the envelope shut; if there is some trace of your saliva I can salvage. I pore over your letters with a magnifying glass, looking for any evidence of YOU: dead skin, DNA, the lovely confusing maze of your fingerprints.

17 April 1995

I've found a patch of sunlight outside the launderette here on Avenue A [New York City] and am writing this to you as my clothes dry. Thanks for your sweet words. You're right—I do think it's important we be good to one another within all this complexity. But at the same time I still can't help feeling resentful of the way you organize your romantic universe, so you get it all—a house, a husband, a dog, plus a boy in every port. It drives me insane thinking of you there with Doug in Venice, wrapped up in all that domesticity. Last night I dreamt we were making love in a tree house built at the top of a telegraph pole. The wires were humming around us as we fucked. But the next time I looked up, there were branches, and Handel's water music was being piped through the branches. Blossoms hung above our heads and fell onto us, gently covering our bodies. I'm glad you're coming back to New York earlier now.

18 April 1995

By the way, I've been flirting with this boy, an architect who just moved to New York from San Francisco. The strange thing is you and I saw him when we were having breakfast together at Café Orlan. Remember the boy with the brilliant blue eyes, icy and clear like Tahoe, and the silvery-gray hair? He's only twenty-six. He told me it went gray overnight, like an unexpected snowfall.

1 May 1995

What am I going to do? I can't bear the thought of being apart from you again, without any plans to see one another. Remember, when we walked past the Starbucks on St. Marks Place, how you said it's somehow comforting to think everyone here will be dead in one hundred years? You were right. I keep thinking of us fucking in the red room in the art theorist's apartment on the corner of Seventh Avenue and Twelfth Street. After we came that night, I went into the bathroom and stood in front of the mirror, examining your dried cum on my face, like a map of sex, trying to read the future in it. I can't stop thinking of that red room. I watched *Rosemary's Baby* last night. It gave me an idea. I'm going to fly over to Venice in the dead of night. I'm going to drug your boyfriend and your dog. I'm going to fuck you like the devil, profanely and sweetly. You'll wake up with something growing inside of you. Everything will taste different.

2 May 1995

Thanks for the phone conversation. Despite all this distance between us, you were very present. That was sweet, but still not enough. All I want is the appropriate time to be given to all the feelings swirling between us. All our rendezvous were wonderful and fine, but I think this intensity between us deserves more than a week or two. I know our situations are different: you and Doug are still so entangled; my world is much more malleable than yours. I don't know, maybe our hearts are too big to fit into this stupid little world. It's interesting living in Brixton with four Danes, my ex-boyfriend and his new boyfriend. I hope this gets to you soon.

4 May 1995

Last night I dreamt we were back in Manhattan. We're wandering down Broadway together, and then somehow I lose sight of you. I find myself on a little side street, with brick paths and rosebushes and two-story red-brick apartment buildings, just like the apartments I lived in for a while back in Perth. I scratch my left hand—my writing hand—on one of the rosebushes. My skin is full of thorns. There's no pain, but I know it's going to take a long time to pull them out, and this is going to delay my catching up with you. I leave the side street, and wander back onto another avenue. I see you a couple of blocks ahead in the distance. But I'm slowly pulling thorns out of my skin, and this takes up all my attention. I lose sight of you again, only to find myself in another section of Manhattan. It's like the moon, all blasted and silver, full of craters. I walk through this moonscape, still pulling the thorns out, one by one; still trying to catch up with you. I woke up from this dream feeling hopeful. If dreams can collapse geography—Manhattan, Perth, the moon—why can't we?

15 May 1995

I've been thinking about our conversation on the phone the other day/night. While we were talking I was being so cautious I didn't allow myself to take in your responses to my challenge. But they're beginning to sink in. If I'm not mistaken, you seem pretty open to my coming to L.A. and our trying things out. Is that correct? I'll wait for your reply to this before I jump to conclusions. Coming back to London has been pretty grim, as I expected. I still feel so raw from what went on between us. I feel like my body is made up of bruises and blushes and tears. But I've been trying to do things to raise my spirits. Took the train down to Brighton yesterday. All the way down I thought of you. I had the strange sensation that I was traveling through more than one country. I look forward to your next letter. I love you. There, I've said it. So much for my being careful with myself. But it's true. Being with you gave me such a feeling of safety and well being. The world felt so warm. Remember when we took off our shirts and lay like lizards in the sun on those rocks in Central Park? I want to feel that kind of warmth again.

25 May 1995

Here is my fourth attempt to write this letter to you. I've been very up and down lately. All this feeling I have for you is so powerful, but confusing: I feel like I'm hanging upside down from a rope attached to the sun, and the rope is swinging me slowly back and forth like a pendulum. It has been good to talk about exactly what is going on between us. And I think to our credit, although it has been hard, we are getting somewhere, despite all the obstacles: distance, expense, time. After I got off the phone with you the other night, I had a dream that you and Doug were on trial, and I was the presiding judge. But then all of a sudden I was also one of the accused, sitting there with you and Doug. We were all dressed in those bright orange jumpsuits prisoners wear and linked together by bright silver handcuffs. Thank you for your beautiful letter. I read it going to work on the tube. It got here incredibly quickly! Brixton must be closer to Los Angeles than Kilburn.

25 June 1995

As I write this you must be sleeping. I wonder what you are dreaming about? I've been thinking a lot about our time together in Tahoe. How sexy the rental car felt. The gradual movement from the blandness of Davis to the wildness. That sinister little German store in the forest where we went to buy candy. It felt like we were Hansel and Gretel. Talking to that forest ranger whose name just happened to be Karen Finley. Driving and touching. Seeing snow for the first time in my life. Being in love for the first time in my life. Sitting in that open-air hot tub, rubbing snow into your pecs. Snow on the trees. The black blindfold falling out of your coat pocket into the snow. All that snow and all that touching, constantly touching. I had a revelation this morning that although we are thousands of miles apart we are still touching each other. Geography presents no obstacle to what is growing between us.

5 July 1995

All the Danes have gone back to Denmark and now I am living with three English girls. I think I am beginning to develop an English accent. If my accent has changed, does that mean the essence of who I am has also changed? Does that mean my tongue is now a different shape? We always obsess about the way time alters us, but what about the effect of space on our bodies? When you see me next, perhaps my tongue will feel different in your mouth, on your skin. I dreamt of you last night, you were wearing your father's sailor suit. I can't wait to see it. Maybe I can try it on?

16 July 1995

I just began writing this letter to you and a letter from you comes through the mail slot in the door. When we're apart and can't fuck, this movement of the letter through the mail slot is our version of sex. It was so sweet to hear your voice flowing electronically from Toronto the other night. I hope all is going well there. Did you find your lake? It's raining here in Brixton. I feel all emotional as I write this to you, like the world is weighing on my shoulders, like Atlas, but it is not a bad feeling. It's a happy, joyous weight.

21 July 1995

I was really sorry to hear in your letter that you've been having such a difficult time with Doug. I have to confess that at the same time as I read the letter I got the biggest boner. I had this dream last night that I was flying over a map down the West Coast of the United States. At first its detail was hidden by thick little white patches of clouds, but then the clouds thinned and I could see all the little black place names with their black dots and the red-ribbon freeways and skinny blue rivers. And then I saw you, standing next to the word "Venice," waving.

28 July 1995

I've been feeling your absence so strongly lately—it's almost more powerful than your presence. Though let me be clear: I will take your presence over your absence any day. As I expressed, I was a little strung out over the prospect of getting enough money together to come to L.A. so soon, so I think the September plan is a good one. It gives me more time, which will then allow us more time. My sister Jeannine offered to help me out. She sent me a beautiful "you've been away a year" card. It certainly has been a year hasn't it? Hearing about the difficult space you and Doug currently find yourselves in, I began noticing an interesting numerology going on. You were twenty-three years old when you met Doug, the age I am now. You guys met thirteen years ago, which is the age difference between us. Talking to you on the phone the other night I felt simultaneously a huge sense of peace and a huge rush—like being engulfed in the certainty of a tidal wave. Los Angeles doesn't get tidal waves, does it?

8 August 1995

I'm sending this to you care of the theater in D.C. I entertained the idea of beginning each sentence, "I cannot tell a lie, I did _____," but it seemed too great a project. Thanks for your beautiful letter. As always I loved getting part of you via red ink on blue paper. I felt real warmth emanating from your words, like little red fires. The thought of you getting mad at those mean people from Adelaide turned me on. Adelaide is known for 1) an excess of churches and 2) an excess of child murderers. My mother (who incidentally was born in Adelaide) is depositing 250 pounds directly into my bank account. Good for the plane ticket to L.A. If I wrote a California guidebook, your body would be listed as a tourist attraction, right next to Disneyland and Universal Studios. I've been jerking off to thoughts of visiting your body, though they are so much more than mere thoughts—the word doesn't do them justice.

12 August 1995

Okay, okay, I cannot tell a lie: I have been seeing a few boys. I was dating Tom, this actor who played a bellboy in this Noël Coward-ish farce at the Drill Hall. The first time we made out was in the dressing room; it was very sexy peeling him out of his red uniform, like peeling an apple. But I've been unfaithful (the question is to whom?). I met this French boy David. He has the manner of an old little bourgeois man but looks like a beautiful child. The other night as we were making love he whispered in my ear "Vive la Australie." And then of course there's Leandro from São Paulo. He speaks very little English, though he articulates the sentence "you're my bitch" very clearly.

13 August 1995

So sweet to receive so much paper from you this week. Your mentioning all those D.C. place names filled me with a great longing to be there with you. I loved hearing about your hallucination of me in Dupont Circle. If you see him again, grab him and kiss him and fuck him. I'm enjoying summer as it fades away. It's actually been hot. The other day I fell asleep in the sun on my belly and got a bad case of sunburn. I wish you were here to peel the strips of skin off my back. But even when it's hot, I feel a chill, because you're not here, like there's a winter in my body. My heart is beating really quickly as I write this to you. Soon, soon, soon.

23 August 1995

I just finished talking on the phone with you. Even though it feels like we're talking in circles sometimes, I still feel like we're getting somewhere. Just like flying around the world in circles gets you to your destination. I like our circles. They are pleasurable circles. Perhaps due to the fact that there is so much pleasure between us. Even after all our difficulties. I have to admit I'm frustrated we have to defer our plans a little. But maybe deferral does the heart good. I want you to be happy in the present, even when we're apart. And somehow all this passion is balanced out by patience. Sitting on the floor talking to you on the phone, I got such a hard-on envisioning you fucking me on the carpet on all fours. As usual I end up wishing you well on a pornographic level. I *will* see you soon.

4 September 1995

How are you as the summer draws to a close? I'm still not used to the short sharp space that constitutes a "summer" here in London, compared to the endlessness of the summers back in Perth. I can already smell winter here, milky and spooky, like sour baby's breath. I saw something beautiful in front of the tube station the other day. Two drunk queer boys with the obligatory shaved heads standing in a puddle of milk, kissing. Right behind them on the wall someone had spray-painted IRA in big red letters. The writing looked a little like yours. My financial problems are slowly sorting themselves out. My lack of $$$ is counterbalanced by the excess of desire I feel toward you. Just to remind you: yes, I still want to try out being in L.A. together. I look at a map of Los Angeles and see the shape of your body imprinted in it like a fossil.

11 September 1995

Thanks for the photograph of you. You look all angular and beautiful. I love that it's a close-up. It was shocking how close you seemed. So tangible. Looking at it made me want to cover your face in counterclockwise kisses. I guess our faces are clocks in a way. When I get to L.A., remind me to change my face-clock to L.A. time. I wonder how we're going to do in the same time zone? I wish I could be there with you on your birthday. I hope this gets to you in time. I wish I could send my body along with this letter, but remember: an aerogramme should contain no enclosure.

19 September 1995

I feel so excited about the prospect of seeing you again. I'm ready for things to be tricky at times, given the complex situation between you and Doug, as well as my inevitable relocation blues. I can't wait to touch you again, to pore over your body, to pour my body into yours. To go swimming together in the Pacific. Thanks so much for offering to pay for my airfare. Someone told me the other day that L.A. is a city without corners—something to do with the mini-malls cutting into the corners, disrupting space. I've always wanted to live in a city without corners. I can't wait to disrupt space with you.

15 October 1995

I'm writing this to you as I wait to get on the plane. I'll be seeing you in approximately thirteen hours. It was dark and foggy when I left the flat this morning. As I walked down the road to the tube stop, two boys emerged out of the fog. They looked like they were just coming back from a night of clubbing. They had their arms around one another. One of them was wearing a sailor's hat. I had the strange feeling of heading off to sea. It made me think of my mum and dad meeting on the ocean liner, the aerogrammes they wrote to one another, which made me think of you. They just called first-class passengers, and I am almost 100 percent sure that Sigourney Weaver got onto my plane. I feel like I'm getting into a spaceship with Ripley. Though in my case I am happy to have this monster growing silently inside of me. Let's order Chinese food in cartons and watch all the *Alien* movies on video. When I see you I am going to kiss you and put this letter directly into your hand.

Crows in
the Hair

Mitch Cullin

When planning a trip from Tucson to Japan, it's important to be aware of several things that I had to learn for myself: don't wear sandals without socks (this might be fine in the dry desert, but when walking in rainy Tokyo you'll end up with horrible blisters on your big and little toes—shoes are preferable); it is taboo to tip anyone, regardless of how good the service has been (if you are among those who feel inclined to tip, bring along a set of postcards from Arizona and offer them instead); on escalators, stand to the left so that others can use the right side for running up the steps (however, when walking on sidewalks stick to the right side, otherwise you're likely to get struck from behind by a bicycle); spend at least two days in Kyoto (one day just doesn't cut it, even if you do find the Ishihara Inn and are shown inside to where Akira Kurosawa wrote many of his later screenplays); no matter how benign a monkey might appear on the island of Miyajima, don't get too close with your camera (he could attack you); if you're hardly versed in the Japanese language, learn a few simple phrases—such as, "Do you speak English?" "Thank you very much." "How much is it?" "Where's the exit?" "Where am I?"—otherwise rely less on phrase books and more on body language (it is, after all, the universal language); when visiting Hiroshima, eat okonomiyaki more than once or twice, but do so at different restaurants (some okonomiyaki will taste better than others); expect to spend a certain amount of your days confused, slightly disoriented, and probably lost (don't panic—the Japanese are quite helpful, even if their directions often tend to be off by a street or a block); and, lastly, if you are planning to go from Tucson to Tokyo, you must reach your destination by airplane (it's almost impossible to arrive by any other means).

As for me, I normally don't fly. For many years, in fact, I refused any suggestion of flying, as it felt somehow counterintuitive to my own sense of self-preservation; the very idea of my body—a relatively minuscule vessel in the universal scheme—getting propelled through a vast, potentially inhospitable expanse was enough to keep my feet planted firmly on the earth. Without question, I knew that there would be no miles spent above the ocean or ground for me, no blue-black firmament from which I might find myself suddenly plunging toward a violent death. And yet to the surprise of those who know me well, I recently did take flight—leaving Tucson, changing planes in Los Angeles, bringing myself and a backpack and my old Minolta camera to Japan (the country of my dreams, a place that had shaped my fiction by virtue of its great writers and had amazed me with its sometimes rich, narrative forms of filmmaking).

In a curious way, my trip was a version of life imitating art. Or, more specifically, it was a novelist traveling to several of the places that one of his characters had already visited. At the moment, however, the novel remains unfinished (the second half already completed, the first half now waiting my attention), although my character's journey across Japan was written months ago: the year being 1947, not 2002, and the protagonist an elderly Englishman who goes by train from Tokyo to Kobe then to Hiroshima and beyond. I, on the other hand, didn't go much farther than Hiroshima, so it's fair to say that my character has still seen more of Japan than I have. Yet by replicating a portion of his journey, I was able to correct a number of inaccuracies that existed in the manuscript. For example, I realized that okonomiyaki is eaten with chopsticks and not by hand, that Hiroshima Castle doesn't sit on a hill, and that I had mistakenly put the Atomic Bomb Dome on the wrong side of Motoyasu-gawa River. But when it came to Shukkeien Garden, I was delighted by how accurately I'd described it; so accurately, in fact, that I found myself effortlessly walking its many paths as if from experience. Of course, in my novel the garden was in terrible disrepair and Hiroshima Castle had been leveled by the atomic blast.

Naturally, my vacation could be viewed as much-needed research, except that wasn't why I went. Even before my current novel was conceived, I'd imagined myself taking this very trip for years but believed I'd only get around to it in the future. Furthermore, I was convinced that the journey would ultimately be attempted without my ever setting foot inside an airplane. In my mind, I envisioned myself heading for Japan via boat, possibly traveling from Vancouver to Osaka on a cruise ship. This, however, was not to be the case. Instead, I braved Singapore Airlines, settling into a window seat, doing so with some grim hope that the plane might actually crash (preferably on the return flight, because I truly wished to see Japan before my swift demise). I'll avoid the details as to why I was hoping for death, other than to mention that in the course of just a few weeks my lover of three years had abruptly left me, as my did desire to write and whatever other tangible reasons I could muster for remaining on this absurd planet.

During those miserable two months preceding my trip, I lost twenty pounds, dropping from the decent weight of 163 pounds to an unhealthy 143 pounds. To ease my depression, I was prescribed various medications—Paxil, Seroquel, Remeron, Clonazepam—all with side effects, mostly drowsiness, although the Paxil not only weakened my sex drive but made having an orgasm pretty much impossible. Then almost as soon as I started the drugs, I stopped cold turkey, deciding that I'd rather suffer the pain on my own. Even so, I began contemplating the best means by which to end my life. Hanging myself seemed difficult and potentially painful. A gunshot to the head might leave me alive but permanently brain damaged. Cutting my wrists was just too messy. Pills were a likely option, but how could I acquire enough for the job? Killing one's self, I realized, was not so clean or so easy, and an incredible amount of determination was needed to do it correctly.

"How about flying?" my therapist suggested.

"I don't fly," I told him.

"Why?"

"I just don't. I'd hate dying in a plane crash."

"You won't fly, but at the same time you can ponder suicide."

"What's your point?"

"Well, if you want to die—but you lack the resolve to do it yourself—why not take your chances on an airplane?"

Fair enough, I thought, already weighing the possibilities.

So, three weeks later, there I was—drifting in the sky and forty-three minutes from Narita Airport, gazing from my airplane window at dusk, studying the orangish, white, dark terrain way below (sunlight and clouds and ocean). Soon I caught sight of land: a mountain silhouetted as evening diminished. Only later did I realize that it had been Mount Fuji that I had seen from my window quickly disappearing into the nighttime. A good omen, I was eventually told, for that to be my first real glimpse of Japan. But throughout my two weeks of travel, I never saw Mount Fuji again, even as I went by bullet train from Tokyo to Kyoto to Kobe to Hiroshima to Kamakura—and then back to Tokyo.

When I think of Tokyo now, it's not the immensity of the city that immediately springs to mind (that odd mosaic of buildings and streets and railroad routes, the curious juxtaposition of old and new—as if everything had arisen by happenstance and yet thrived nonetheless—somehow recalling the strange, otherworldly creations of Antonio Gaudi) or the brightness of the city after dusk (alleys aglow with electric lanterns, bar or noodle-shop marquees, flashing pachinko parlor signs, and those huge electronic billboards high above Shinjuku or Shibuya or Ikebukuro), which reminds me some-what of the Las Vegas strip at night. I don't easily summon to mind the darkness that exists amongst all that glimmer or the haphazard yet apparently symbiotic relationship between fast-walking pe-destrians and even faster vehicles. No, when I think of Tokyo now, I think of the elusive crows that appeared every morning. They were larger than any crows I'd seen in America, with massive heads and bodies, periodically crying out in the dull, murky sky. There were thousands of them, making their presence known at dawn, rum-maging through the remnants of the previous night, and using their massive beaks to tear into trash bags. By evening they vanished com-pletely, waiting for the night to conclude and the streets to empty briefly. Every morning they returned by early light, waking me with their echoing, disquieting cries. Again and again I tried photograph-ing them as I strolled from the Grand House Chang Tee in Ikebu-kuro to the nearby Excelsior Cafe; but, as if on cue, they scattered before the camera could capture them. I shot twenty-seven rolls of black-and-white film in Japan, with thirty-six exposures per roll—and only once was I able to capture a crow: the creature bolting into flight from a streetlight just as my shutter snapped.

All the same, I captured a good many other images with my old Minolta, that trusted piece of equipment that I'd retire with dignity upon my return to Arizona, ceremoniously putting it away in the closet and never using it again. I'll mention now that my Minolta has a name, the same name my computer has and the same name my first truck had; the camera has been called Seymour since I was in high school. So, in some regard, the trip was as much for Seymour as it was for me: for nearly twenty years it was my camera of choice, but at last, age was beginning to take its toll (the numerous scuffs and scratches on my favorite lens, a slightly purplish tint to all my black-and-white shots). But as I no longer felt capable of creating fiction, the Japan trip allowed me to rediscover the joy of photography, a serious hobby that I'd put aside when I began writing fiction over fifteen years ago. The beauty of photography—as opposed to the act of fiction writing—is that it asks the artist to look beyond himself while still allowing a singular worldview to be expressed. Photography is, without a doubt, the most selfless of all art forms, and because I felt plagued by my own personal problems and self doubt, there was no better traveling companion than sturdy, reliable Seymour.

Among the hundreds of shots Seymour gave me were those of a monk begging for yen in front of Shinjuku Station, of a policeman blowing a tuba in Kyoto, of an androgynous teenager simultaneously playing keyboards and trumpet in Kobe, and a of street sign simply stating in English: WELCOME TO HIROSHIMA. On the island of Miyajima, I photographed a monkey who—after I'd leaned in too close—proceeded to scream at me, attack my leg, and push me away; this episode being the single xenophobic experience of my entire trip, and one that amused the other tourists around me—all of whom were Asian. Still, Seymour and I survived this harsh rebuke, and, in hindsight, I suspect if a stranger ever tried getting that close to me with a camera, I might react in a similar manner.

My trip, however, wasn't merely a photographic excursion into a land that I'd only read about and seen in movies. It wasn't designed or intended solely as an escape from my troubles, and yet I brought with me the desire for forgetting: to remove my thoughts from the desert, to pull myself away from the complicated pangs of heartache. In reality, I wished to be completely alone for the first time in my life—alone without a familiar language, wandering around in a unique country where I'd be forced to navigate the distances on my own. Like some improbable character in a novel, I longed to be a living ghost, moving as if unseen among the living. I also wanted to grasp the differences between loneliness and aloneness, so I could come home with a better understanding of those two similar but unrelated states of being. Ultimately, I wished to reenter the desert transformed—a man who could accept his solitary fate while, at the same time, knowing he wasn't alone on the earth or in the universe.

After the initial culture shock wore off, I wrestled with my loneliness in the evenings, usually in whichever hotel room I was staying in that night. I knew that upon returning to Tucson I'd be grappling in much the same manner—with the TV on, drinking beer from a can, stretched out on a bed or a couch. Yet for now, this parallel world— where the hotel rooms were smaller than my dining room, the bathtubs were compact and deep, the television shows were entertaining but unintelligible—was good enough for me. Some hotels provided sex channels, but a TV card had to be purchased in advance for a thousand yen. The sex appeared like visions from another realm. Genitals were blotted out by computer-generated patterns, with only a sperm trail allowed as the sole indicator of the sex act—the stuff squirted across chins, or between breasts, or on stomachs. What little arousal I felt was dampened by slight intoxication and thoughts of home. I didn't want sex in Japan, or human companionship. I wanted solitude and peace of mind. More often than not, I dozed off with the TV still on, the images playing like half-remembered dreams as I slept: baseball games, endless news reports about Japanese citizens abducted by North Koreans, programs warning of impending bad weather. In the morning I'd stir, feeling hopeful, either listening for the crows or hearing them. Another day of travel and exploration was about to begin. I was almost always out of the hotels by dawn, heading for breakfast, then a coffee shop, and then a train station.

But while watching people move down sidewalks, eat side by side in cramped noodle shops, press together on crowded trains, I began sensing in the Japanese something that I felt was lacking in myself: a kind of wide, personal inward space—a place where the self could take refuge when faced with so many people and so little outward space. On trains I saw strangers pushed against each other, sleeping or reading or in thought, seemingly unaware of their bodies touching; in those moments, I imagined, they were somewhere else, somewhere within and away from the physical world. Americans, on the other hand, especially those of us from the desert Southwest, view personal space in outward terms, in the miles and miles of open land around us. In other words, our sense of inward space is usually determined by the amount of outward space that is available to us. Not so with the Japanese, a race who apparently revere the natural world more than most Americans do, and yet who live mostly in dense, humid, over-populated cities; for them the wide open spaces are carried within. I craved for such space inside myself—rather than the tangled, narrow confines of my psyche—and I believed I might discover it somewhere along my travels.

In hindsight, I was probably a pilgrim without a point, seeking needed information but not knowing what questions to ask or what kind of answers should be sought. Perhaps I hoped that just by arriving by myself in Japan—going alone from city to city, making little eye contact, never acknowledging other Caucasians when I encountered them—the answers would come like meager waves of satori, briefly revealing themselves to me here and there. Then one evening, as I walked deep in thought from my hotel in Ikebukuro toward Babiron Studio (an underground samba bar I'd discovered when roaming the alleyways at night), a young woman emerged from the shadows; crossing toward me, she asked, "You need a message?"

My god, I thought, this is it: "Yes," I said, almost desperately, "I need a message. What is it?"

"No," she said, shaking her head. "A massage—you need a massage?"

"Oh," I replied, smiling politely. "Thank you, but no—no massage. Message, yes. Massage, no."

She returned my smile, shrugging as she moved past me. I would get no message or massage that evening, just beer.

Aimless soul-searching aside, I maintained the agenda of a tourist. There were graves I wished to pray beside, post-modern monuments I longed to gaze upon, and holy statues I hoped would give me some direction in my life (regardless of how vague or undeserved the instructions might be). In Kawasaki, I was allowed into a private cemetery where I was escorted to the grave of the actor Toshiro Mifune, his tombstone adorned with offerings of empty beer cans and wilted flowers. In Kita-Kamakura—a short distance from the train station—I walked up mossy steps near the parking lot of Engaku-Ji Temple, finding the resting place of the train-loving director Yasujiro Ozu; his black marble, cube-like tombstone etched with a single character: nothingness. How fitting, I thought, for Ozu to be buried so close to railroad tracks—and how fitting, too, that those same tracks soon took me the short distance to Kamakura.

At the Tourist Information Center in Kamakura Station, I asked an elderly woman to direct me toward the cemetery where another famous director was buried. She consulted a blue binder that was kept behind the counter, her finger sliding down a list of deceased names until the right one was found. Then she showed me a map of the city, pointing at Anyo-in Temple. "Mr. Kurosawa is sleeping under the ground here." In reality, Akira Kurosawa is not buried at that particular temple. He is buried a short distance from the temple, at the far end of a rather plain, unassuming cemetery—his tombstone being smaller and less notable than Mifune's and Ozu's. But after some effort—asking oblivious strangers for proper directions, then seeking the help of the temple's groundskeeper—I was finally able to locate him. For a while I remained beside his grave, thanking him quietly for the movies that had transported my imagination and had moved me in ways that are difficult to articulate. Later that night, I returned to his grave with two beers, gradually pouring the contents of a Sapporo over his tombstone as I drank from the other. Again I gave thanks, squatting there in the nighttime—just me and Kurosawa and the moon. By moonlight I tidied his plot, clearing pebbles and leaves from his grave. And before leaving, I slipped a few stones into my pocket—three black stones from Kurosawa's grave, one for each character on his tombstone. From Ozu's grave I'd taken a single black stone; from Mifune's I'd also taken away a single black stone, although it looked more rugged than the others, which seemed somehow befitting considering the samurai he'd played.

My visit to Mifune's grave occurred before starting my journey from Tokyo to Hiroshima. The visits to the graves of both Ozu and Kurosawa came after Hiroshima, as my trip was drawing to a close. By the time I arrived to stay the night in Kamakura, I had spent several days in Tokyo, a day in Kyoto, a day in Kobe, and three days in Hiroshima. Each city provided its own preferred means of transportation:

in Tokyo it was trains, in Kyoto it was buses, in Kobe it was walking, and in Hiroshima it was trolley cars.

It was while staying in Hiroshima the rain began to fall in earnest, and the skies became gray, punctuated on occasion by clear patches. The weather in Japan, it seemed, could change on a dime: one hour breezy and wet, the next partly cloudy and calm; it was like west Texas weather. I spent the first two days avoiding the Atomic Bomb Dome and Peace Memorial Park altogether, busying myself instead with exploring art museums, eating okonomiyaki, and making a side trip to Miyajima. My friends in the Tucson band Calexico had recently performed in Hiroshima, and both Joey and John had mentioned the city's intense aura, as if to suggest that the devastating energy and violence of Hiroshima's past was still palpable. Yet I felt none of what they spoke of, at least not initially. Instead, I found the city to be modern and working class, with a slightly eastern European quality (maybe it was the trolley cars or the long bridges crossing all those urban rivers). The happiest hours of the entire trip were spent on nearby Miyajima, as I bicycled around the island, periodically passing school children who waved and giggled at this carefree, grinning American. "Kon-nichi-waaaaaaaaa," I'd say when peddling by, speaking in the deliberately exaggerated drawl of a Texan. Then from behind I'd hear their laughter, and inevitably I was answered by two or three voices, each trying out his or her version of Tex-Jap: "Kon-nichi-waaaaaaaaaa—!"

But having spent two relaxing days avoiding the Atomic Bomb Dome—and everything else that addressed Hiroshima's destruction—on my final day I could no longer stay away. Early on that last morning, Seymour and I found ourselves circling the building, photographing it from every imaginable angle. At first it seemed unimportant even to photograph the dome, simply because it had been photographed ad infinitum over the decades and any shot I took could only be cliché. Except, I reminded myself, there was nothing cliché about Hiroshima, and, indeed, there was no other site in Japan that I'd wanted to see more than the Atomic Bomb Dome. Only then did that palpable aura find me—making itself known while I began snapping shot after shot after shot.

Afterwards, I went to Peace Memorial Park and mingled with a tour group of Chinese. We studied the thousands of paper cranes left as offerings to the dead. We photographed trees that had survived the bombing and continued to thrive. We filed into the Peace Memorial Museum, where, finally, I was able to see my place in the atomic devastation: two large scale models of Hiroshima sat beside each other; one showed the city prior to the bombing, the other showed the city after the explosion—and studying that second model, I was able to find the exact location of my hotel, a black, charred, radiated, desolate patch of earth. I left the tour group and the museum in an uneasy, somber mood. But no sooner had I emerged into light than I heard Japanese pop music blaring from a riverboat. Crossing the bridge to exit the park, I paused to watch a young artist with an orange mohawk as he sketched the dome from a distance. Crude as his artwork was, I ended up buying three of his crayon sketches (the tori in Miyajima, the Atomic Bomb Dome, Hiroshima Castle) for three hundred yen each. He was grateful, and so was I.

Later that evening, I went again to the dome. As I sat quietly before the building, captivated by a crane that stood tall on the steel grid of the dome itself, I realized that my body was suddenly at the epicenter of the modern age. Everything that I knew or understood or treasured had resonated from this very point, spreading out across the planet—all my favorite art and books and movies, all the technology that continually evolves at an accelerated pace, as well as the darkest, deepest fears of the human race. In comparison to what the building represented, my own problems and pointless despair seemed irrelevant. If nothing else, I was alive, and I was lucky to be alive; aware of this, I hoisted Seymour for one last shot of the building, photographing it in dusk's fading light. Then I started for my hotel, deciding it was better to keep going forward and not look back.

Here, I suppose, is where my narrative should conclude. However, I want to relate something else. I want to mention the rain that fell hard and fast upon my return to Tokyo (it had started before I departed Kamakura, as I stood before the statue of the Great Buddha Daibutsu)—and the wind that yanked umbrellas from hands or turned them inside-out. Assuming it was typical Tokyo weather and unable to read the local newspapers, I was oblivious to the fact that the worst typhoon to hit Tokyo since World War II was blowing through the city. Once more I was staying at the Grand House Chang Tee, and that night the wind raged above my top-floor room, sounding like a freight train. I drank beer while watching TV, and then I slept. And then I dreamed: cowering in a dark corner, covering my face, I was hiding from the two crows that flitted above my head, their claws tangled in my hair; I was terrified to move, but finally I jumped up and ran—with the crows digging their claws into my skull, their immense wings abruptly flapping and whisking me from the ground.

When I woke the following morning, I heard them in the distance, calling out in the aftermath of Typhoon Higos. That previous night, a couple had been electrocuted by downed power lines, an Osaka security guard had been killed by falling glass, somewhere else a woman had been swept into the sea when she went to view the typhoon's approach, and off the coast of Japan, an Indonesian sailor had jumped from his ship to escape the onslaught of waves. But I'd been lifted above the disaster by crows, which later that morning circled above me as I went for noodles and then coffee. At last the storm had passed, leaving a flawless blue sky in its wake and the remains of umbrellas strewn along the sidewalks. Soon, I knew, it'd be as if the storm had never come at all. Soon, I realized, Japan would seem no more real to me than my vivid dream of the crows, and I'd again find myself surviving on my own in the desert. And yet, for a while at least, I was content with the sudden realization that we are born alone, that we die alone, and that living provides us with the rare opportunity to truly love and to be loved; that, I suspect, is the only thing I know for certain.

Then, while sipping my coffee at the Excelsior Cafe and reading a short story by Haruki Murakami, my eyes stopped on a single sentence: *"No matter how far you travel, you can never get away from yourself," Shimao said.* How true, I found myself thinking. How perfectly true. And so I shut the book, preferring instead to gaze outside, mindful of the crows that were beyond the window and which were just now sorting through the debris of the storm's widespread havoc—their long, curved beaks pecking at the messes created by both man and nature. Sitting there, my coffee growing cold, I could have stared at them all morning.

Contributors

BRIAN BOULDREY has written six books and edited six anthologies, including three volumes of *Best American Gay Fiction*. His edited collection *Wrestling with the Angel: Faith and Religion in the Lives of Gay Men* won a Lambda Literary Award and his memoir *Monster: Adventures in American Machismo,* was a Lambda finalist. His latest novel is *The Boom Economy: Or, Scenes from Clerical Life.* He is a visiting assistant professor in creative writing at Northwestern University.

MITCH CULLIN, his writing described by *the New York Times* as "brilliant and beautiful . . . rhythmic and telling," is the author of six highly acclaimed books, including *Tideland* and *From the Place in the Valley Deep in the Forest.* His short fiction has been widely anthologized, most recently in *Best American Gay Fiction 2* and *Gay Fiction at the Millennium.* He currently resides in the San Gabriel Valley, where he continues to live and work with Peter I. Chang.

EDWARD FIELD began writing poetry during World War II, when, as a navigator in the 8th Air Force, he flew twenty-five missions over Germany. In 1992, he received a Lambda Literary Award for *Counting Myself Lucky: Selected Poems 1963–1992.* His other honors include the Lamont Award, the Shelley Memorial Award, and an Academy Award for the documentary *To Be Alive,* for which he wrote the narration. He and his partner Neil Derrick, longtime residents of Greenwich Village, have written *The Villagers,* a best-selling historical novel about their community. Soon to be published are his literary memoirs, *The Man Who Would Marry Susan Sontag, and Other Intimate Literary Portraits.*

MACK FRIEDMAN is the author of *Strapped for Cash: A History of American Hustler Culture.* His work has also appeared in the anthology *Obsessed.* He lives in Pennsylvania, where the rivers run iron oxide, and is currently working on a new novel scheduled to be published in 2005.

PHILIP GAMBONE is an award-winning essayist, journalist, and fiction writer living in Boston. He teaches Chinese history at the Park School in Brookline, Massachusetts, and writing at Harvard University. His previous work includes *Beijing: A Novel, Something Inside: Conversations with Gay Fiction Writers,* and a book of stories, *The Language We Use up Here.*

RIGOBERTO GONZÁLEZ is the author of *So Often the Pitcher Goes to Water until It Breaks,* a selection of the National Poetry Series; *Soledad Sigh-Sighs,* a children's book; and *Crossing Vines,* a novel. His memoir, *Butterfly Boy,* is scheduled to be published in 2005.

RAPHAEL KADUSHIN is the humanities acquisitions editor at the University of Wisconsin Press, and the co-founder and editor, along with Joan Larkin and David Bergman, of the Living Out series of gay and lesbian autobiographies. He is a contributing editor at *Bon Appétit* and contributor to a range of periodicals, including *National Geographic Traveler, Islands, National Geographic,* and the *Chicago Tribune.* His work is also represented in a variety of anthologies, including *Men on Men 5, Best Food Writing 2001,* and the recently published *Through the Lens: National Geographic Greatest Photographs.*

WAYNE KOESTENBAUM is the author of five books of prose, most recently *Andy Warhol,* and three books of poetry, most recently *The Milk of Inquiry.* His second book of prose, *The Queen's Throat: Opera, Homosexuality, and the Mystery of Desire,* was nominated for a National Book Critics Circle Award. He is a professor of English at the CUNY Graduate Center and lives in New York City.

MATTHEW LINK works with Arthur Frommer at Newsweek's *Budget Travel* magazine. He is the author of *Rainbow Handbook Hawaii,* and has contributed to the anthologies *Gay Tourism: Culture, Identity, and Sex* and *ReCreations: Religion and Spirituality in the Lives of Queer People.* He writes travel pieces for *Newsweek, Time, The Advocate,* and *Out* and has appeared on NBC. Matthew grew up on his father's sailboat in the Pacific, and describes himself as a "born traveler," having visited over sixty countries.

MICHAEL LOWENTHAL is the author of the novels *Avoidance* and *The Same Embrace.* The recipient of fellowships from the Bread Loaf and Wesleyan writers' conferences, the Massachusetts Cultural Council, and the Hawthornden International Retreat for Writers, he has also written for the *New York Times Magazine, New York Times Book Review,* and *Washington Post Book World,* among many other publications. A member of the Executive Board of PEN New England, he teaches creative writing at Boston College and also works as a private manuscript consultant. He can be contacted through his Web site, www.MichaelLowenthal.com.

Contributors

J. S. MARCUS was born in 1962. He grew up in Milwaukee, Wisconsin, and graduated from the University of Wisconsin–Madison. He is the author of two books: *The Art of Cartography*, a short story collection; and a novel, *The Captain's Fire*. His fiction has appeared in *The New Yorker* and *Harper's*. His essays and articles have appeared in the *New York Times*, the *New York Review of Books*, and *Lingua Franca*. He is the recipient of a number of prizes and fellowships, including the Whiting Writer's Award and a senior fellowship at the Remarque Institute of European Studies at New York University. Currently he lives in Berlin, where he is completing his second novel.

DAVID MASELLO is New York editor of *Art & Antiques* magazine and the recently named editor in chief of *Out Traveler*. His essays and poetry have been published in many periodicals and anthologies, including the *New York Times*, *San Francisco Chronicle*, *Boston Globe*, *Newsweek*, *Massachusetts Review*, *Travel & Leisure*, and *Book*. His essay, "Double Vision," was included in *The Man I Might Become: Gay Men Write about Their Fathers*. He is also the author of two books about architecture and public art.

ALISTAIR MCCARTNEY was born in Perth, Western Australia, in 1971. His work has appeared in such publications as *The James White Review*, *Fence*, *Mirage Periodical #4*, *4th Street*, and *Aroused: A Collection of Erotic Writing*. He is currently working on two books: a poetic experimental encyclopedia, *The End of the World Book* and a novella about Freud, *The Life of Nerves*. He received an MFA in creative writing from Antioch University, Los Angeles, where he currently teaches creative writing and literature. He has lived with his partner Tim Miller in Los Angeles since 1995.

TIM MILLER is the author of the books *Body Blows: Six Performances* and *Shirts & Skin* and his performance texts have appeared in the play collections *O Solo Homo* and *Sharing the Delirium*. He teaches performance at the University of California, Los Angeles, School of Theater and is co-founder of Performance Space 122 in New York City and Highways Performance Space in Santa Monica, California. In 1990, he was awarded a solo performer fellowship by the National Endowment for the Arts and became known as one of the "NEA Four" when the grant was withdrawn under political pressure. He lives in Los Angeles with his partner Alistair McCartney. Tim Miller can be reached at his Web site http://hometown.aol.com/millertale/timmiller.html

ROBERT TEWDWR MOSS was a journalist of astonishing versatility. He first made his mark as diary editor of the books section of the *London*

Sunday Times. He also contributed to magazines as varied as *Tatler, Women's Journal, Harper's, Queen,* and *Africa Events.*

BOYER RICKEL's books include *Taboo,* a collection of autobiographical essays, and *arreboles,* a book of poems. A recent NEA poetry fellow, he is the assistant director of the University of Arizona Creative Writing Program.

BRUCE SHENITZ is the executive editor of *Out.* His edited collection, *The Man I Might Become: Gay Men Write about Their Fathers,* won a Lambda Literary Award for Best Nonfiction Anthology.

COLM TÓIBÍN is the author of a number of travel books and five novels, including *The Blackwater Lightship,* which was shortlisted for the Booker Prize in 1999.

EDMUND WHITE has written sixteen books, including a trilogy of autobiographical novels. His most recent novel is *Fanny: A Fiction.* He teaches writing at Princeton University.